For all those who engage in the process of research, writing, and publication.

– MB, A

"Keep writing. Keep doing it and doing it. Even in the moments when it's so hurtful to think about writing."

– Heather Armstrong, 2006

Getting Your Research Paper Published

A Surgical Perspective

Edited by

Mohit Bhandari, MD, PhD
Department of Surgery
Department of Clinical Epidemiology and Biostatistics
McMaster University
Hamilton, Ontario, Canada

Anders Joensson, MD, PhD
On behalf of the OTCF Stryker GmbH
Schönkirchen/Kiel, Germany

Associate Editors:

Bernd Robioneck, PhD
Vice President
R&D and Technical Marketing
Stryker Trauma Company Ltd.
Schönkirchen, Kiel, Germany

Emil H. Schemitsch MD, FRCSC
Head
Division of Orthopaedic Surgery
University of Toronto
St. Michael's Hospital
Toronto, Ontario, Canada

Managing Editor:

Sheila Sprague, MSc
Program Manager
Department of Clinical Epidemiology and Biostatistics
McMaster University
Hamilton, Ontario, Canada

With contributions by
Lars C. Borris, Ole Brink, Dianne Bryant, Jason W. Busse, Chad Coles, Peter V. Giannoudis, Richard Gould, Kyle Jeray, Paul Karanicolas, George M. Kontakis, Jacqelyn Marsh, Tara Mastracci, George Mathew, Eric Morrison, Bradley Petrisor, Rudolf W. Poolman, Lyndsay Somerville, Stephanie Tanner, Daniel Vena, Scott Wingerter, Cheryl Wylie, Rad Zdero, Boris A. Zelle

127 illustrations

Thieme
Stuttgart · New York

Library of Congress Cataloging-in-Publication Data is available from the publisher.

Illustrations by Karin Baum, Paphos, Cyprus

© 2011 Georg Thieme Verlag,
Rüdigerstrasse 14, 70469 Stuttgart, Germany
http://www.thieme.de
Thieme New York, 333 Seventh Avenue,
New York, NY 10001, USA
http://www.thieme.com

Cover design: Thieme Publishing Group

Typesetting by Hagedorn Kommunikation GmbH, Viernheim, Germany

Printed by Officin Andersen Nexö, Zwenkau, Germany

ISBN 978-3-13-149991-2   1 2 3 4 5 6

Acknowledgments

The Editors would like to sincerely thank Dr. Thomas Einhorn for writing the foreword. Also Sarah Resendes, Mandy Tam, Farrah Naz Hussain, Brian John Chan, Meaghan Zehr, and Gerald Sung for their assistance in the preparation of this book.

Foreword

Like most skills, scientific writing is something that is learned and continuously improved over the course of a career. To the academician, it is an essential skill without which success can never be attained. To the clinical practitioner, it can be an inherent gift to be called upon when an opportunity to contribute new knowledge presents itself. However, as the quality and complexity of basic and clinical science continue to evolve, the requirements for scientific writing become more demanding. Journals have adopted standards for measuring quality and levels of evidence and now have a more consistent way of knowing when an article is worthy of communication to its readers. Authors, on the other hand, are challenged by increasingly rigid criteria for organizing their data and drawing meaningful conclusions.

The title of this book states its purpose. It is meant to be a guide. More importantly, it is meant to be a practical guide, one that can be used as a tutorial as well as a reference. It begins with a chapter that is almost rhetorical in its title, "Why Should We Publish Papers?" The writer needs to think about the importance and purpose of what he or she is doing. Will the published article advance knowledge? Will it raise new questions that require further exploration? Will it change clinical practice? If it will do none of these, perhaps it shouldn't be written. This opening chapter addresses the responsibility of authorship.

A good part of this book addresses the basic principles of scientific writing, presenting them in a structured and organized way. It provides lots of tips, "dos and don'ts," and identifies the essential elements of scientific writing in a "what you need to know" manner. It provides direction on the use of statistics and when a statistician is needed. It distinguishes the role of the statistician from one who just "crunches numbers" to one who is part of the intellectual process of study design. Importantly, it provides clear direction on the role of the author and the qualifications for authorship. It addresses the question of ethics in scientific writing, not only in terms of communicating the truth but also in maintaining credibility over the course of a career.

The maturation process for a successful scientific writer can be long and arduous. Along the way, there are problems, pitfalls, missteps, and failures. Picking oneself up, dusting oneself off, and moving forward after a paper or grant application has been rejected is something we must all learn to do. This book should make that experience a little easier. One of the really nice features of this book is that, in addition to the practical guide for writing a paper for publication, there is a section about the presentation of research findings, learning how to write an abstract, learning how to prepare a PowerPoint or poster presentation, and learning how to be consistent when presenting and publishing results. The importance of this latter skill can be greatly underestimated.

As a researcher, the greatest way to share knowledge with the scientific community and to establish oneself as a scientist is through publication in academic journals. Those who are fortunate enough are able to learn the process of academic writing through valuable mentorship and experience. However, there is no formal process for those who have not had the opportunity for such mentorship. Writing a research paper for publication is what we consider to be one of the most essential steps in the practice of clinical research. Consequently, this second book was developed to provide an easy-to-follow guide for surgeons wishing to contribute to the scientific community, but lacking adequate guidance and familiarity to successfully do so.

Although the process of publication is often daunting and time consuming, the benefits of publishing your work often far outweigh the costs. This unique book has been written by surgical experts and is designed to provide a roadmap for the challenging, yet rewarding process of academic publication and presentation in surgery. It includes excellent tips on the principles of writing and provides a detailed description of the requirements for preparing to submit an academic manuscript to a peer review journal. A thorough overview of the review process as well as guidelines for interacting with journal editors will provide you with the required skills and confidence to see your manuscript through the review process. This book concludes with advice on the proper presentation of research findings, including both podium presentations and poster presentations at academic meetings. We are confident that this text will smoothly guide you to successful publication and presentation of your academic research.

Nothing is more gratifying than seeing your work published. It is the closure of a loop that involves substantial effort, commitment, and dogged attentiveness to detail. In the final analysis, communicating what you know with enough evidence to justify a treatment, intervention or the making of a diagnosis is a contribution of enormous impact. This book provides the vision to help achieve that goal.

Thomas A. Einhorn, MD
Boston, Massachusetts

Preface

Evidence-based medicine requires the application of best evidence to optimize patient care. Critical to the advancement of the core principles of evidence-based medicine is the timely publication of important studies to guide patient care. Without wide dissemination of research findings, important advances in patient care may not be realized and potentially beneficial therapies under-utilized. As a clinical researcher, publication of research is critical for several reasons including knowledge transfer, academic advancement, development of new collaborations, and impact on patient care. Publishing research increases the awareness of an investigator's findings, prevents publication bias, increases the quality and credibility of the paper, and prevents the use of preliminary data from abstracts. The critical last step to the translation of a well-constructed and executed clinical study is the writing of the final manuscript for publication. Unfortunately, the majority of research fails to get published—often for one of two reasons: 1) authors not submitting their manuscripts for publication and 2) rejection of manuscripts from peer-reviewed journals.

To optimize the translation of evidence into practice, the results of clinical research studies needs to be efficiently and effectively disseminated to health care practitioners. Realizing the challenges to writing a paper for publication, we have carefully presented a practical guide to *Getting Your Research Paper Published*. We focus on surgeons given the historical challenges of publishing research in the surgical subspecialty. This textbook is the culmination of years of experience among experienced authors in both conducting research and disseminating research results. The first section of the book stresses the importance of disseminating research results and discusses many of the challenges faced when reporting the results of surgical trials. The second section of the book provides practical steps for writing a manuscript, determining authorship, and submitting a manuscript to an academic journal for publication. We also describe journal requirements and the peer review process. The final section of the book focuses on presenting research findings at specialty meetings. All aspects of the book center around the core theme of *Getting Your Research Paper Published* and provide critical context to publishing, responding to journals, and presenting findings of your research to a broader audience at meetings.

Throughout the text we have maintained a standardized approach that includes a number of innovate strategies to make the book easy to read and interpret. Jargon Simplified sections provide simple definitions of terminology that may not be familiar to the reader and Key Concepts sections highlight the most important issues described in each chapter. The Reality Check boxes highlight real life examples of the concept being discussed, which provides a practical context to the chapters. Our text provides the key principles for disseminating research results, preparing manuscripts for publication, and presenting research findings, and is unique in its approach of "practical advice for working clinical researchers."

Mohit Bhandari
Anders Joensson

List of Contributors

Lars C. Borris, MD
Aarhus University Hospital
Department of Orthopaedics
Section of Traumatology
Aarhus, Denmark

Ole Brink, MD
Aarhus University Hospital
Department of Orthopaedics
Section of Traumatology
Aarhus, Denmark

Dianne Bryant, PhD
Assistant Professor
School of Physical Therapy
University of Western Ontario
Elborn College
London, Ontario, Canada

Jason W. Busse, PhD
Assistant Professor
Department of Clinical Epidemiology and Biostatistics
McMaster University
Hamilton, Ontario, Canada

Chad Coles, MD, FRCSC
Assistant Professor
Division of Orthopaedic Surgery
Dalhousie University
Halifax, Nova Scotia, Canada

Peter V. Giannoudis, MD
Professor
Department of Orthopaedic and Trauma Surgery
University of Leeds
Leeds, UK

Richard Gould, MBChB(Hons)
Surgical Directorate
University Hospital of North Staffordshire
Stoke-on-Trent, UK

Kyle Jeray, MD
Program Director, Director of Research
Department of Orthopaedic Surgery
Greenville Hospital System
Greenville, SC, USA

Paul Karanicolas, MD, PhD
Department of Surgery
Memorial Sloan-Kettering Cancer Center
New York, NY, USA

George M. Kontakis, MD
Associate Professor
Department of Orthopaedics and Traumatology
School of Medicine University Hospital
Iraklion, Crete, Greece

Jacquelyn Marsh, BHSc
Faculty of Health Sciences
University of Western Ontario
Elborn College
London, Ontario, Canada

Tara M. Mastracci, MD, MSc
Assistant Professor
Department of Vascular Surgery
The Cleveland Clinic Foundation
Cleveland, OH, USA

George Mathew, MD
Department of Orthopaedic Surgery
Hamilton General Hospital
Hamilton, Ontario, Canada

Eric Morrison, BSc
Department of Clinical Epidemiology and Biostatistics
McMaster University
Hamilton, Ontario, Canada

Bradley Petrisor, MD, MSc, FRCSC
Assistant Professor
Department of Surgery
McMaster University
Hamilton, Ontario, Canada

Rudolf W. Poolman, MD, PhD
Joint Research
Department of Orthopaedic Surgery
Onze Lieve Vrouwe Gasthuis
Amsterdam, The Netherlands

Lyndsay Somerville, MSc, PhD (candidate)
Faculty of Health Sciences
University of Western Ontario
Elborn College
London, Ontario, Canada

Stephanie Tanner, MSc
Clinical Trials Research Coordinator
Department of Orthopaedic Surgery
Greenville Hospital System
Greenville, SC, USA

Daniel Vena, BSc
Department of Clinical Epidemiology and Biostatistics
McMaster University
Hamilton, Ontario, Canada

Scott Wingerter, MD, PhD
Resident Physician and Orthopaedic Surgeon
Department of Orthopedic Surgery and Rehabilitation
The University of Mississippi Medical Center
Jackson, MS, USA

Cheryl Wylie, BSc
Research Associate
Department of Clinical Epidemiology and Biostatistics
McMaster University
Hamilton, Ontario, Canada

Rad Zdero, PhD
Research Director
Martin Orthopaedic Biomechanics Lab
St Michael's Hospital
Toronto, Ontario, Canada

Boris A. Zelle, MD
Department of Orthopaedic Surgery
University of Pittsburgh School of Medicine
Pittsburgh, PA, USA

Table of Contents

Observing, Bending, and Breaking Rules

Much of the advice in this book comes into the class of "best practice" as distilled from the authors' experience and intellectual appreciation of the methods and mores of scientific communication. As such it is of general applicability and will guide you faithfully through the process of preparation and publication of your research paper.

But as the authors point out, each journal to which you are likely to submit also has its own peculiarities and stipulations, both as to what must be submitted and how, and also as to small (perhaps seemingly trivial) matters of presentation (headings to be used, forms of references and citation, and so on). As the authors also stress repeatedly, you should thoroughly familiarize yourself with those rules and observe them to the letter, and should not attempt even to bend them a little if you want your submission to be considered with the fewest obstacles. Some of the specific stipulations mentioned may conflict with the more general advice: the general advice will always be good advice, but it should always be refined by specific requirements from your target journal.

There is rather more room for maneuver where matters of "style" are concerned. Some of these of course are embedded in national linguistic practices. Spelling of the English language differs between the two major "camps" of American English and the traditions of British English that still predominate in large areas that were historically influenced by British practice; and there are intermediate cases such as represented by Canadian English spelling among others.

This book (Chapter 18) gives advice on grammar and punctuation based on "different sources that are very thorough on the subject matter," and also indicates some of the differences in spellings that predominate. This manual is based on American sources. There are national (or transatlantic) differences even in the placement of periods and commas with quotation marks, whether those quotation marks should be single or double, and attitudes to the use of plural or singular pronouns when referring to organizations or other "corporate" entities. And there is ample scope for variability in the degree to which relatively recent developments in the use of language are considered acceptable. Thus there are "rules" that can be bent to various degrees short of fracture, and with circumspection.

You will accordingly find instances in this book where "rules" laid down in one part are apparently broken in another. And of course, because of the use of material cited for illustration from a variety of published sources, you will encounter examples of British spelling. Various usages and styles employed even counter the publisher's own Style Guide (such as the discipline-specific preference for the spelling "orthopaedic," whereas Webster[1] cites "orthopedic" as the standard and journals are mentioned with "orthopedic" in their titles). These are not "inconsistencies" but rather illustrations that it is not possible to lay down simple (simplistic) absolute "rules" in the complex field of human communication.

The emphasis of this book is always on the practical matter of putting your ideas and findings as clearly and forcefully as possible. Where the actual writing is concerned in this endeavor, as long as you appreciate which rules must be observed and which can tolerate some bending, the advice of the august Chicago Manual of Style can be applied to the rest:

Break a rule when it doesn't work.[2]

References

1. *Webster's Third New International Dictionary, Unabridged.* Merriam-Webster, 2002. Available at: http://unabridged.merriam-webster.com. Accessed November 2, 2009
2. *The Chicago Manual of Style Online.* 15th ed. paragraph 8.170. Available at: http://www.chicagomanualofstyle.org. Accessed November 2, 2009

1

Why Should We Publish Papers?

George M. Kontakis, Peter V. Giannoudis

Summary

As a researcher, one of the best ways to share your knowledge with the scientific community and establish yourself as a scientist is through publication. The publication of papers in peer-reviewed journals is vital to the ongoing advancement of the different disciplines of medicine and to one's own academic or professional position. In this chapter we will discuss the significance and benefits of publishing research, the nature of publication, and the qualities required to be a good author.

Introduction

During the beginning of a residency program, an orthopaedic resident will first obtain knowledge of his or her discipline by observing senior doctors and by studying the appropriate textbooks. Soon, the resident will become familiar with specialty journals, which include published articles submitted from researchers from all over the world. Initially, the resident may be attracted by review articles, which summarize current knowledge, by interesting case reports, or by technical notes. In addition, by participating in journal "clubs," residents will find excitement, especially when a research group from elsewhere is publishing an article that challenges current knowledge or supports a new practice based on experimental or clinical research methodology.[1]

Gradually, as the resident's knowledge increases, he or she becomes more interested in primary research articles. Some residents will continue to use primary research literature to improve their clinical practice throughout their professional life, while others may also become members of a research group to participate in the evolution of the science.[1,2]

This scenario could be representative for most orthopaedic surgeons. Becoming a researcher in the surgical specialty requires commitment, knowledge, and frequently additional formal training in health research methodology. When this is combined with clinical practice, researchers will generate questions, giving birth to new ideas. A scientific question may be structured as a hypothesis; its validation (or rebuttal) will thus add new knowledge and contribute to scientific progress.[2] As Gerald Piel, the editor responsible for expanding *Scientific American* worldwide, stated, "Science is dead without publication."[3]

Key Concepts: Scientific Questions
A scientific question may be structured as a hypothesis and evidence supporting or rebutting it will add new knowledge and promote scientific advancement.

The Significance of Communication

Even before the era of civilization, people always tried to find ways to express themselves and communicate with others. Tools of communication developed over the ages from shouts and dances, to symbols and languages. Communication was established in both the verbal and written forms. It is on the written form (i.e., publication through research papers) that the scientific community has relied to communicate with the rest of the world.

Why is communication important? For one thing, we live our lives by gathering information from the environment that surrounds us. We modulate ourselves by interacting with others and also build our character through such interactions. Even in nature, existence is made possible only when the various parts of ecosystems interact. Ground, water, plants, animals, and energy: each would not be sustained if they all did not interact and work together. Humans would be inadequate if they did not interact with each other.

Secondly, communication also advances the evolution of ideas and contributes to the development of our civilization. Imagine what would have happened if major historical figures had not shared their ideas. Although a concept may not always be accepted immediately, it can at least provide the first steps for action. Ultimately, action always causes reaction and inactivity causes misery.[4]

Sharing ideas among the scientific community is the most crucial step toward progress. Opinions are exchanged and issues are faced in a more productive way. Hard work leads to conclusions; a conclusion is an idea, and an idea locked up in the mind of even the most brilliant person is worthless. An idea not shared is worth nothing, whereas a shared one is precious. So instead of being afraid to expose ourselves, it is better to take the chance and express our ideas as a possible contribution to the ongoing evolution of science.[5]

Key Concepts: Publishing Research Papers
Publishing our papers is a way to communicate with others among the scientific community and throughout the entire world.

The Significance of Disseminating Information

Research results are also presented at scientific meetings where other professionals can evaluate and scrutinize the study methodology. Attendance at scientific meetings is important because there researchers can be informed about the latest developments in their field. For presentations introducing new methodology, authors have the chance to discuss their findings with their colleagues, to have its efficacy examined, and perhaps even to have it applied widely. Although scientific meetings can be beneficial for you as a researcher to discuss your already published work, scientists should also consider such meetings as an opportunity to be exposed to other concepts presented by other professionals.[6] The rapid pace of advances in medicine and surgery makes it incredibly important to keep informed about the latest discoveries. Attending academic meetings is one strategy for keeping current with advances. However, scientists need to go beyond attending meetings and announcing research results. They should seek validity for their research and try to demonstrate their skills to the scientific community through a published article on significant scientific inquiries. Evidence of a researcher's contribution to their field comes only through formal publication of their work.[6] Furthermore, by publishing an article, a researcher will have the opportunity to be cited as a reference in a future presentation or publication, which makes an author of a published paper more frequently noted. In addition, published work can become the foundation for writing research grants leading to potential acquisition of funds and allowing continuation of a research program. As you can see, there are several very strong incentives behind publication.[7]

In today's technological world, simple and convenient telecommunications allow ideas to travel globally with a simple click of a button. Is it not, therefore, worthwhile to discover something unique and share it with others? The broadcasting of information may have varied effects on different individuals: some people may only read your article, while others may be influenced to alter the way they think, the way they practice, and even to implement appropriate changes into their lives.

Incentives for Scientific Research

Ideally, scientific research should advance with clinical practice. For many, surgery is mainly an art, but this conception is not wholly valid—surgery requires the combination of art and science.[1] Surgical skills, as an art, are obtained through proper education and practice, but a proper education requires both scientific research and a profound commitment to science. As well, the local work environment may influence a researcher's specific interest. Young

surgeons may be stimulated to do research in certain directions by their seniors, and the senior members need to inspire and guide inexperienced surgical trainees in their pursuit of scientific research.[8]

Key Concepts: Education
A proper education requires involvement in scientific research as well as the "internal flame" of devotion to science.

Usually, members of the academic surgical community are encouraged and expected to participate in research programs; however, many surgeons are based outside the university environment, which poses difficulties for them to become involved. Nowadays, participation in research projects is considered by the national health care systems as an integral part of a surgeon's professional and academic medical career. Furthermore, participation in research projects helps develop discipline and encourages collaboration between professionals taking part. Team work is of paramount importance for the growth of scientific maturity.[2] But participation in research groups and completion of a project are insufficient in themselves. Results of studies need to be disseminated in the scientific community to allow evaluation and retesting of the findings, and for improvements in the future.[2]

Key Concepts: Participation in Research
- Participation in research projects is nowadays constantly assessed both for an academic career and for a professional career in the national health care system.
- Presentation of our findings and ideas at scientific meetings is not enough to gain identification, validity, and funding.

Peer-Reviewed Journals

The researcher who publishes his or her work in peer-reviewed journals is at an advantage in terms of author identity, validity, and opportunities for collaboration compared with one who chooses not to publish. Moreover, the continual increase in the number of journal subscribers is proof that there is a significant demand for the sharing of knowledge through publication. Publishing articles helps build authors' reputations as a reliable resource and it gives them greater credibility compared with researchers who do not have publications. In reality, authors are often perceived not solely on the basis of the quality of their work but also by the number of publications they have. By searching the medical literature via the Internet, we are able to quantify a researcher's citations, and to use this as a means to measure the success and status of a researcher. Nonetheless, a researcher's prestige depends ultimately on both the quantity and the quality of their published articles.[9]

The Nature of Publication

Competition

The process of publishing an article among members of the surgical community is quite competitive. Each team must be coordinated, well-organized, and consistent, as well as reliable, to rise above the competition. Competition provokes and maintains a constant interest in the field of research: when an individual or a team of researchers publish their work, it may stimulate other researchers either to express their opinions on the published result or to develop a similar research program. In this way, competition always exists and works as a driving force toward scientific advancement.[10]

Today's researchers are judged by the quality of their published articles; thus each researcher is constantly trying to gain respect by continuously presenting innovative ideas. This mentality can be compared with the philosophy of athletics—the faster and stronger is always on top. Similarly, surgeons leading in research initiatives have the chance to prove their abilities not only through taking care of patients but also by excelling within this kind of competition.[10]

Criticism

While authors may achieve validity, acceptance, and appreciation from their publications, they also gain the benefit of criticism. By publishing, they invite others to make suggestions on their research. The opinions, experiences, or criticisms of others may influence a researcher's approach and lead to adoption of new methods or prompt them to change their attitudes. One can, therefore, make use of constructive criticism to improve one's work, one's scientific endeavors, and one's ability to express oneself. The ability to recognize and appreciate valuable constructive criticisms, and set them apart from insignificant comments, is important to avoid wasting time. Proactively taking part in the discussion of ideas in published work can be one of the best ways to promote lifelong learning.[11,12]

Key Concepts: Lifelong Learning
• Publication of articles means expressing the quality of our thought and consolidating the corpus of our personal effort.
• Taking an active part in broad "discussions" by publishing work and ideas can be one of the best ways to promote lifelong learning.

Satisfying Demands

Adequate evidence is necessary to convince those involved in science. Accordingly, a proper published article should contain experimental and clinical data to validate the conclusions of a study. Additionally, references are supplied so that readers can cross-reference other papers to authenticate what is written. Since science is based on evidence from experiments that can be repeated over and over again, a published article is a proper vehicle for persuading orthopaedic surgeons. An author needs to work hard, gaining significant insight on their subject matter, to produce a publication that can convince others of their individual contribution to scientific progress. The demand for rigorous publications is high, and researchers face increasing demands to publish high-quality research.[13]

Key Concepts: Scientific Method
Since science is based on evidence and on experiments that can be carried out over and over again, a published article is a proper source for persuading the scientific/medical community at large

Excitement as Motivation

Junior surgeons who begin reading published articles find great interest in the rapid way they acquire knowledge. An article can easily become the subject of debate or a common topic of work, engendering and necessitating continuous effort in their being more informed about the latest progress of that subject. As their knowledge continues to develop, they will become more enthusiastic and have a greater urge to contribute to the exchange of ideas. This enthusiasm drives them to become more knowledgeable and they will eventually consider undertaking research work seriously. As you may recall from childhood, it was easier to gain and maintain knowledge through games. We participate in games, then acquire the desire to win. Likewise, junior surgeons start participating in the "challenge" of publishing their articles when they feel wise enough to do so. Throughout this procedure, a young doctor's knowledge is consistently expanding, which produces a satisfying feeling like that of winning and an excitement to propel them even deeper into research.[14]

When it comes to senior members of the research collaborative, the initial feeling of excitement is obviously decreased and competition is what motivates them to keep going. However, by being competitive, they inspire young surgeons to work hard and enter the world of sharing ideas. Besides, there is no game without competition and there is no competition without excitement. Also, while temporal actions are notable, written documents transcend time and can always be used as evidence of our abilities and our work. This adds to our excitement and motivates us mentally and physically. It is clear that there are many personal and inter-professional benefits in sharing research through publications.[15]

Prerequisites for Publication

Scientific Resources

An author who publishes an interesting article that reflects a well-organized research project may obtain funding help from external partners. As we all know, much medical research requires state subsidy, which is not easy to obtain. One way to attract this kind of help is by presenting a piece of worthy work. By publishing their efforts, researchers demonstrate their personal devotion to what they do. They attempt to persuade the scientific community that their research group has a deep understanding in their research field. This may trigger interest from external partners and induce them to contribute to the extension and development of the research. For example, scientists who aim to investigate a specific field need to convince potential funding sources that they are the most suitable to carry out this research work. They need to become a well-organized scientific team, members of a prominent laboratory, and developers of a promising scientific project. The best proof of all these qualifications is published work.[16]

Why is funding so important? Action is needed to transform thoughts into reality, and in most cases an extended period of time is required to produce results. During this period, a lot of laboratory work, material, accoutrement, as well as personnel are needed; thus, the scientific team surely needs support or subsidy. When this is provided, the team becomes stronger and more alert to producing further research, and the team is more integrated, providing a greater impetus toward scientific progress. A strong research team needs also to have a passion for excellence, to be dedicated to success, and to be committed to their chosen research field.[17] These qualities are demonstrated by the publication of articles and presentation of results, making it more likely that support will be found.

Organization of Thought

Effectiveness in the research field calls for a mind with organized thought. In creating and publishing an article much concentration is required from the authors to gather their thoughts and propositions in such a way as to ensure that readers understand the intention behind their publication. The shaping of a paper can be a great challenge! It takes a lot of personal energy to give birth to assumptions, analyze concepts, and organize a frame of expression.

Putting our thoughts into words helps us identify and clarify the real meaning of our thoughts and brings us closer to our objectives. A well-organized mind offers continuously new and promising ideas to all fields; this is especially true for doctors, since they need to keep their mind in good shape to confront challenges posed by patients. It can be very difficult to create an article that involves marshalling a large number of thoughts, and the shaping of a paper can be a great challenge.[18]

Practice in the organization of thought also offers many personal benefits. Consider a mind in good shape as a significant aid to achieving and maintaining internal balance. Persons in harmony with themselves can be efficient in many domains and therefore offer much more to the rest of mankind.

> **Key Concepts: Written Documents**
> Action always counts but is ephemeral. Written documents persist through time and can always be used as a proof of our abilities.

Consolidation of Work

In scientific work, there is a specific process to be followed to maximize the chances of success. First, scientists need to investigate a formulated hypothesis and attempt to substantiate their ideas. This must be a thorough, and thus often lengthy, process to ensure the quality of their findings. The validation of their efforts is then accomplished by the sharing of their work with others. Publication of articles is one way of sharing information, and it is the means through which authors consolidate their efforts into a quality document. When scientists intend to publish their results, they should always have timeliness and scheduling at the back of their minds so as to make their published work exclusive.[19] It is also equally important for them to overcome challenges in their research and improve upon their work. Through publications, scientists can endorse the uniqueness of their approach to a major topic of interest within the scientific community, or present a brand new idea to achieve a breakthrough.

Discipline

Discipline is a virtue that can be achieved through various means. It is one of the main components of a personality as well as one of the main features that contribute to success. An author wanting to complete a well-framed article in a specific time needs to be disciplined and compliant with both self-imposed rules and the requirements and stipulations of the publishers. No progress is made without hard work. Authors must be willing to dedicate a significant portion of their personal life—sacrificing personal time, family time, time for enjoyment and relaxation—to obtain their objective. Preparing a publication allows and requires researchers to practice the art of self-discipline, and this skill can also be applied to other aspects of daily life. Deadlines and rules imposed by the journal of publication are another issue. The researcher must learn to work according to demands. Authors should organize their manuscripts to the best of their ability to increase the probability that their work will be published. Anxiety also plays a factor in compliance because authors are anxious when waiting to find out whether their article has been accepted. Through this process, a scientist improves himself or herself and becomes more mature.[20]

> **Key Concepts: Discipline**
> When working on publishing articles, one has to practice discipline and consequently learns to be disciplined in daily life.

Conclusion

Each of you may be able to bring to mind an example of a published article that greatly changed or influenced your view of the world. Among the pages of the journals in your collection, you can always find several that have captured your attention. The feeling of satisfaction that you have when you read an article of interest is something valuable. Some articles may have even discouraged you from studying a certain field, and turned your interest toward another. Furthermore, with a simple search on the Internet, you can easily gather information from opinion leaders, and be able to network with other professionals to broaden their knowledge and your own.

Undoubtedly you will have devoted a great deal of time and effort in gaining knowledge in your chosen scientific field, and a part of your wisdom stems from reading articles. Now you may have the ability to share your acquired knowledge with the world by publishing articles of your own. Your article can be the start of something new and innovative; even if the results are not the desired ones, you should be aware that your paper can make a change even if it is impermanent. By publishing, you will always assert what you deserve: a role in research, identification, opportunities, competition, criticism, excitement, funding, discipline, interaction, and so much more. For those who have never dared publish their work: take the chance. For the rest of you: keep working for your personal development.

Suggested Reading

Rennie D, Flanagin A, Yank V. The contributions of authors. JAMA 2000;284(1):89–91

Yank V, Barnes D. Consensus and contention regarding redundant publications in clinical research: cross-sectional survey of editors and authors. J Med Ethics 2003;29(2):109–114

References

1. Schmidt HG, Norman GR, Boshuizen HPA. A cognitive perspective on medical expertise: theory and implication. Acad Med 1990;65(10):611–621
2. Colliver JA. Research strategy for problem-based learning: cognitive science or outcomes research. Teach Learn Med 1999;11(2):64–65
3. Satya-Murti S Interpreting the medical literature. JAMA 2006;296(11):1410–1411
4. Kurtz MJ, Eichhorn G, Accomazzi A, Grant CS, Demleitner M, Murray SS. The effect of use and access on citations. Inform Process Manage 2005;41(6):1395–1402
5. Gartfield E. Citation indexes for a science: a new dimension in documentation through association of ideas. Science 1955; 122(3159):108–111
6. Mirowski P, Van Horn R. The contract research organization and the commercialization of scientific research. Soc Stud Sci 2005;35(4):503–548
7. Yank V, Barnes D. Consensus and contention regarding redundant publications in clinical research: cross-sectional survey of editors and authors. J Med Ethics 2003; 29(2):109–114
8. Regehr G, Norman GR. Issues in cognitive psychology: implications for professional education. Acad Med 1996; 71(9):988–1001
9. Fontanarosa PB, Glass RM, De Angelis CD. Thanking authors, peer reviewers, and readers—constancy in a time of change. JAMA 2000;283(15):2016–2017
10. Cariaga-Lo LD, Richards BF, Hollingsworth MA, Camp DL. Non-cognitive characteristics of medical students: entry to problem-based and lecture based curricula. Med Educ 1996;30(3):179–186
11. Rennie D, Flanagin A, Yank V. The contributions of authors. JAMA 2000;284(1):89–91
12. Gomez-Alonso J. Author! Author! JAMA 2004;292(15):1815, author reply 1816
13. Riis P. Scientific dishonesty: European reflections. J Clin Pathol 2001;54(1):4–6
14. Hren D, Sambunjak D, Ivanis A, Marusić M, Marusić A. Perceptions of authorship criteria: effects of student instruction and scientific experience. J Med Ethics 2007;33(7):428–432
15. Martin B. How to succeed in publishing articles by really trying: some notes for postgraduates. Postgraduate Reporter 1995;3(1):14
16. Pitkin RM, Branagan MA, Burmeister LF. Accuracy of data in abstracts of published research articles. JAMA 1999; 281(12):1110–1111
17. Schauder D. Electronic publishing of professional articles: attitudes of academics and implications for the scholarly communication industry. J Am Soc Inf Sci 1994;45(2):73–100
18. Horton R. The hidden research paper. JAMA 2002;287(21):2775–2778
19. Benos DJ, Fabres J, Farmer J, et al. Ethics and scientific publication. Adv Physiol Educ 2005;29(2):59–74
20. Bates T, Anić A, Marusić M, Marusić A. Authorship criteria and disclosure of contributions: comparison of 3 general medical journals with different author contribution forms. JAMA 2004;292(1):86–88

2

Presented but Never Published: Why Research Papers Are Not Being Published

Cheryl Wylie, Sheila Sprague

Summary

Publication rates (see Jargon Simplified for definition) in orthopaedic research range anywhere from 11% to 78%. Publishing research increases the awareness of an investigator's findings, prevents publication bias, increases the quality and credibility of the paper, and prevents the use of preliminary data from abstracts. The two primary causes of low publication rates include authors not submitting their manuscripts for publication or the rejection of manuscripts from peer-reviewed journals. In this chapter we discuss various methods to increase the likelihood of publication by arranging timeline goals, developing a budget, ensuring a methodologically sound paper, and conducting a thorough review of the literature. By reading the ideas presented in this chapter and learning to research with proper techniques, researchers like yourself will learn to avoid common mistakes in the publication process and help contribute to the orthopaedic literature by publishing your article.

Introduction

The primary purpose of research is to discover new and important information and to share this knowledge with others. The distribution of new orthopaedic discoveries is most effectively done through publication in top research journals such as the *Journal of Bone and Joint Surgery*, *Journal of Orthopaedic Trauma*, or *Clinical Orthopaedics and Related Research*. Publication of findings allows the investigator to complete an extensive analysis of the results and experience the peer-review process, ensuring the production of a quality report. Unfortunately, not all research gets published, for many reasons.

Publication rates represent the percentage of presentations at national meetings that result in a published journal article that can be found in a literature search. This is a very common measure used when examining unpublished research. When studies are presented at major meetings, it can be assumed and expected that a complete paper will follow. However, it is hard to estimate the number of research studies that do not even make the presentation stage; thus, reported publication rates may be higher than the true publication rates.

Key Concepts: Research Timeline
A researcher's typical timeline for conducting research begins with a study design, followed by data collection, data analysis, presentation of the results at a major international orthopaedic meeting, and then full publication of these findings in an established research journal.

Jargon Simplified: Publication Rates
Publication rates represent the percentage of presentations at national meetings that result in a published journal article that can be found in a literature search.

A study conducted in North America based on the abstracts presented at the 63rd Annual Meeting of the American Academy of Orthopaedic Surgeons in 1996 found that from the abstracts presented only 34% produced full-text publications.[1] An influential study conducted by Hamlet et al. in 1997 analyzed the general trends in orthopaedic research publication and estimated that 1465 presentations were made at the Annual Meetings of the American Academy of Orthopaedic Surgeons in 1990, 1991, and 1992.[2] Of those presentations, the publication rate of the abstracts from the meetings was found to be only 46%.[2] The average time to publish an article was 20 months after presentation.[2] There was a gradual increase in the total number of published presentations each month following the meeting until a plateau was reached approximately 3 years following the presentation at the meeting (**Fig. 2.1**).[2]

Hamlet et al. (1997) also reviewed the top journals with publications from this meeting, and found the *Journal of Bone and Joint Surgery* (24%) to come first, followed by *Clinical Orthopaedics and Related Research* (16%) in terms of publication rates achieved (**Table 2.1**).[2]

Lastly, Hamlet et al. (1997) looked at overall publication rates for each specialty in orthopaedics and found the basic-science category to score the highest, with 64% (**Table 2.2**).[2] Next to follow were spine (53%), foot-and-ankle (52%), and pediatrics (48%). Kwong et al. (2007) conducted a similar study comparing publication rates of orthopedic specialties, but focused on the anatomical areas that are most often published.[3] Their results indicated that the proximal femur had the most published research, followed by general orthopaedics, and then the tibia (**Fig. 2.2**).[3] Kwong et al. reported that 40.3% of the abstracts had a corresponding published article that they were able to find in a PubMed or Embase search.[3]

Table 2.1 Rate of publication of papers presented according to journals[2]

Journal	No. of papers (*N* = 668)	Percentage
Journal of Bone and Joint Surgery (American Volume)	161	24
Clinical Orthopaedics and Related Research	106	16
Spine	63	9
Journal of Pediatric Orthopaedics	51	8
Journal of Orthopaedic Trauma	46	7
Journal of Arthroplasty	43	6
Journal of Bone and Joint Surgery (British volume)	38	6
American Journal of Sports Medicine	35	5
Orthopaedics	19	3
Journal of Hand Surgery	15	2
Journal of Spinal Disorders	14	2
Arthroscopy	13	2
Foot and Ankle	9	1
American Journal of Orthopaedics	7	1
Journal of Orthopaedic Research	6	1
Orthopaedic Clinics of North America	5	0.7
Plastic and Reconstructive Surgery	5	0.7
All other journals	32	5

Source: Hamlet WP, Fletcher A, Meals RA. Publication patterns of papers presented at the Annual Meeting of The American Academy of Orthopaedic Surgeons. *J Bone Joint Surg Am* 1997;79(8):1138–1143. Reprinted with permission.

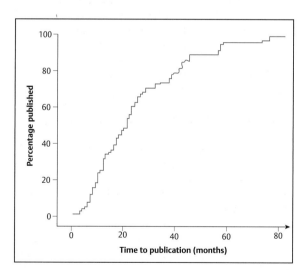

Fig. 2.1 Rate of publication of 91 oral presentations published after a congress.[3] (From Kwong Y, Kwong FNK, Patel J. Publication rate of Trauma abstracts presented at an International Orthopaedic conference. Injury 2007;38(7):745–749. Reprinted with permission.)

Table 2.2 Rate of publication of papers presented according to subspecialty[2]

Subspecialty	No. published/ no. presented	Percentage
Basic science	18/28	64
Spine	110/206	53
Foot and ankle	16/31	52
Pediatrics	95/199	48
Sports	72/150	48
Arthroplasty	218/500	44
Oncology	29/69	42
Hand	28/72	39
Trauma	82/210	39
Composite average	**668/1465**	**46**

Source: Hamlet WP, Fletcher A, Meals RA. Publication patterns of papers presented at the Annual Meeting of The American Academy of Orthopaedic Surgeons. *J Bone Joint Surg Am* 1997;79(8):1138–1143. Reprinted with permission.

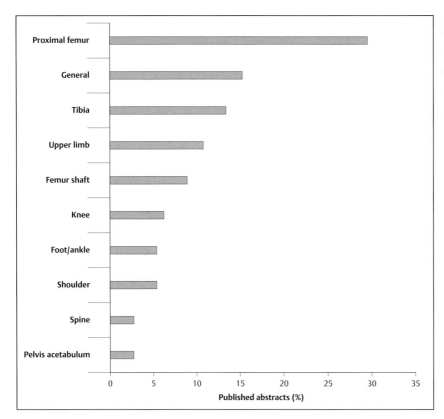

Fig. 2.2 Distribution of specialty of published abstracts (%).[3] (Data from Kwong Y, Kwong FNK, Patel J. Publication rate of Trauma abstracts presented at an International Orthopaedic conference. *Injury* 2007;38(7):745–749. Reprinted with permission.)

Sprague et al. (2006) conducted a similar study and found that 34.2% of the 465 abstracts presented at the 1996 Annual Meeting of the American Academy of Orthopaedic Surgeons were followed by the publication of a complete report, according to their Medline search.[4] This means that approximately 60% of potentially beneficial studies are either rejected by journals or discontinued by the authors. However, keep in mind that publication rates being reported in the literature are fairly low and inconsistent from year to year. The objective of this chapter is to investigate the reasons behind low publication rates and their subsequent impact on the field of scientific research. Lastly, we will make several useful recommendations to help you avoid common pitfalls in publishing a paper in the orthopaedic field.

Why Unpublished Research is a Problem

If more than 60% of all abstracts are "missing," this could pose major problems to the realm of scientific research. Publishing your research will increase the awareness of an investigator's findings, prevent publication bias, enhance the quality and creditability of the paper, and reduce the use of preliminary data from abstracts. Despite this loss, 53–63% of chapters in major orthopaedic textbooks rely solely on results from abstracts presented at international meetings.[1]

Key Concepts: Benefits of Publishing Research
1. It increases the awareness of an investigator's findings.
2. It may change clinical practice.
3. It prevents publication bias.
4. It increases the quality and creditability of the paper.
5. It helps to prevent the subsequent use of preliminary results.

The most important reasons for pursuing publication of research are to increase awareness of the investigator's research and the aim of making a difference in clinical practice. This is usually done through a journal readership, either through journal club meetings or an individual reading routine. With publication of one's results in well-known scientific journals, the research is available to more people than a scientific meetings could ever offer. Since the purpose of most orthopaedic research is to discover new treatments, to improve existing treatments, or to confirm or reject treatment ideas that already exist, the impact of these studies is of great importance to many orthopaedic surgeons and allied health professionals. Thus, it can be said that not publishing results found, however mundane the authors may believe them to be, can be unethical. Professionals in orthopaedics rely on these journals to keep up to date in their field of specialization, and often change their clinical practice according to the results of research. By not publishing significant findings, authors are withholding important information, and subsequently physicians may not be able to offer the best possible treatment for their patients, leading to suboptimal treatment policies.[5]

Prevention of publication bias is another benefit of publishing research findings. When authors' results are negative, they often believe that their findings are not as important as positive results, and fail to proceed with the publishing process. This will cause a shift in the results of meta-analyses or systematic reviews, because current data will overestimate treatment effects when not all authors publish their findings.[5] Redundant publication is becoming a major problem in orthopaedic research, as in many other surgical areas, which can be partly prevented by the proper publication of studies. Unknowing repetition of studies is a waste of time, money, and effort, which hinders the progress of scientific research. Eck et al. (2007) concluded that the rate of redundant publication in the general surgery literature is approximately 14%.[6] Luckily, this rate is a little lower in orthopaedics. The *Journal of Bone and Joint Surgery* had a 3.15% redundancy rate, the *Journal of Orthopaedic Trauma* 0%, the *Journal of Spinal Disorders* 2.9%, and *Spine* 3.12%.[6] However, these statistics only include published papers; the true redundancy rate will be much higher when unpublished research is included.

> **Jargon Simplified: Publication Bias**
> Publication bias occurs when the publication of research results depends on their nature and direction. This typically arises from the tendency for researchers and editors to handle experimental results that are positive (the authors found something) differently from results that are negative (the authors found that something did not happen) or inconclusive.

> **Jargon Simplified: Redundant Publication**
> A redundant publication is "one which duplicates previous, simultaneous, or future publications by the same author or group or, alternatively, could have been combined with the latter into one paper."[7]

When research is published in a high-quality journal, it goes through a peer-review process. This process exists to ensure that only high-quality research is being published, thus improving the creditability of published studies. The same cannot be said for abstracts presented at meetings, which is the third reason why authors should publish their results. Abstracts presented at meetings do go through a peer-review process, which provides these meetings with credibility, but this process is not nearly as rigorous as the journal publication peer-review process. Journals are much more in-depth and detailed, which allows readers to assess for themselves the validity of the

published investigations.[4] From there, the reader can make critical analyses of the impact of the study, its generalizability, and whether or not it applies to their practice or other research they are working on.

> **Jargon Simplified: Peer Review**
> Peer review is the process of subjecting an author's research work to the review of others who are experts in the same field. It is a means of screening and selecting manuscripts for publication in journals and enforcing the application of standards required for high-quality research. According to Turner (2003), "peer review depends on five core attributes: fairness in reviewing, appropriate expertise, identifiable reviewers, timely reviews, and helpful critiques."[8]

Many presentations at major orthopaedic meetings present only preliminary results, which may differ from the final results of the study.[9] Reports of studies that present only preliminary results should be interpreted cautiously. Several studies have demonstrated discrepancies between abstracts presented at meetings and final publication reports.[10] Additionally, Guryel et al. (2005) found that 19% of published reports differed in one or more aspects of study design or authorship when compared with the presented abstract.[9] The most common change was sample size (20.4%), more so with studies that had a longer lag time between their presentation and publication.[9] Other changes included authorship (16.1%) and results (10.9%) (**Table 2.3**).[9] Some changes, such as authorship, may not impact the audience's use of the information presented, however some changes—such as the results—are crucial. Abstracts at meetings do not have the same creditability as peer-reviewed published articles, and centering changes in a physician's practice on abstracts is not recommended. If no published results are reported after the abstract, the audience is left to rely on the information presented, which might have changed without them ever knowing.

Table 2.3 Consistency of data and study design between published full text articles and initial abstracts[9]

	Total number	Percentage of full text articles
Objectives	0/137	0
Design	2/137	1.5
Outcome	3/137	2.2
Sample number	28/137	20.4
Analysis	4/137	2.9
Results	15/137	10.9
Authorship	22/137	16.1

Source: Guryel E, Durrant AW, Alakeson R, Ricketts DM. From presentation to publication: the natural history of orthopaedics abstracts in the United Kingdom. *Postgrad Med J* 2006;82 (963):70–72. Reprinted with permission.

Orthopaedics versus Other Specialties

As already indicated, orthopaedic research currently has a problem with unpublished research, but what about other types of medical research? Peng et al. (2006) conducted a study comparing publication rates among various surgical specialties and found that most specialties had similar publication rates.[11] Orthopaedics had an average of approximately 48%, which was similar to those of otolaryngology (approximately 51%), anesthesiology (50%), pediatrics (44%), and family medicine (48%) (**Table 2.4**).[11] Ophthalmology had a slightly higher average publication rate of approximately 59%. However, some other areas, including gastrointestinal and emergency medicine and radiology, have lower publication rates. As you can see, orthopaedic research does not particularly stand out among other specialties, but this only means that the problem is consistent throughout medicine. Fortunately, studies have been done looking into why this occurs, and

from here on, recommendations can be made in attempts to increase publication rates.

Why Papers Don't Get Published

There are two major reasons why papers don't get published: (1) authors do not submit their manuscripts for publication, or (2) authors submit their manuscripts for publication but they are rejected by the journals. Sprague et al. (2003) reviewed this topic and found that only 63% of authors submitted manuscripts for publication (**Table 2.5**).[4] This means that approximately 37% of authors did not even attempt to get their papers published. This section looks into the reasons why authors are not submitting their manuscripts, and at some of the major factors that result in rejection of manuscripts.

Table 2.4 Comparison of publication rates among annual meetings of medical and surgical specialties[11]

Author (year)	Specialty	Society meeting	Year(s)	Publication rate (%)
Peng (2005)	Otolaryngology	AAO-HNS annual meeting	1999	52
Larian (2001)	Otolaryngology	AAO-HNS annual meeting	1993–1995	32
Roy (2001)	Otolaryngology	Otorhinolaryngological Research Society	1978–1995	69
Scherer (1994)	Ophthalmology	American Academy of Ophthalmology	1988-1989	61
		Association of Research in Vision and Ophthalmology		
Juzych (1991)	Ophthalmology	Association of Research in Vision and Ophthalmology	1985	57
		American Academy of Ophthalmology	1984	64
Bhandari (2002)	Orthopaedics	American Academy of Orthopaedic Surgeons	1996	34
Yoo (2002)	Orthopaedics	American Orthopaedic Society for Sports Medicine	1990–1994	68
		Arthroscopy Association of North America	1990–1994	51
Jackson (2000)	Orthopaedics	Pediatric Orthopaedic Society of North America	1991–1994	45
Hamlet (1997)	Orthopaedics	American Academy of Orthopaedic Surgeons	1990–1992	46
Yentis (1993)	Anesthesiology	American Society of Anesthesiologists	1985	50
		International Anesthesiology Research Society		
		Anaesthesia Research Society Canadian Anaesthetists' Society		
Li (2004)	Emergency Medicine	Society of Academic Emergency Medicine	1999–2001	38
Carrol (2003)	Pediatrics	Pediatric Academic Society Meeting	1989–1999	44
Eloubeidi (2001)	Gastrointestinal	American Society of Gastrointestinal Endoscopy	1994	25
Elder (1994)	Family Medicine	Society of Teachers of Family Medicine	1988	48
		North American Primary Research Group		
Marx (1999)	Radiology	American Society of Neuroradiology	1993	37
		Radiology Society of North America	1993	33

Source: Peng PH, Wasserman JM, Rosenfeld RM. Factors influencing publication of abstracts presented at the AAO-HNS Annual Meeting. *Otolaryngol Head Neck Surg* 2006;135(2):197–203. Reprinted with permission.

Table 2.5 Publication status of the research at 5 years after abstract presentation[4]

Status of research	No. of respondents (%)
Published	36.2
Accepted for publication (in press)	3.5
Under consideration by a journal	7.0
Submitted but rejected	16.1
Never submitted for publication	35.7
Not recalled by investigator	1.5

Source: Sprague S, Bhandari M, Devereaux PJ, et al. Barriers to full-text publication following presentation of abstracts at annual orthopaedic meetings. *J Bone Joint Surg Am* 2003;85(1):158–163. Reprinted with permission.

Authors Who Don't Submit for Publication

Failure of surgeons to submit manuscripts to journals for publication is the most commonly reported reason why publication rates are so low after presentations at meetings. There are various reasons for this, the most common being lack of available time and resources.[3–5,12,13] Most researchers in orthopaedics are surgeons who have a clinical practice as well as an interest in research. Because of this, many orthopaedic surgeons start projects, progress to the presentation stage, but find it too time-consuming to submit a final manuscript. Thus, due to time constraints, they are prone not to publish their findings. Also, funding can become an issue, and many authors reported that a lack of resources is a barrier to full-text publication.[3,5,13] In fact, Kyzyzanowska et al. (2003) demonstrated that external funding was associated with a higher probability of full-text publication.[5] Sponsorship is also a significant predictor of publication rates and the time needed for a paper to be published. Studies have shown that papers are published sooner when associated with major sponsorship such as that by large pharmaceutical companies.[5] Furthermore, investigators who practice at academic centers achieved better success then those who were not affiliated with them, with a difference in publication rate of 76% to 17%, respectively.[4] This may be due to funding or to other benefits, such as a recognizable name and reputation.

Even when an author of a paper manages his or her time appropriately, other barriers may get in the way of submitting a manuscript. Problems with coauthors are another commonly reported reason for failure to publish or for delay in publication of full-text papers.[3,4,12,13] Sprague et al. (2003) found that 19.7% of the researchers they surveyed reported that responsibility for writing a manuscript belonged to a coauthor, which is why their manuscript had yet to be submitted to a journal.[4] Coauthor difficulties are further demonstrated by the number of author changes found between presentation and publication. Approxi-

mately 60% of all final full-text publications indicated different authors during presentation at meetings.[4] When problems arise among co-investigators, project roles are disturbed and possible work time is wasted. It therefore becomes very inefficient for all parties involved when the research team does not work well together, and ultimately contributes to a lower publication rate.

Abstract meetings are useful for authors to present their current work and get opinions from peers in their profession. However, negative responses from a meeting may lead to pessimism about one's chances of having a manuscript accepted by a journal, causing many researchers to decide not to submit their research to publishers. Weber and colleagues (1998) found that 20% of the researchers who failed to submit manuscripts did so because they believed that their papers were unlikely to be accepted by journals.[12] Many of these researchers had not been accepted to present their abstract at a meeting, which may discourage these workers from continuing their research. Interesting, though, was the finding that researchers from institutions ranking higher in federal grant dollars experienced this more often than those from lower-ranking institutions. It appears that researchers from high-ranking institutions may feel greater pressure to produce high-quality papers; if they believe they are going to be rejected by a journal, they may choose to not submit one at all to avoid possible embarrassment.

Another common belief is that negative results do not get published as often as positive results. Because of this, 4% of authors in Weber et al.'s study,[12] and 4.2% in Sprague et al.'s study,[4] did not submit their findings; this is a problem because it skews meta-analysis and systematic reviews, leading to an overestimation of treatment effects.[5] To abolish any existing myths, study outcomes (positive or negative) were actually found to have no effect on publication rates.[13] Some researchers also believe that their results are not important enough to publish (1.4%) or that they have insufficient interest to readers (1.4%), resulting in fewer submissions for full-text publication.[4] In addition, some researchers discover part way through their project that studies or findings similar to their own work have already been published (4.2%).[4] Overall, these factors lead to nonsubmission of manuscripts, which can at times be easily avoided.

There is considerable pressure on developing orthopaedic surgeons to conduct research and present their findings at meetings. Presenting abstracts gives surgeons in training more exposure and improves their chances of progressing to a higher level of medical training. However, when this happens, surgeons tend to lose their desire to continue with their publication because they are by then undergoing higher surgical training and no longer place as much emphasis on their earlier findings.[3] Another common complaint is that the peer-review process of publication is too slow and time-consuming, and that it hinders the free flow of information.[3] Surgeons presenting their investigation at scientific meetings have the tendency to move on to another study without ever publishing their findings because of this slowness of the peer-review process. This is, of course, problematic since some reviewers of abstracts are unqualified, and may interpret or bias the investigators' findings incorrectly.[3]

Lastly, many of the studies looking at the reason for non-publication of research found that authors were not at the stage to submit because the study was still ongoing. Most articles that reviewed the issue of publication rates allowed authors at least 5 years to submit a manuscript to a journal after presentation at a meeting.[3] This is more than sufficient, since most studies are published only 2 years after presentation. Nonetheless, longer ongoing studies can arise due to continued entry of patients into a study protocol, extended periods of data analysis, or continued revision of the final manuscript.[4] Whatever the reason, prolonged publication time is associated with lower priority, which then results in fewer publications.[4]

Key Concepts: Reason Why Researchers Don't Submit Their Manuscripts to Journals
1. Lack of available time and resources.
2. Problems with coauthors.
3. Pessimism about chances of publication.
4. Findings are negative, results are not important, or results are not contributing something new to the field.
5. Surgical trainees' lack of commitment after progress to higher training.
6. Slow peer-review process.
7. The study is still ongoing.

Articles Rejected for Publication

Approximately 63% of the researchers who responded to the questionnaire of Sprague et al. (2003) had submitted an article to a journal for publication; however, 25% of these articles were rejected.[4] Several investigators have looked into the reasons for rejection of manuscripts submitted to scientific journals. Bordage (2001) discussed the reasons for rejection as well as reasons for acceptance. They reported that the top reasons for rejection of manuscripts were inappropriate or incomplete statistics, over-interpretation of results, small sample size, confusing text, and inaccuracies or inconsistencies in the reporting of data.[14] Typically journals accept high-quality manuscripts and the characteristics of these manuscripts include focusing on important and relevant problems, having a valid design, being well written, and including an up-to-date review of the literature. Pierson (2004) also investigated the reasons for manuscript rejection and after reviewing the literature and came up with his top reasons for manuscript rejection.[15] The reasons are discussed in the following sections.

Failure to Revise and Resubmit after Peer Review

The peer review process can seem ruthless to many authors, but it is of the utmost importance. The peer review process ensures that each article conveys its message accurately, unambiguously, and as convincingly as possible.[15] All manuscripts submitted to a journal go through a peer-review process, and almost all are returned to the author with comments for improvement. The majority of published manuscripts have been substantially improved as result of peer-review comments, but not all authors revise their work. Submitting manuscripts without revision can lead to a high chance of rejection. When resubmitting a manuscript, authors should indicate the peer reviewer's comments and whether or not each of these revisions has been addressed.[15]

Poor Study Design

Poor study design is a fatal flaw once the manuscript has been written. Study design must be addressed at the time the research is planned, not during data manipulation or the writing process. Poor study design consists of using the wrong model or study design, collecting data in a manner that would not allow a meaningful examination of the hypothesis, or making too few measurements to permit confident conclusions to be drawn.[15]

A very interesting study done by Peng et al. (2006) looked into specific factors related to a study's design and publication rates specific to each of these factors. The complete analysis of these results is summarized in **Table 2.6**.[11] Some key findings from this study include a positive association between success of publication and the use of statistical analysis, any research award received, and presence of a control group.[11] Also demonstrated was that increased publication rate correlates with oral presentation, and the number of authors involved. Although not significantly, more level 1 and 2 studies were published when compared with levels 3 and 4. Many of these factors contribute to the fact that most of the studies published are of complex study designs, with multicenter studies and increased sample size.[11] These studies are typically higher-level studies, with many authors, and a definite control group. This shows the importance of good study design when publishing your paper.

Jargon Simplified: Level of Evidence for Therapeutic Studies
Level 1
- High-quality randomized controlled trial with statistically significant difference or no statistically significant but narrow confidence intervals

Level 2
- Lesser-quality randomized controlled trial (e.g., <80% follow-up, no blinding, or improper randomization)
- Prospective comparative study

Level 3
- Case–control study
- Retrospective comparative study

Level 4
- Case series

Table 2.6 **Bivariate analysis of factors related to publication status for 388 abstracts[11]**

Factor	Level	Publication status	
		Unpublished (%)	Published (%)
Presentation type	Oral	37	63
	Poster	61	39
Authors	Mean (SD)	1.3	1.4
Sample size	Median (IQR)	52	79
Direction of inquiry	Retrospective	59	41
	Prospective	42	58
	Cross-sectional	44	56
Control group	Present	39	61
	Absent	56	44
Statistical analysis	Present	33	67
	Absent	59	41
Level of evidence	Level 1	35	65
	Level 2	38	62
	Level 3	52	48
	Level 4	61	39
	Level 5	33	67
Case report	Yes	74	26
	No	46	54
Grant support	Yes	32	68
	No	52	48
Research award	Yes	10	90
	No	51	49
Reported outcome	Positive	44	56
	Negative	50	50

CI, confidence interval, IQR, interquartile range, SD, standard deviation.
Source: Peng PH, Wasserman JM, Rosenfeld RM. Factors influencing publication of abstracts presented at the AAO-HNS Annual Meeting. *Otolaryngol Head Neck Surg* 2006;135(2):197–203. Reprinted with permission.

Lack of New or Useful Knowledge

Ehara and Takahashi (2007) conducted a study looking at the reasons for manuscript rejection among various countries and found that anywhere from 44% to 76% of all rejections were due to a lack of new or useful knowledge.[16] This includes a lack of clinical relevance, or old knowledge with no new or useful material. Determining the benefit of the research should be one of the first things done when beginning a research project; research cannot enhance and benefit the state of knowledge in a field if it does not provide an explanation to an as yet unanswered question.

Inadequate Description of the Methods

Inadequate description of the methods used is often responsible for outright rejection of a manuscript.[15] This typically means a lack of description of what was done in the study. Specifically in orthopaedics, failure to provide sufficient detail of the selection of patients for an operative procedure is a common pitfall for authors. The Methods section should be clear and concise, and needs to indicate exactly what patient inclusion and exclusion principles were used when recruiting patients, and how are they justified in answering the research question.[17]

The reader should be able to repeat the study if desired, so study design, apparatus used, and procedures followed must be made clear.[15] A diagram, photograph, or survey instrument is also recommended.

Suboptimal Reporting of Results

The most common mistake authors make in reporting results is slipping interpretive comments into the Results section of the manuscript.[15] The Results section is there to report straightforward documentation of what was found, with no summarization of percentages or generalizations. The most effective way to present results is through a table or figure.

Getting Carried Away with the Discussion

The importance of the Discussion section is to explain what the results of the study mean.[15] Authors often get carried away and begin to overemphasize the importance of their work. The discussion should be used to explain how the findings fit in with previous work, point out limitations, and speculate cautiously how the results may extend current understanding.[15]

Poor Writing

Scientific context is cognitively demanding of the reader, and thus the writing style of the author should be simple and concise. Many authors think they have to impress their readers with flowery or deliberately complicated writing. In actuality this will be detrimental to the author in the end, when readers are having a hard time understanding the paper.[15] Poor writing prevents readers from understanding and grasping the author's message, which contradicts the purpose journals serve in our scientific community.

Not Following Instructions

Each journal has specific guidelines for submission, but many authors fail to use this guide and submit unacceptable manuscripts. Many authors' manuscripts may not even be read if required items are missing, wasting the editor's time but even more the author's time. Even when all requirements are present, improper formatting compared with the journal's requirements may also result in immediate rejection of a manuscript.

Submitting to the Wrong Journal

Each journal has a specific area that it reports on, and submitting a manuscript with a topic outside of a journal's range is an automatic invitation to rejection.

> **Key Concepts: Reasons Why Articles May Be Rejected**
> 1. Failure to revise and resubmit after peer review.
> 2. Poor study design.
> 3. Lack of new or useful knowledge.
> 4. Inadequate description of the methods.
> 5. Suboptimal reporting of results.
> 6. Getting carried away in the discussion.
> 7. Poor writing.
> 8. Not following the journal's own specific instructions.
> 9. Submitting to am inappropriate journal.

Recommendations

There are many factors that can enhance publication rates. The following section provides several recommendations that can be implemented by authors to improve publication rates.

Define Adequate Clinical Research Times to Make Timeline Goals

The most commonly reported reason for not submitting manuscripts to journals is a lack of time.[3–5,12,13] When deciding to do research, it is important to plan out your timeline wisely. Each investigator should have a set of realistic goals for different stages of their research. The key factor to reaching these goals is determining how much time should be spent away from clinical responsibilities, to focus solely on research.[4] Depending on the author, the overall daily time devoted to research and writing could be as little as 10%, or as much as 80%. It is up to the author to determine what is adequate for himself or herself, and to follow through with it. It is recommended that the author plan specific writing times or days to prepare a manuscript effectively in a timely manner. Getting help from other surgeons is also common, especially if that surgeon is specialized in a specific area of the manuscript.

Plan and Maintain a Budget

Before starting a project, an investigator should know exactly how much it is going to cost to complete the planned research, and where the funding will be coming from. Common areas of financial resource include, but are not limited to, government grants, industry sponsorship, and foundation/association grants. All authors should arrange with their sponsor when and how they will receive their funding, so that investigators are not stopped part way through due to an insufficient budget.

Assemble a Good Team

Difficulty with coauthors was a frequently given reason why authors had not submitted manuscripts to journals.[4] A group of co-investigators with common goals and commitment to the completion of the research is crucial to avoiding complications down the road. It is also important to define each investigator's role and responsibility before the project begins, to limit confusion. Predetermining an authorship guideline is the most effective way of doing this. Each author is aware of their responsibilities before agreeing to help in the study, which helps to minimize problems later.

Ensure a Methodologically Sound Research Paper

Manuscripts should be methodologically sound, with adequate detail regarding the methods and the reported outcomes. Remember, level 1, high-quality randomized controlled trials are more likely to be published than level 4 case series on the same topic.[11] Therefore, ensure that your study design is addressed at the beginning and that the most appropriate type is chosen for your best interest. The commonest ways to avoid design flaws are by knowing what the literature on your topic says, by seeking advice from experts, and by consulting a biostatistician.

Key Concepts: Benefits of a Biostatistician

Including a biostatistician or someone with formal research methodology training is the easiest and best way to ensure the manuscript is sound. They should assist the author from the beginning of the initial protocol to the final manuscript, making sure all areas are covered. Ensuring adequate sample size, units of analysis, and determinants of both clinical importance and statistical significance are the responsibilities of a biostatistician.

Submit Properly to an Appropriate Journal

Submission to the wrong journal or not following instructions are common reasons for rejection that can easily be avoided. Reading the journal to which submission is planned will give an author a sample of what material is typically published in the journal. From there, he or she can assess whether their manuscript is appropriate for this journal. Once a journal is chosen, authors should read the guidelines on formatting and review the submission requirements to ensure they are meeting all mandatory requests.

Conduct a Thorough Review of the Literature

A study has shown that 44–76% of authors find prior to submission of their manuscripts that their findings will not contribute any new knowledge to the literature.[16] Review of the literature is an extremely important step in research, and can be very beneficial to the investigators' current research as well. Not only is it useful to make sure that the study will add new and important information, but it can also be used to establish the context of the study as well as a sound methodology.[4]

Avoid Presenting Preliminary Data

Many studies were still ongoing 5 years after their presentation at a major orthopaedic meeting, and this was most often because only preliminary results were ready for presentation at the time of the meeting. This causes great discrepancies between the presentation and the published results, which is generally not recommended. Therefore, avoid presenting preliminary data at meetings, and instead wait until all subjects have been enrolled and concrete data are established before making findings public. Research meetings should only accept completed research for presentation, to avoid this problem altogether.

Reduce Pressure on Surgical Trainees to Publish

As mentioned earlier, there is a lot of pressure on surgical trainees to publish data and get their name known. Unfortunately, this results in many papers being incomplete when these trainees move on to higher surgical training and have no time to finish manuscripts. Therefore, it is recommended that pressure on these individuals to publish should be reduced. If trainees do choose to investigate with a research group, they should remain as a co-investigator, letting other investigators who have a strong interest in the study take over when the trainees move on to higher surgical training. In this way, trainees gain experience with publication, but no studies are left on the shelf, forgotten.

Key Concepts: Recommendations for Increasing Publication Rates

1. Define adequate clinical and research time to make timeline goals.
2. Plan and maintain a budget.
3. Assemble a good team (coauthors).
4. Ensure a methodologically sound research paper.
5. Submit properly to an appropriate journal.
6. Conduct a thorough review of the literature.
7. Avoid presenting preliminary data.
8. Reduce pressure on surgical trainees to publish.

Conclusion

Knowledge of why publication rates are low will hopefully aid researchers in avoiding the common errors outlined in this chapter. Through proper research techniques, we can anticipate an increase in orthopaedic publication rates. Thus, by taking the first step to prepare high-quality protocols and manuscripts, we can expect to change the trend of orthopaedic publication rates. The next chapters will discuss how this can be done.

Suggested Reading

Cowell HR. Preparing manuscripts for publication in The Journal of Bone and Joint Surgery: responsibilities of authors and editors. A view from the editor of the American volume. J Bone Joint Surg Am 1993;75(3):456–463

Peng PH, Wasserman JM, Rosenfeld RM. Factors influencing publication of abstracts presented at the AAO-HNS Annual Meeting. Otolaryngol Head Neck Surg 2006;135(2):197–203

Pierson DJ. The top 10 reasons why manuscripts are not accepted for publication. Respir Care 2004;49(10):1246–1252

Sprague S, Bhandari M, Devereaux PJ, et al. Barriers to full-text publication following presentation of abstracts at annual orthopaedic meetings. J Bone Joint Surg Am 2003;85-A(1):158–163

References

1. Bhandari M, Devereaux PJ, Guyatt GH, et al. An observational study of orthopaedic abstracts and subsequent full-text publications. J Bone Joint Surg Am 2002;84-A(4):615–621
2. Hamlet WP, Fletcher A, Meals RA. Publication patterns of papers presented at the Annual Meeting of The American Academy of Orthopaedic Surgeons. J Bone Joint Surg Am 1997;79(8):1138–1143
3. Kwong Y, Kwong FNK, Patel J. Publication rate of Trauma abstracts presented at an International Orthopaedic conference. Injury 2007;38(7):745–749
4. Sprague S, Bhandari M, Devereaux PJ, et al. Barriers to full-text publication following presentation of abstracts at annual orthopaedic meetings. J Bone Joint Surg Am 2003;85-A(1):158–163
5. Krzyzanowska MK, Pintilie M, Tannock IF. Factors associated with failure to publish large randomized trials presented at an oncology meeting. JAMA 2003;290(4):495–501
6. Eck JC, Nachtigall D, Hodges SD, Humphreys SC. Redundant publications in the orthopedic literature. Orthopedics 2007;30(1):60–62
7. Schein M, Paladugu R. Redundant surgical publications: tip of the iceberg? Surgery 2001;129(6):655–661
8. Turner L. Promoting F.A.I.T.H. in peer review: five core attributes of effective peer review. J Acad Ethics 2003;1(2):181–188
9. Guryel E, Durrant AW, Alakeson R, Ricketts DM. From presentation to publication: the natural history of orthopaedic abstracts in the United Kingdom. Postgrad Med J 2006;82(963):70–72
10. Smith WA, Cancel QV, Tseng TY, Sultan S, Vieweg J, Dahm P. Factors associated with the full publication of studies presented in abstract form at the annual meeting of the American Urological Association. J Urol 2007;177(3):1084–1088, discussion 1088–1089
11. Peng PH, Wasserman JM, Rosenfeld RM. Factors influencing publication of abstracts presented at the AAO-HNS Annual Meeting. Otolaryngol Head Neck Surg 2006;135(2):197–203
12. Weber EJ, Callaham ML, Wears RL, Barton C, Young G. Unpublished research from a medical specialty meeting: why investigators fail to publish. JAMA 1998;280(3):257–259
13. Sanossian N, Ohanian AG, Saver JL, Kim LI, Ovbiagele B. Frequency and determinants of nonpublication of research in the stroke literature. Stroke 2006;37(10):2588–2592
14. Bordage G. Reasons reviewers reject and accept manuscripts: the strengths and weaknesses in medical education reports. Acad Med 2001;76(9):889–896
15. Pierson DJ. The top 10 reasons why manuscripts are not accepted for publication. Respir Care 2004;49(10):1246–1252
16. Ehara S, Takahashi K. Reasons for rejection of manuscripts submitted to AJR by international authors. AJR Am J Roentgenol 2007;188(2):W113–6
17. Cowell HR. Preparing manuscripts for publication in The Journal of Bone and Joint Surgery: responsibilities of authors and editors. A view from the editor of the American volume. J Bone Joint Surg Am 1993;75(3):456–463

3

What is the Quality of the Published Orthopaedic Literature?

Daniel Vena, Sheila Sprague

Summary

This chapter begins by introducing the concept of evidence-based medicine and relating it to quality orthopaedic literature. An important differentiation is made between the quality of reporting and the quality of the trial. We look at how study designs can be ranked based on a hierarchy of evidence. Evaluation of study quality is explained through the description of three currently used quality assessment tools: the Detsky scale, the Jadad scale, and the CONSORT statement, as well as brief descriptions of other systems. The chapter finishes off with summaries of current quality assessment endeavors by different groups, all using the different quality assessment tools mentioned, to provide an idea of what quality orthopaedic literature exhibits according to the criteria given in each scale.

Introduction

To make appropriate clinical decisions about patient care, orthopaedic surgeons should use the highest-quality evidence that is available. Unfortunately, orthopaedic surgeons have traditionally relied on lower levels of evidence, such as case series and expert opinion pieces, to make important clinical decisions.

The process of integrating a practitioner's clinical knowledge and judgment with the best available evidence is known as evidence-based medicine (EBM).[1] To practice EBM properly, a clinician must formulate clinical questions relevant to the clinical decision to be made, acquire information regarding the clinical questions via a literature search, appraise the quality of the acquired literature, apply the results that qualified according to the quality criteria to the clinical situation, and finally, act on what was learned on the patient or clinical issue.[2]

To create reliable studies that orthopaedic surgeons may use to assist in their practice, investigators must ensure they are producing high-quality research with quality evidence. The higher the quality, the less the bias, and the more confidence orthopaedic surgeons will have in applying the results of the study to their patients. If quality reporting is practiced by all investigators, it will allow for a simpler and more successful decision-making process among orthopaedic surgeons.[3]

The purpose of this chapter is to review the quality of published orthopaedic literature and discuss its significance. Additionally, the chapter will outline some of the tools for critical appraisal of medical scientific literature. With this background knowledge, you will develop an appreciation for high-quality orthopaedic research and, it is hoped, motivation to practice it in reporting and trial design in your own future research.

> **Key Concepts: High-Quality Evidence**
> High-quality evidence is what must guide orthopaedic surgeons in their practice. The use of high-quality evidence has implications not only for future research but also for the welfare of patients.

Quality of the Trial versus Quality of the Published Report

It is important to differentiate between the actual quality of a trial and the quality of its reporting in a published article. The quality of the trial is of primary interest, sometimes referred to as the scientific quality, and it may be defined as the likelihood of the trial design to generate unbiased results and approach the therapeutic truth.[4] This definition focuses on the *methodological* quality of the study.[5]

Quality reporting may be defined as providing information on the trial design, conduct, and analysis to the reader.[5] Quality *of* reporting moves away from the information contained within the report and toward assessing the completeness of the reporting.[6] This allows the reader to evaluate the methodology of a trial and determine whether the results can be applied to their patients.

Assessing the Study Design

To determine which evidence qualifies as being of the highest quality, there is a system that places evidence into appropriate rankings. This is referred to as a hierarchy of evidence, which is primarily based on research design.[2]

Determining the type of study is the first step in placing a study into a hierarchy of evidence. **Randomized controlled trials** (RCTs) are considered the highest level of evidence and **case series** are toward the bottom of the hierar-

Table 3.1 Strengths and weaknesses of different study designs[3]

Study design	Observational				Randomized
	Case report	Case series	Case control	Cohort	RCT
Strengths	Description of general characteristics and distribution of disease		Can calculate or estimate odds ratios and relative risk		Control for known and unknown variables
	Description of complications associated with surgical treatment		Can assess outcomes with multiple etiologic factors		Blinding
	Provide information of rare disease entities or associations		Can do studies in short time and inexpensively		More accurate estimate of truth
	May be hypothesis-generating				
Weaknesses	Retrospective		Recall bias		Difficult to randomize some surgical interventions
	Inherent biases in study methodology may over- or underestimate the truth		Measurement bias		Unable to blind treating surgeon to intervention
	Nongeneralizable		No control over unknown variables		May need very large number, necessitating involvement of numerous centers

Source: Petrisor BA, Keating J, Schemitsch E. Grading the evidence: levels of evidence and grades of recommendation. *Injury* 2006;37 (4):321–327. Reprinted with permission.

chy. Bounded by these upper and lower limits of study designs are **case–control** and **cohort design**. **Table 3.1** describes the strengths and weaknesses of each type of study design.[3]

Jargon Simplified: Study Design
- **Randomized controlled trial (RCT)**—"Experiment in which individuals are randomly allocated to receive or not receive an experimental preventative, therapeutic, or diagnostic procedure and then followed to determine the effect of the intervention."[2]
- **Meta-analysis RCT**—"An overview that incorporates a quantitative strategy for combining the results of several studies into a single pooled or summary estimate."[2] The studies included in this type of meta-analysis are high-quality RCTs.
- **Case–control study**—"A study designed to determine the association between an exposure and outcome in which patients are sampled by outcome (that is, some patients with the outcome of interest are selected and compared to a group of patients who have not had the outcome), and the investigator examines the proportion of patients with the exposure in the two groups."[2]
- **Cohort study**—"Prospective investigation of the factors that might cause a disorder in which a cohort of individuals who do not have evidence of an outcome of interest but who are exposed to the putative cause are compared with a concurrent cohort who are also free of the outcome but not exposed to the putative cause. Both cohorts are then followed to compare the incidence of the outcome of interest."[2]
- **Case series**—"A study reporting on a consecutive collection of patients treated in a similar manner, without a control group. For example, a surgeon might describe the characteristics of an outcome for 100 consecutive patients with cerebral ischemia who received a revascularization procedure."[2]

The quality of literature is also important for meta-analyses. Rigorous methodologies are often formulated for the conduct of an effective meta-analysis. These methodologies can go to waste if quality research is not utilized. A common response from researchers regarding meta-analysis is skepticism about combining results from numerous poorly designed and poorly conducted studies. Methodological flaws of individual poor-quality studies may be hidden behind the methodology employed in the meta-analysis, making the unreliability of those studies hard to identify.[7]

While each design is important in its own way, when it comes to conducting a quality orthopaedic trial to aid in clinical decision making, the most trustworthy are high-quality RCTs. The RCT decreases bias by controlling for known and unknown prognostic variables and is known as the trial that is "the least likely to be wrong."[8] The remainder of this chapter focuses on RCTs and the scales and checklists presented in this chapter are for assessing quality of RCTs since they often produce the highest-quality evidence with the least bias.

Key Concepts: Quality of Literature
Study design alone does not give an accurate indication of the quality. A randomized controlled trial with poor reporting and methods can have less reliable outcomes than some high-quality cohort studies.
The most reliable research is high-quality RCTs or meta-analyses of RCTs that use high-quality homogeneous RCTs.

Assessing the Study Quality

To assess a study's quality, one must look not only at the design of the study but also at the methodology used by the researcher. A study whose methodology displays rigor and transparency will often represent the truth most accurately. Several scales exist to assess the methodologies and provide a score based on randomization, statistical analysis, blinding, concealment, intention-to-treat principle, and other aspects of the study. The scales presented provide insight as to what a report must include to qualify as being of quality. Detsky presents a scale in checklist format to assess the methodology of an RCT and other study designs[7]; Jadad's scale reviews the study by using a series of questions,[9] and the CONSORT statement provides a checklist and flow diagram guiding the author on how to effectively report a methodology and the study results.[10]

Jargon Simplified: Assessing the Study Quality

- **Concealment**—"Randomization is concealed if the person who is making the decision about enrolling a patient is unaware of whether the next patient enrolled will be entered in the treatment or control group. If randomization was not concealed, patients with better prognoses may tend to be preferentially enrolled in the active treatment arm resulting in exaggeration of the apparent benefit of therapy (or even falsely concluding that treatment is efficacious)."[2]
- **Blinding**—"The participant of interest is unaware of whether patients have been assigned to the experimental or control group. Patients, clinicians, those monitoring outcomes, judicial assessors of outcomes, data analysts, and those writing the paper can all be blinded or masked. To avoid confusion the term *masked* is preferred in studies in which vision loss of patients is an outcome of interest."[2]
- **Intention-to-treat principle**—"Analyzing patient outcomes based on the group into which they were randomized regardless of whether they actually received the planned intervention. This analysis preserves the power of randomization, thus maintaining that important unknown factors that influence outcome are likely equally distributed in each comparison group."[2]

Reality Check: Intention to Treat

The systematic omission of specific patients from their assigned treatments can detrimentally influence the effect of randomization. After randomization, the patients should ideally receive the treatment they were randomized to. If the patient is randomized to the control arm, in which case there is no treatment, they should not receive the treatment.[11]

There are situations where a patient is randomized to the treatment, but is excluded because of a technical difficulty that does not allow for the treatment to take place. Technical difficulties can be that the patient is too sick, or is suffering from the outcome of interest already (for example, stroke, deep venous thrombosis). Excluding these patients makes the treatment appear better than it actually is, since the patients who are more sick, and difficult to work with, are all being excluded.[11] Instead these patients should be treated depending on what they are randomly allocated to, thereby creating an equal distribution of unknown prognostic factors in the treatment and control arms.[11]

Detsky Scale

The Detsky quality assessment index originated from concerns regarding variation of the quality of individual studies being included in meta-analysis research. The index presented in **Table 3.2** was generated while assessing RCTs; however, Detsky and his colleagues "believe many of the principles are generalizable overviews of epidemiological and clinical studies using other designs."[7]

The Detsky quality index is a 15-item index created to assess the methodological quality of a study. It contains a variety of questions in the following critical categories:
1. Randomization.
2. Outcome measures.
3. Eligibility criteria and reasons for patient exclusion.
4. Interventions.
5. Statistical issues.

Each category is given an equal weighting of 4 points; the final category contains one extra question for negative trials (those in which the findings were found to be insignificant): Were confidence intervals or post hoc power calculations performed? Therefore, studies are scored out of 20 or 21 for positive or negative trials, respectively.[7] It is also important to note that the Detsky scale does not measure literary quality, importance, relevance, originality, or other attributes of the trial.[12]

Jadad Scale

Jadad and his colleagues also developed an instrument to assess quality of clinical trials (**Table 3.3**).[9] The aims of the instrument are to assess the scientific quality of any clinical trial in which pain is an outcome measure or in which analgesic interventions are compared for outcomes other than pain, as well as to allow for the consistent and reliable assessment of quality by raters with different backgrounds for judging purposes. It was stated at the end of the paper, however, that, due to the general nature of the final quality assessment tool, it may be adapted for use on any RCT and not just those on pain. An example of this adaptation is described below in the section summarizing the quality assessment study performed by Gummesson et al.[15] A rigorous methodology was employed to deter-

Table 3.2 Detsky quality scale for randomized trials[7]

1	(a)	Were patients assigned to treatments randomly		Yes
				No
	(b)	Description of randomization		Adequate
				Partial
				Inadequate
	(c)	Do you believe there could have been bias in treatment assignment (e.g., if clinicians were not blind to treatment assignment before enrolling patient in trial?)		Yes
				No
2	(a)	Was there a description of the criteria for measuring outcomes?		Yes
				No
	(b)	Were the criteria objective?		Yes
				Partial
				No
	(c)	Were the outcome assessors blind to treatment received		Yes
				No
3	(a)	Were the inclusion/exclusion criteria clearly defined?		Yes
				Partial
				No
	(b)	Do we know how many patients were excluded in the trial (not enrolled for logistical reasons, refused consent, not eligible)?		Yes
				Partial
				No
4	(a)	Was the therapeutic regimen fully described for the treatment group?		Yes
				Partial
				No
	(b)	Was the therapeutic regimen fully described for the control group?		Yes
				Partial
				No
5	(a)	Is there a statistical analysis?	Test stated	Yes
				No
			p-value	Yes
				No
	(b)	Is the statistical analysis appropriate?		Yes
				Partial
				No
	(c)	If the trial is negative, were confidence intervals or post-hoc power calculations performed?		Yes
				No
				N/A
	(d)	Was there a sample size justification before the study?		Yes
				No

Source: Detsky AS, Naylor DC, O'Rourke K, et al. Incorporating variations in the quality of individual randomized trials into meta-analysis. *J Clin Epidemiol.* 1992;45(3):255–265. Reprinted with permission.

Table 3.3 Jadad quality scale[9]

Instrument to Measure the Likelihood of Bias in Pain Research Reports

This is not the same as being asked to review a paper. It should not take more than 10 minutes to score a report and there are no right or wrong answers.

Please read the article and try to answer the following questions (see attached instructions)

1. Was the study described as randomized (this includes the use of words such as randomly, random, and randomization)?

2. Was the study described as double blind?

3. Was there a description of withdrawals and dropouts?

Scoring the items

Either give a score of 1 point for each "yes" or 0 points for each "no." There are no in-between marks

Give 1 additional point if:	For question 1, the method to generate the sequence of randomization was described **and** it was **appropriate** (table of random numbers, computer generated, etc.)
and/or	If for question 2, the method of double blinding was described **and** it was **appropriate** (identical placebo, active placebo, dummy, etc.)
Deduct 1 point if:	For question 1, the method to generate the sequence of randomization was described **and** it was **inappropriate** (patients were allocated alternately, or according to date of birth, hospital number, etc.)
and/or	For question 2, the study was described as double blind but the method of blinding was **inappropriate** (e.g., comparison of tablet versus injection with no double dummy)

Source: Jadad AR, Moore RA, Carroll D, et al. Assessing the quality of reports of randomized clinical trials: is blinding necessary? *Control Clin Trials* 1996;17(1):1–12. Reprinted with permission.

mine a suitable scale for assessing quality. It involved the use of raters all with different backgrounds including researchers, clinicians, professionals from other disciplines, and members of the general public. The end result was an instrument with which to measure the likelihood of bias in pain research reports, more commonly known as the Jadad scale. However, ultimately, the Jadad scale is applicable to all RCTs, including RCTs in orthopaedics.[9]

A limitation of the Jadad scale that forces the need for it to be adapted for quality assessment of surgical trials is the need for a double-blinded study. In studies comparing orthopaedic surgical interventions, it is often impossible to blind the surgeon to achieve double blinding. In this case, the Jadad scale must be modified to grade a study according to whether or not it had "blinding" rather than "double blinding." In addition, the Jadad scale grades a paper on whether or not the word "randomized" is mentioned. However, consideration should be given to the method of randomization used and whether it was performed appropriately. These adaptations make the Jadad scale an appropriate option for the quality assessment of surgical interventions.

Jargon Simplified: Double-blind

A study is double-blind when two parties are blinded to the participants' group allocation (e.g., patients and outcome assessors, patients and investigators, and so on).

The CONSORT Statement

For an RCT to exhibit quality in its reporting, it must convey to the reader pertinent information regarding the design, conduct, analysis, and generalizability of the trial. If an RCT report is composed in this manner, bias will be removed and practitioners may use these reports to guide their practice. However, the analysis of evidence produced over the past 30 years has proved the situation to be quite the opposite of that just described.[10]

A group called the Standards of Reporting Trials (SORT) that met in 1993 provided the framework for reconciling the recurring issue of poor reporting of published biomedical research. In May 1994, another group, the Asilomar Working Group on Recommendations for Reporting of Clinical Trials in Biomedical Literature, independently set out to discuss similar issues regarding the reporting of clinical trials.[10]

In September 1995, nine members of both groups including editors, clinical epidemiologists, and statisticians met in Chicago to merge ideas and produce a working tool for improving the quality of reporting. The result was the Consolidated Standards of Reporting Trials (CONSORT) statement —a flow diagram and checklist concerned mainly with methods, results, and discussion that identifies key pieces of information necessary to evaluate the validity of a report. Four years later, in 1999, the same group met again with the intent to revise the original CONSORT checklist and flow diagram. In May 2000, a revised CONSORT statement was finalized. The revised statement includes a 22-item checklist (**Table 3.4**) and a flow diagram (**Fig. 3.1**).[13]

When the CONSORT statement is followed properly, it will not only provide guidance on improving quality but will encourage transparency in reporting the methods and results so that reports of RCTs can be interpreted both readily and accurately.[13] In addition, the flow diagram is helpful in guiding the author through the phases of an RCT.

The primary purpose of the CONSORT statement is to help authors improve the quality of simple two-group parallel RCT reports. However, the philosophy of the statement may be applied to any study design. Furthermore, it encourages transparency in reporting the methods and results, so that RCT reports can be interpreted both readily and accurately. One should expect the release of additional statements specific to other designs.[13]

For the specific purpose of improving understanding to ensure its use in reporting, three members of the CONSORT group and members for some checklist items made up the Revised CONSORT Statement for Reporting Randomized Trials: Explanation and Elaboration. It describes, in detail, the parts of the CONSORT statement and provides references from which checklist items were adopted.[13] The document is available for download from the CONSORT Web site at: http://www.consort-statement.org/consort-statement/.

Other Systems

Other systems in place are developed to score evidence, such as the Oxford Center for Evidence-Based Medicine (OCEBM), the Scottish Intercollegiate Guidelines Network (SIGN), and the American College of Chest Physicians (ACCP).[3] Adaptations of the Oxford system are commonly used by orthopaedic journals to assign a level of evidence to a study.

GRADE System

The most modern system in place, developed to address the shortcomings of other systems (mentioned above) was recently established by the GRADE working group. They essentially produced and improved systems for grading evidence of multiple studies looking at the same intervention, to essentially determine a grade of recommendation for that intervention.[3]

The GRADE system grades evidence by first considering the level of evidence and scoring it as high, moderate, low, or very low, depending on the study design and where it falls in the hierarchy of evidence. Following this, the studies must be analyzed for consistency of results, consistency of target population, and similarity of interventions. If inconsistencies arise, this will bring the grade of recommendation down.[3]

Table 3.4 CONSORT checklist[13]

PAPER SECTION and topic	Item #	Description
TITLE & ABSTRACT	1	How participants were allocated to interventions (e.g., "random allocation," "randomized," or "randomly assigned").
INTRODUCTION		
Background	2	Scientific background and explanation of rationale.
METHODS		
Participants	3	Eligibility criteria for participants and the settings and locations where the data were collected.
Interventions	4	Precise details of the interventions intended for each group and how and when they were actually administered.
Objectives	5	Specific objectives and hypotheses.
Outcomes	6	Clearly defined primary and secondary outcome measures and, when applicable, any methods used to enhance the quality of measurements (e.g., multiple observations, training of assessors).
Sample size	7	How sample size was determined and, when applicable, explanation of any interim analyses and stopping rules.
Randomization:		
Sequence generation	8	Method used to generate the random allocation sequence, including details of any restrictions (e.g., blocking, stratification)
Allocation concealment	9	Method used to implement the random allocation sequence (e.g., numbered containers or central telephone), clarifying whether the sequence was concealed until interventions were assigned.
Implementation	10	Who generated the allocation sequence, who enrolled participants, and who assigned participants to their groups?
Blinding (masking)	11	Whether or not participants, those administering the interventions, and those assessing the outcomes were blinded to group assignment. If done, how the success of blinding was evaluated.
Statistical methods	12	Statistical methods used to compare groups for primary outcome(s); Methods for additional analyses, such as subgroup analyses and adjusted analyses.
RESULTS		
Participant flow	13	Flow of participants through each stage (a diagram is strongly recommended). Specifically, for each group report the numbers of participants randomly assigned, receiving intended treatment, completing the study protocol, and analyzed for the primary outcome. Describe protocol deviations from study as planned, together with reasons.
Recruitment	14	Dates defining the periods of recruitment and follow-up.
Baseline data	15	Baseline demographic and clinical characteristics of each group.
Numbers analyzed	16	Number of participants (denominator) in each group included in each analysis and whether the analysis was by "intention-to-treat." State the results in absolute numbers when feasible (e.g., 10/20, not 50%).
Outcomes and estimation	17	For each primary and secondary outcome, a summary of results for each group, and the estimated effect size and its precision (e.g., 95% confidence interval).
Ancillary analyses	18	Address multiplicity by reporting any other analyses performed, including subgroup analyses and adjusted analyses, indicating those prespecified and those exploratory.
Adverse events	19	All important adverse events or side effects in each intervention group.
DISCUSSION		
Interpretation	20	Interpretation of the results, taking into account study hypotheses, sources of potential bias or imprecision and the dangers associated with multiplicity of analyses and outcomes.
Generalizability	21	Generalizability (external validity) of the trial findings.
Overall evidence	22	General interpretation of the results in the context of current evidence.

Source: Moher D, Shulz KF, Altman DG. The CONSORT statement: revised recommendations for improving the quality of reports of parallel group randomized trials. *BMC Med Res Methodol* 2001;1:2. Reprinted with permission.

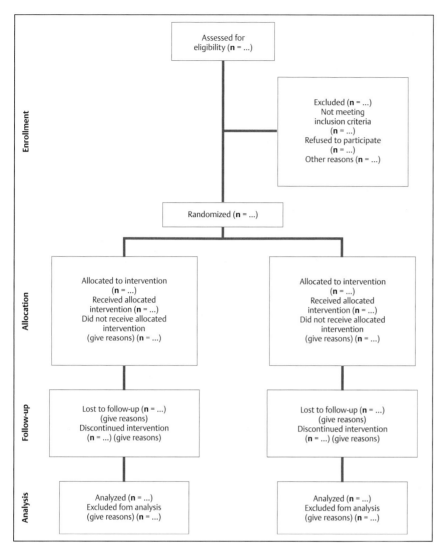

Fig. 3.1 The CONSORT flow diagram.[13] (From Moher D, Shulz KF, Altman DG. The CONSORT statement: revised recommendations for improving the quality of reports of parallel group randomized trials. *BMC Med Res Methodol* 2001;1:2. Reprinted with permission.) An extra box per intervention group relating to care providers can be added if necessary. Details on this can be found on the Consort statement website at http://www.consort-statement.org.

The GRADE system also assesses the benefit versus the harm of the intervention in question. For example, if one study showed that the intervention had potentially dangerous side-effects, then the strength of recommendation regarding that intervention would fall. If, on the other hand, other RCTs addressed this "dangerous side-effect" as a secondary outcome, a different grade of recommendation would result.

Current Quality of Published Orthopaedic Literature

This section focuses on the actual quality of orthopaedic literature. Several published studies have assessed this.

In 2002, Bhandari et al. evaluated the quality of the reporting of RCTs from 1988 to 2000 in the *Journal of Bone and Joint Surgery*. In addition, they identified factors that were associated with study quality, and reported the reliability of a simple system for scoring the quality.[12]

Under a rigorous methodology, a manual search of 2468 articles was performed and 72 of them met the eligibility criteria. An article was considered eligible if it was described as a randomized trial and published in the *Journal of Bone and Joint Surgery* between January 1988 and December of 2000. The Detsky quality scale was employed on the included articles under blinded conditions to evaluate the quality of the included trials.

Each study was independently reviewed by two raters for methodological quality under blinded conditions. The Detsky scale **(Table 3.2)**, composed of five broad categories, was used to score each study. Each category is given equal weights of four points each, with an additional point in the final section for negative trials. Thus, the total possible scores for positive and negative trials are 20 and 21, respectively. To standardize, the final score was transformed to be out of 100. For example, 12 out 20 is 60 out of 100, or

Table 3.5 Transformed quality score (0% to 100%) according to type of intervention[12]

Type of intervention	No. of studies	Mean and standard error (%)	Range (%)
Drug	26	72.8 ± 2.4	50.0–95.4
Surgery	30	63.9 ± 2.5	28.0–81.0
Nonsurgical therapy	16	67.3 ± 3.5	40.0–90.0
Overall	72	68.1 ± 1.6	28.0–95.4

Source: Bhandari M, Richards R, Sprague S, Shemtisch E. The quality of reporting of randomized trials in the Journal of Bone and Joint Surgery from 1988 through 2000. *J Bone Joint Surg Am* 2002;84(3):388–396. Reprinted with permission.

60%. Studies with a score of 75% or greater were considered to be of high quality.

The group found that the number of randomized trials increased from 1988 to 2000; three-quarters of the included articles were from the preceding seven years. As for scientific quality, the mean transformed score for the 72 studies was 68.1% ± 1.6%; specifically, surgical trials scored 63.9%. **Table 3.5** and **Table 3.6** display, respectively, the quality scores of the different intervention types and the proportion of the trials that met individual Detsky scale criteria.

Numerous other results are discussed in the paper that are beyond the scope of this chapter; however, some important points to note are that a significantly greater proportion of drug trials were reported as being double-blinded compared with surgical trials, even though double blinding of the outcome assessors, patients, or data analysts could have been achieved in at least two-thirds of the surgical trials. In addition, 98% of the trials described a randomized trial, but less than half reported concealed randomization. This meant that it was possible for the majority (59%) of the included trials to have investigators who knew to which treatment a patient would be allocated.

The quality of published fracture care literature was analyzed using the Consolidated Standards of Reporting Trials (CONSORT) as an assessment tool. Studies identified as being published in the English language involving patients with fractures that were randomly allocated to alternative treatments were considered eligible. These articles were scored on how well they conformed to the criteria described in the CONSORT checklist and flow diagram.[14]

Items within the CONSORT considered to be critical elements in the reporting of trials were:

1. Identification of the study as a randomized controlled trial.
2. Use of a structured abstract.
3. Statement of inclusion and exclusion criteria.
4. Statements of planned interventions and their timing.
5. Description of the randomization method, including concealment.
6. Description of primary and secondary outcome measures.

7. Rationale and methods for statistical analyses and whether the results were analyzed as originally assigned.
8. Completeness of follow-up.
9. Statement of the estimated effect of the intervention on the primary and secondary outcome measures, including a point estimate and measure of precision.
10. Statement of results in absolute numbers.
11. Deviations from the study protocol.[14]

A total of 196 studies from 32 medical journals were eligible for inclusion. The proportion of trials that adhered to specific items on the CONSORT checklist is listed in **Table 3.7**. Over 70% of the included RCTs failed to meet at least half of the CONSORT criteria. Further, more than two-thirds of the studies met four or fewer of the more

Table 3.6 Proportion of the 72 trials that met the Detsky quality scale criteria[12]

Component of scale	Met criterion (%)	Did not meet criterion (%)
Randomization		
Patients randomly assigned	97.5	2.5
Methods of randomization described	68	32
Randomization concealed	40.5	59.5
Outcomes		
Outcomes described	95.8	4.2
Outcomes objective	41.7	58.3
Outcome assessors blind	44.4	55.6
Eligibility		
Eligibility criteria well defined	61.1	38.9
Reasons for excluding patients described (withdrawals/dropouts)	9.7	90.3
Therapy fully described		
Treatment arm	85	15
Control arm	80	20
Statistical issues		
Test stated and *P*-values given	90.3	9.7
Statistical analysis appropriate	89	11
If negative trial, 95% confidence intervals given or post hoc power calculation performed	2	98
Sample size	6	94

Source: Bhandari M, Richards R, Sprague S, Shemtisch E. The quality of reporting of randomized trials in the Journal of Bone and Joint Surgery from 1988 through 2000. *J Bone Joint Surg Am* 2002;84(3):388–396. Reprinted with permission.

Table 3.7 Proportion of the included studies that met the CONSORT statement criteria adapted to fracture care[14]

CONSORT questions	No. of studies (*N* = 196)
Title	
1. Identify study as a randomized trial	76 (38.8%)
Abstract	
2. Use a structured format	15 (7.7%)
Introduction	
3. (a) State prospectively defined hypothesis and clinical objectives	73 (37.2%)
(b) State prospectively planned subgroup or covariate analyses	23 (11.7%)
Methods	
4. Planned study population, together with inclusion/exclusion criteria	153 (78.1%)
5. Planned interventions and their timing	194 (99.0%)
6. (a) Primary and secondary outcome measure(s)	173 (88.3%)
(b) Minimum important difference(s)	3 (1.5%)
(c) How the target sample size was projected	6 (3.1%)
7. (a) Rationale and methods for statistical analysis	40 (20.4%)
(b) Detailed main comparative analyses and whether they were analyzed as originally assigned	2 (1.0%)
(c) Mere mention of any statistical analysis	86 (43.9%)
8. Prospectively defined stopping rules	2 (1.0%)
Assignment	
9. Unit of randomization (hip, individual, cluster, geographic)	116 (59.2%)
10. Method used to generate the allocation schedule	93 (47.4%)
11. Method of allocation, concealment, and timing of assignment	47 (24.0%)
12. Method to separate the generator from the executor of assignment	38 (19.4%)
Masking	
13. (a) Describe mechanism, similarity of treatment characteristics, allocation schedule control, and evidence for successful masking (blinding) among participants, person doing intervention, outcome assessors, and data analysts	9 (4.6%)
(b) Blinding of outcomes (patients or surgeons) if applicable	22 (11.2%)
Results	
Participant Flow and Follow-up	
14. (a) Provide a trial profile and/or diagram summarizing participant flow, numbers and timing of randomization, assignment and interventions	33 (16.8%)
(b) State completeness of follow-up and measurements for each randomized group	116 (59.2%)
Analysis	
15. State estimated effect of intervention on primary and secondary outcome measures, including a point estimate (i.e., mean, odds ratio, relative risk, etc.)	12 (6.1%)
16. State results in absolute numbers when feasible (20 of 40 hips, not 50%)	158 (80.6%)
17. Present summary data and appropriate descriptive and inferential statistics in sufficient detail to permit alternative analyses and replication	187 (95.4%)
18. Describe prognostic variables by treatment group and any attempt to adjust for them	11 (5.6%)
19. Describe protocol deviations from the study as planned, together with the reasons	10 (5.1%)
Comment	
20. State specific interpretation of study findings, including sources of bias and imprecision (internal validity) and discussion of external validity, including appropriate quantitative measures when possible	14 (7.1%)
21. State general interpretation of the data in light of the totality of the available evidence	184 (93.9%)

Source: Bhandari M, Guyatt GH, Lochner H, Sprague S, Tornetta P. Application of the consolidated standards of reporting trials (CONSORT) in the fracture care literature. *J Bone Joint Surg Am* 2002;84(3):485–489. Reprinted with permission.

significant elements of the CONSORT statement mentioned above. A well-designed, well-reported surgical trial should meet all of the CONSORT criteria.[14] The study found that there was some improvement in reporting since CONSORT was first introduced, but there still needs to be an improvement in the quality of published orthopaedic literature overall.[14]

Gummesson and colleagues also assessed the change in the quality of reporting in RCTs over time. This group's evaluation was specific to upper-extremity disorders published in four hand surgical and orthopaedic journals during an 11-year period. They also go on to discuss the types of outcome measures used in the trials, though this will not be discussed here. Studies were considered eligible if they were RCTs, and compared treatment methods for upper-extremity disorders among an adult population between the years 1992 and 2002 in any of the following four journals: the *Journal of Hand Surgery* (American Volume), the *Journal of Hand Surgery* (British and European Volume), the *Journal of Bone and Joint Surgery* (British Volume), the *Journal of Bone and Joint Surgery* (American Volume). This was achieved through a PubMed search, and a study was considered eligible only if in the title, abstract, or list of indexed terms it was stated that the trial was randomized and the aim of the study was to evaluate the treatment of any kind of upper-extremity condition.[15]

The quality scale used to assess eligible RCTs was a modified version of the Jadad scale (**Table 3.8**). This scale assessed the trial's randomization and blinding, and patient withdrawals and dropouts. The final quality score for each study ranged between 0 and 5.[15] A total of 92 articles met all of the eligibility criteria covering a variety of upper-extremity disorders. Details of the results of this study can be found in **Table 3.9**, but some general points are stated here. The median scale score calculated for the 92 included articles was 2 (in a range of 0–5). Interestingly enough, the median score for articles published between 1992 and 1996, the years before the CONSORT was published, was 1; between 1997 and 2002, the median score was 3. Furthermore, the *Journal of Bone and Joint Surgery* (American Volume), the only journal that enforces the CONSORT statement as a guideline, received a score of 5—a significantly higher score than any of the other journals. Looking at **Table 3.10**, we see that trailing the *Journal of Bone and Joint Surgery* (American Volume), with a median score of 2.5 is the *Journal of Hand Surgery* (American Volume), then the *Journal of Bone and Joint Surgery* (British Volume) with 2, and finally, the *Journal of Hand Surgery* (British and European Volume) with a score of 1.[15]

Table 3.8 Modified Jadad scale for quality assessment of studies on upper-extremity disorders[15]

Item	Points
Randomization	
Study described as randomized	+1
Randomization method described and appropriate	+1
Randomization method described and inappropriate	−1
Randomization method not described*	−1
Blinding	
Study described as double blind (or single blind*)	+1
Blinding method described and appropriate	+1
Blinding method described and inappropriate	−1
Blinding method not described	0
Study not described as blind	0
Withdrawals and dropouts	
Withdrawals and dropouts described	+1
Withdrawals and dropouts not described	0

* Scale modifications used in this study.
Source: Gummesson C, Atroshi I, Ekdahl C. The quality of reporting and outcome measures in randomized clinical trials related to upper-extremity disorders. *J Hand Surg Am* 2004;29(4):727–733. Reprinted with permission.

Table 3.9 The number of articles for each item of the modified Jadad scale[15]

Jadad scale items	JBJS Am n	JBJS Br n	JHS Am n	JHS Br n
Randomization				
Study described as randomized	14	21	16	41
• Randomization method described and appropriate	11	11	7	11
• Randomization method described and inappropriate	2	3	8	8
• Randomization method not described*	1	7	1	22
Blinding				
Study described as double blind (or single blind*)	9	6	8	10
• Blinding method described and appropriate	9	5	7	7
• Blinding method described and inappropriate	0	0	1	0
• Blinding method not described	0	1	0	3
Study not described as blind	5	15	8	31
Withdrawals and dropouts				
Withdrawals and dropouts described	14	19	13	31
Withdrawals and dropouts not described	0	2	3	10

Source: Gummesson C, Atroshi I, Ekdahl C. The quality of reporting and outcome measures in randomized clinical trials related to upper-extremity disorders. *J Hand Surg Am* 2004;29(4):727–733. Reprinted with permission.

Table 3.10 **Final Jadad scores for the quality of reporting of RCTs at differing time periods**[15]

Time period	n	JBJS Am Median (Range)	n	JBJS Br Median (Range)	n	JHS Am Median (Range)	n	JHS Br Median (Range)
1992–2002	14	5 (1–5)	21	2 (0–5)	16	2.5 (0–5)	41	1 (0–5)
1992–1996	4	1 (1–5)	8	1.5 (1–5)	5	2 (0–5)	11	1 (0–3)
1997–2002	10	5 (3–5)	13	3 (0–5)	11	3 (1–5)	30	1 (0–5)

Source: Gummesson C, Atroshi I, Ekdahl C. The quality of reporting and outcome measures in randomized clinical trials related to upper-extremity disorders. *J Hand Surg Am* 2004;29(4):727–733. Reprinted with permission.

Finally, Dulai et al. conducted a study with the purpose of reviewing the quality of RCTs published in journals known to be most influential to pediatric orthopaedic surgeons in Canada.[16] To determine which articles would be included in the evaluation, a method was designed to determine which journals are most influential to the practices of pediatric orthopaedic surgeons in Canada. This was achieved through three fellowship-trained pediatric orthopaedic surgeons producing a list of journals they found most influential. This list was embedded into a larger one and used to survey pediatric orthopaedic surgeons across the country. Once the most influential journals were determined, the group conducted a literature search in Medline, Embase, and the Cochrane Database of RCTs from these journals. Additional inclusion criteria were that the articles had to be published between January 1995 and September 2005, with a patient sample younger than 18 years at the time of enrollment; the study design had to be described as an RCT; and the topic of the paper had to involve orthopaedic patients. Finally, to ensure a thorough search, a manual search was conducted. The Detsky scale was employed for quality assessment; this may be found in **Table 3.2** and its use in quality assessment has been described in earlier sections.[16]

A total of seven journals were identified as eligible: *Journal of Pediatric Orthopaedics, Journal of Pediatric Orthopedics Part B, Journal of Bone and Joint Surgery* (American Volume), *Journal of Bone and Joint Surgery* (British Volume), *Spine, Journal of the American Academy of Orthopaedic Surgeons,* and the *Canadian Journal of Surgery.* No eligible studies were found in the last two journals mentioned, so out of the remaining five journals a total of 36 eligible studies were identified. The mean Detsky score for eligible articles ranged from 71% in the *Journal of Bone and Joint Surgery* (American Volume) to 43% in the *Journal of Pediatric Orthopaedics* Part B.[16]

The mean percentage score on the Detsky scale was 53% with a 95% confidence interval and a range of 46–60%. The number of studies that were considered of high quality (a Detsky score ≥75%) was 7, or 19%. It was not possible to determine which journal provided the most reliable articles since the *Journal of Pediatric Orthopaedics* had significantly more eligible articles simply because the entire journal is composed of pediatric cases. Such a low score for quality was attributed to the rarity with which RCTs are conducted

in pediatric orthopaedics due to the practical obstacles often encountered when performing such studies. The group concluded that although the use of RCTs and better-quality reporting are observed in the latter of the years analyzed, improvement still needs to be made in the quality of published pediatric orthopaedics.[16]

In conclusion, it was made clear in all of the above studies assessing the quality of published orthopaedic literature that, despite recent improvements and movement toward RCT study designs, it is still not enough. Investigators conducting research studies in orthopaedics need to concentrate on creating satisfactory study design, complemented with acceptable reporting. Furthermore, investigators need to publish their work with higher quality standards in mind so that the worth of their studies can be fully appreciated. Finally, it is also incumbent on the editors of journals to be more stringent about studies they consider acceptable to be included for publishing.

Key Concepts: Elements of Quality Research
When attempting to produce quality research, it is critical to practice and/or concisely report the following elements: randomization, structured abstract, clear statement of inclusion and exclusion criteria, statements of planned interventions and their timing, the randomization method and concealment, primary and secondary outcome measures, statistical analyses, completeness of follow-up, estimate of effect of intervention, statement of results in absolute numbers, and deviations from the study protocol .

Conclusion

Significant efforts continue to be made to help improve the quality of published orthopaedic literature. Scales and checklists have been developed as a result of these efforts to act as a guideline for quality research. Numerous high-impact journals such as the *Journal of the American Medical Association, Lancet,* and the *British Medical Journal* have insisted on researchers following these guidelines. This is a step in the right direction, but enforcement of the checklists is still an issue.[17] The next step needs to be a standardized reporting outline that must be completed for a study even to be considered for publication.

This chapter has identified what elements a methodology must include to be considered of high quality and how to properly report it. It is now up to the reader to read further into the topic and incorporate their findings into their own research practice.

Suggested Reading

Begg C, Cho M, Eastwood S, et al. Improving the quality of reporting of randomized controlled trials. The CONSORT statement. JAMA 1996;276(8):637–639

Dulai SK, Slobogean BL, Beauchamp RD, Mulpuri K. A quality assessment of randomized clinical trials in pediatric orthopaedics. J Pediatr Orthop 2007;27(5):573–581

Guyatt GH, Rennie D, eds. User's Guides to the Medical Literature: A Manual for Evidence-based Clinical Practice. Chicago, IL: AMA Press; 2002

Moher D, Schulz KF, Altman DG; CONSORT. The CONSORT statement: revised recommendations for improving the quality of reports of parallel group randomized trials. BMC Med Res Methodol 2001;1:2

Poolman RW. Moving towards Evidence-based Orthopaedic Surgery. Amsterdam: Buijten & Schipperheijn; 2007

References

1. Sackett DL, Rosenberg WM, Gray JA, Haynes RB, Richardson WS. Evidence based medicine: what it is and what it isn't. BMJ 1996;312(7023):71–72
2. Guyatt GH, Rennie D, eds. User's Guides to the Medical Literature: A Manual for Evidence-based Clinical Practice. Chicago, IL: AMA Press; 2002
3. Petrisor BA, Keating J, Schemitsch E. Grading the evidence: levels of evidence and grades of recommendation. Injury 2006; 37(4):321–327
4. Oxman AD, Guyatt GH. Validation of an index of the quality of review articles. J Clin Epidemiol 1991;44(11):1271–1278
5. Moher D, Jadad AR, Nichol G, Penman M, Tugwell P, Walsh S. Assessing the quality of randomized controlled trials: an annotated bibliography of scales and checklists. Control Clin Trials 1995;16(1):62–73
6. Poolman RW. Moving towards Evidence-based Orthopaedic Surgery. Amsterdam: Buijten & Schipperheijn; 2007
7. Detsky AS, Naylor CD, O'Rourke K, McGeer AJ, L'Abbé KA. Incorporating variations in the quality of individual randomized trials into meta-analysis. J Clin Epidemiol 1992; 45 (3):255–265
8. Sackett DL, Haynes RB, Guyatt GH, Tugwell P. Clinical Epidemiology: A Basic Science for Clinical Medicine. Boston, MA: Little, Brown, and Company; 1991.
9. Jadad AR, Moore RA, Carroll D, et al. Assessing the quality of reports of randomized clinical trials: is blinding necessary? Control Clin Trials 1996;17(1):1–12
10. Begg C, Cho M, Eastwood S, et al. Improving the quality of reporting of randomized controlled trials. The CONSORT statement. JAMA 1996;276(8):637–639
11. Bhandari M, Deveraux PJ. Issues in the design and conduct of randomized trials in surgery. Evid Based Med 2004;2(4):6–12
12. Bhandari M, Richards RR, Sprague S, Schemitsch EH. The quality of reporting of randomized trials in the Journal of Bone and Joint Surgery from 1988 through 2000. J Bone Joint Surg Am 2002;84-A(3):388–396
13. Moher D, Schulz KF, Altman DG; CONSORT. The CONSORT statement: revised recommendations for improving the quality of reports of parallel group randomized trials. BMC Med Res Methodol 2001;1:2
14. Bhandari M, Guyatt GH, Lochner H, Sprague S, Tornetta P III. Application of the consolidated standards of reporting trials (CONSORT) in the fracture care literature. J Bone Joint Surg Am 2002;84-A(3):485–489
15. Gummesson C, Atroshi I, Ekdahl C. The quality of reporting and outcome measures in randomized clinical trials related to upper-extremity disorders. J Hand Surg [Am] 2004; 29 (4):727–734, discussion 735–737
16. Dulai SK, Slobogean BL, Beauchamp RD, Mulpuri K. A quality assessment of randomized clinical trials in pediatric orthopaedics. J Pediatr Orthop 2007;27(5):573–581
17. Mills EJ, Wu P, Gagnier J, Devereaux PJ. The quality of randomized trial reporting in leading medical journals since the revised CONSORT statement. Contemp Clin Trials 2005;26(4): 480–487

4

Common Pitfalls in the Reporting of Surgical Results

Rudolf W. Poolman

Summary

This chapter discusses some of the limitations and pitfalls that are commonly found in the reporting of surgical trials. For example, many studies fail to report all of the methodological safeguards that they utilize to help reduce bias. In addition, studies often report analyses that were not presented in the original study protocol. This may result in data dredging in an effort to find positive results. Frequently, the primary outcome of interest is not identified as such, leading to multiple outcomes being analyzed and reported. Failure to adjust for multiple endpoints will result in erroneous significant findings. In this chapter, these and other notorious errors made when reporting surgical data are identified and discussed.

Introduction

This chapter will describe some of the common errors and misconceptions that are reproduced in the surgical literature. Several publications reveal poor quality of reporting, particularly in the surgical literature.[1-23] Investigators are responsible for reporting the findings of their study and revealing as much information about their trial as possible. Recent studies suggest that researchers did use methodological safeguards but failed to report them in their manuscript.[22,24] The lack of disclosure of this information is one of the problems leading to poor reporting quality, a key element of the criteria used in judging a trial's merit. With this in mind, it is clear that reporting in trials needs improvement.

Why Is Clear Reporting So Important?

If you fail to report your trial in a clear and concise manner, readers may conclude that your study was likewise poorly designed and conducted. You, of course, know this was not the case. Accordingly, readers should be informed about the internal and external validity of your investigation, which should be reflected in a clear manuscript.

The *internal validity* of a trial is the extent to which bias (systematic error) is reduced in clinical trials.[25] This form of bias includes *selection bias* (biased allocation of groups), *performance bias* (unequal provision of care apart from

treatment under investigation), *detection bias* (biased measurement of outcome), and *attrition bias* (bias resulting from the number of and management of deviations from protocol and loss to follow up).[25] **Figure 4.1** shows where biases are typically present in the trial flow and how they can be prevented.

Jargon Simplified: Types of Bias Possible in Studies
- **Selection bias**—"Biased allocation to comparison groups."[25]
- **Performance bias**—"Unequal provision of care apart from treatment under evaluation."[25]
- **Detection bias**—"Biased assessment of outcome."[25]
- **Attrition bias**—"Bias resulting from the number and management of deviations from protocol and loss to follow up."[25]

The *external validity* of a trial is the degree to which results of trials offer a correct basis for generalization to other situations.[25] When considering the external validity of a study, you need to consider the following:
- *Patient characteristics* such age, sex, severity of the condition treated, risk factors, and co-morbidities
- *Treatment regimens* including surgical technique and concomitant treatments
- *Settings* including the level of care (primary to tertiary) and experience and specialization of surgeons
- *Modalities of outcomes* such as the type or definition of end points and length of follow-up[25]

Key Concepts: Items to Consider When Assessing External Validity
To ensure external validity, consider patient characteristics, treatment regimens, settings, and modalities of outcomes.

The most common error in reporting trial design and results is failure to include a clear description of measures taken to ensure internal and external validity of the study conducted. The investigators may have used methodological safeguards but failed to report them.[22,24] If you do not present your results in a clear fashion, the readers will not be able to know whether your results can be generalized for use in their clinical practice.[26,27]

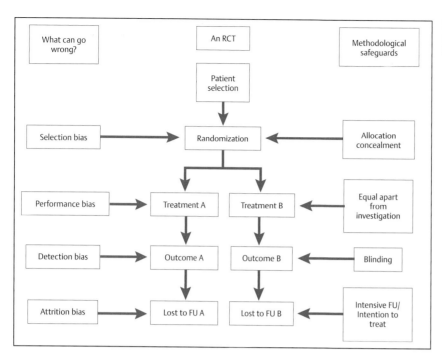

Fig. 4.1 Sources of bias in trials and safeguards to prevent them. FU, follow up.

> **Key Concepts: The Most Common Error in Trial Reports**
> Failure to describe specific actions taken to establish and maintain internal and external validity of the study is the error most frequently made in trial reporting.

Measures to Improve Reporting of Research Results

Initiatives taken by journal editors help to overcome shortcomings in reporting.[28] Moreover, CONSORT, which stands for Consolidated Standards of Reporting Trials, covers a range of initiatives developed by the CONSORT Group to alleviate the troubles arising from inadequate reporting of randomized controlled trials (RCTs).[5,29] The CONSORT group developed a checklist to help authors during the preparation of their work, detailing critical points on methodological safeguards to prevent bias (see **Table 3.4**).

CONSORT was developed for pharmaceutical trials. Surgical trials are another matter, wherein surgical expertise is the crux. A checklist better suited for surgical intervention is the Checklist to Evaluate a Report of a Non-Pharmacological Trial (CLEAR NPT), which was recently developed using consensus among surgeons, epidemiologist, and other collaborators in systematic reviews (**Table 4.1**).[30] Finally, this group's efforts resulted in the CONSORT NPT extension (**Table 4.2**). This extension is added to the CONSORT checklist, and clarifies specific issues when assessing surgical trials, such as blinding issues, the complexity of the surgical procedure, and the influence of care providers' expertise in the procedures under investigation and volume of care of centers on treatment effect. Moreover, the CONSORT flow diagram was modified to include data on the number of surgeons and centers in each treatment arm and the number of patients treated by each surgeon.[31] (The extended checklist and flow diagram can be downloaded for noncommercial purposes from the CONSORT web site http://www.consort-statement.org.)

Due to limitations on publication space, editors may request that manuscripts be shortened. In this case it is wise to ask the editor to publish only the essential details of your trial in the manuscript and to display any excluded information online. Several journals offer this feature of supplementary material online. Furthermore, open-access online journals, such as Biomed Central (BMC series) have no space restrictions.

Common Errors and Misconceptions

Classically, the IMRaD format (which stands for Introduction, Methods, Results, and Discussion) is used in the mainstay of publications reporting trials in biomedical journals.[26,27] Each section is open to errors and will be discussed individually below.

Introduction

In the Introduction section you will provide the background information on your work. Next, you will describe the scientific problem at hand resulting in a research question. Many manuscripts rejected for publication fail to report a *null hypothesis* and subsequent *aim of the study*.

Table 4.1 Final checklist of items to assess quality of randomized controlled trials of nonpharmacologic treatment (CLEAR NPT)[30]

1. Was the generation of allocation sequences adequate?	Yes
	No
	Unclear
2. Was the treatment allocation concealed?	Yes
	No
	Unclear
3. Were details of the intervention administered to each group made available[a]?	Yes
	No
	Unclear
4. Were care providers' experience or skill[b] in each arm appropriate[c]?	Yes
	No
	Unclear
5. Was participant (i.e., patients) adherence assessed quantitatively[d]?	Yes
	No
	Unclear
6. Were participants adequately blinded?	Yes
	No, because blinding is not feasible
	No, although blinding is feasible
	Unclear
6.1. If participants were *not adequately blinded*	
6.1.1. Were all other treatments and care (i.e., co-interventions) the same in each randomized group?	Yes
	No
	Unclear
6.1.2. Were withdrawals and lost to follow-up the same in each randomized group?	Yes
	No
	Unclear
7. Were care providers or persons caring for the participants adequately blinded?	Yes
	No, because blinding is not feasible
	No, although blinding is feasible
	Unclear
7.1. If care providers were *not adequately blinded*	
7.1.1. Were all other treatments and care (i.e., co-interventions) the same in each randomized group?	Yes
	No
	Unclear
7.1.2. Were withdrawals and lost to follow-up the same in each randomized group?	Yes
	No
	Unclear

(Continued)

Table 4.1 Final checklist of items to assess quality of randomized controlled trials of nonpharmacologic treatment (CLEAR NPT)[30] (Continued)

8. Were outcome assessors adequately blinded to assess the primary outcomes?	Yes
	No, because blinding is not feasible
	No, although blinding is feasible
	Unclear
8.1. If outcome assessors were *not adequately blinded*, were specific methods used to avoid ascertainment bias (systematic differences in outcome assessment)[e]	Yes
	No
	Unclear
9. Was the follow-up schedule the same in each group[f]?	Yes
	No
	Unclear
10. Were the main outcomes analyzed according to the intention-to-treat principle?	Yes
	No
	Unclear

Source: Boutron I, Moher D, Tugwell P, et al. A checklist to evaluate a report of a nonpharmacological trial (CLEAR NPT) was developed using consensus. *J Clin Epidemiol* 2005;58(12):1233–1240. Reprinted with permission.

[a] The answer should be "yes" for this item if these data were either described in the report or made available for each arm (reference to a preliminary report, online addendum, etc.).

[b] Care providers' experience or skill will be assessed only for therapist-dependent interventions (i.e., interventions where the success of the treatment are directly linked to care providers' technical skill). For other treatment, this item is not relevant and should be removed from the checklist or answered "unclear."

[c] Appropriate experience or skill should be determined according to published data, preliminary studies, guidelines, run-in period or a group of experts and prespecified in the protocol for each study arm before the beginning of the survey.

[d] Treatment adherence will be assessed only for treatments necessitating iterative interventions (e.g., physiotherapy that supposes several sessions, in contrast to a "one-shot" treatment such as surgery). For one-shot treatment, this item is not relevant and should be removed from the checklist or answered "unclear"

[e] The answer should be "yes" for this item if the main outcome is objective or "hard" or outcomes were assessed by a blinded or at least an independent endpoint review committee or outcomes were assessed by an independent outcome assessor trained to perform the measurements in a standardized manner or the outcome assessor was blinded to the study purpose and hypothesis.

[f] This item is not relevant for trials in which follow-up is part of the question. For example, this item is not relevant for a trial assessing frequent versus less frequent follow-up for cancer recurrence. In these situations, this item should be removed from the checklist or answered "unclear."

Table 4.2 CONSORT NPT extension checklist of items for reporting trials of nonpharmacologic treatments, with examples[31]

Section
Title and abstract
Item 1
Standard CONSORT* Description
How participants were allocated to interventions (e.g. "random allocation," "randomized," or "randomly assigned")
Extension for Nonpharmacologic Trials
In the abstract, description of the experimental treatment, comparator, care providers, centers, and blinding status
Examples of Good Reporting Based on Extension
Objective: To compare the primary therapist model (PTM), provided by a single rheumatology-trained primary therapist, with the traditional treatment model (TTM), provided by a physical therapy (PT) and/or occupational therapy (OT) generalist, for treating patients with rheumatoid arthritis (RA).
Methods: Eligible patients were adults requiring rehabilitation treatment who had not received PT/OT in the past 2 years. Participants were randomized to the PTM or TTM group. The primary outcome was defined as the proportion of clinical responders who experienced a > or = 20% improvement in 2 of the following measures from baseline to 6 months: Health Assessment Questionnaire, pain visual analog scale, and Arthritis Community Research and Evaluation Unit RA Knowledge Questionnaire.

(Continued)

Table 4.2 CONSORT NPT extension checklist of items for reporting trials of nonpharmacologic treatments, with examples[31] *(Continued)*

Methods
Participants
Item 3
Standard CONSORT Description
Eligibility criteria for participants and the setting and locations where the data were collected
Extension for Nonpharmacologic Trials
When applicable, eligibility criteria for centers and those performing the interventions
Example of Good Reporting Based on Extension
All participating centres ... were major neurosurgical centres, treating large numbers of patients after aneurysmal subarachnoid haemorrhage (SAH), each centre treating between 60 and 200 cases annually ... Centres had to have expertise in both neurosurgical and endovascular management of ruptured aneurysms. Only accredited neurosurgeons with experience of aneurysm surgery were permitted to manage patients in the trial. Endovascular operators had to have done a minimum of 30 aneurysm treatment procedures, before they were permitted to treat patients in the trial.
Interventions
Item 4
Standard CONSORT Description
Precise details of the interventions intended for each group, and how and when they were actually administered
Extensions for Nonpharmacologic Trials
Precise details of both the experimental treatment and comparator
Item 4A
Extensions for Nonpharmacologic Trials
Description of the different components of the interventions and, when applicable, descriptions of the procedure for tailoring the interventions to individual participants
Examples of Good Reporting Based on Extension
The exercise training program ... consisted of 2 approximately 3-month-long phases of exercise training. The initial phase of exercise was designed to prepare the participants for progressive resistance training and also to minimize injury. Exercises during the first 3-month phase (phase 1) were conducted by a physical therapist using a group format (2–5 participants/group) and were designed to enhance flexibility, balance, coordination, movement speed, and, to some extent, strength of all major muscle groups. Twenty-two exercises formed the basis of this program (protocol available from the authors). The exercises were made progressively more difficult by increasing the number of repetitions and/or by performing the exercises in more challenging ways. When safely able, participants also exercised on a stationary bicycle or treadmill. Participants attempted this exercise for minimum of 5 minutes and progressed to a maximum of 15 minutes. The treadmill speed or bicycle resistance was set at the highest comfortable setting that was safe for the participant. A formal aerobic exercise training protocol was not performed. Exercise sessions lasted 45 to 90 minutes (with breaks), depending on the participant's ability and tolerance, which increased over the course of phase 1. During the second exercise phase (phase 2), progressive resistance training was added. One-repetition maximum (1-RM) voluntary strength was measured on each of 6 different exercises (knee extension, knee flexion, seated bench press, seated row, leg press, and biceps curl), which were performed bilaterally on a Hoist weightlifting machine (Hoist Fitness System, San Diego, Calif). Initially, the participants performed 1 to 2 sets of 6 to 8 repetitions of each exercise at 65% of their 1-RM. By the end of the first month of weight training, they progressed to 3 sets of 8 to 12 repetitions performed at 85% to 100% of the initial 1-RM. The 1-RM measurements were repeated at 6 weeks and used to progressively increase each individual's exercise prescription. Participants continued to perform a shortened version of the phase 1 exercises and the treadmill or stationary bicycle warm-up exercise ....
The [control] treatment follows the same format [as experimental treatment], i.e., 10 weekly 90-min sessions. The therapist helps the patients identify daily stresses and discusses them in a supportive non-directive mode. No instructions for exposure are included. If the patient brings up trauma-related issues, the therapist gently redirects her to discuss other material.

(Continued)

Table 4.2 CONSORT NPT extension checklist of items for reporting trials of nonpharmacologic treatments, with examples[31] *(Continued)*

Item 4B

Extensions for Nonpharmacologic Trials

Details of how the interventions were standardized

Example of Good Reporting Based on Extension (Reference)

The usual practices of surgeons performing optic nerve decompression surgery were determined through literature review and through a survey of study surgeons. These practices were described in the protocol as a series of 31 steps, only six of which were required to be performed so as to ensure adequacy of the surgery as well as safety of the patient. The remaining steps could be performed according to surgeon preference as they did not directly affect either patient safety or adequacy of surgery. Each study surgeon signed a written commitment to adhere to the six required steps, which were: general anesthesia, medial approach, no mechanical static traction, subarachnoid dissection if no cerebrospinal fluid release was seen following fenestration of the optic nerve sheath, no more than 7 minutes of sustained traction on the globe at any one time and rest periods of at least 2 minutes following any 7-minutes period of globe traction.

Item 4C

Extension for Nonpharmacologic Trials

Details of how adherence of care providers with the protocol was assessed or enhanced

Examples of Good Reporting Based on Extension

All therapy sessions are videotaped … A senior clinician who is independent of … treatment delivery will rate 10% of the videotapes using measures adapted from several randomized clinical trials of psychotherapy …; the 10% figure was chosen arbitrarily in an attempt to ensure an adequate sample of information from each treatment condition.

Sample size

Item 7

Standard CONSORT Description

How sample size was determined and, when applicable, explanation of any interim analyses and stopping rules

Extension for Nonpharmacologic Trials

When applicable, details of whether and how the clustering by care providers or centers was addressed

Examples of Good Reporting Based on Extension

The study was designed to enroll 8 participants for each of 4 therapists at the 12 participating sites … Sample size was computed on the basis of our primary hypothesis, that PE [prolonged exposure] will be more effective than PCT [present-centered therapy] for the treatment of PTSD [posttraumatic stress disorder] due to military-related trauma in women as measured by the CAPS [clinician-administered PTSD scale] at 3 months posttreatment. Although treatment is delivered on an individual basis, each participant cannot be assumed to generate independent observations because participants are clustered within therapists. Thus, the computed sample size, based on the unpaired t-test statistic, was inflated by a factor, $f = 1 + (m-1)\rho$, to achieve the variance that one would have anticipated had there been no clustering. The cluster size (m) is 8 (participants/therapist), and the intraclass correlation coefficient (ρ) was estimated from prior studies to be in the range of .10 to .15, which in turn yields a sample size inflation factor of 1.7 to 2.05. With an estimated sample size of 384, this study has 85% to 90% statistical power to detect an effect of $d = .50$ at $\alpha = .05$, two tailed ….

Randomization-sequence generation

Item 8

Standard CONSORT Description

Method used to generate the random allocation sequence, including details of any restriction (e.g., blocking, stratification)

Extension for Nonpharmacologic Trials

When applicable, how care providers were allocated to each trial group

(Continued)

Table 4.2 CONSORT NPT extension checklist of items for reporting trials of nonpharmacologic treatments, with examples[31] *(Continued)*

Example of Good Reporting Based on Extension

At each of the 12 sites, 4 female therapists were randomly assigned to deliver either PE [prolonged exposure] or PCT [present-centered therapy] (*n* = 2 per condition per site) ... By design, each therapist treats 10 participants: 2 training cases during a 6-month run-up period, and 8 randomized cases during 2 years of recruitment.

Pancreaticoduodenectomy [in both experimental and control group] was performed by just 3 experienced surgeons who had done more than 40 pancreaticoduodenectomies with either the conventional [control treatment] or the binding pancreaticojejunostomy [experimental treatment].

The patients were randomly selected for one of two operative procedures: open reduction and internal fixation or external fixation and limited internal fixation. The six attending orthopaedic surgeons who performed the operations had been assigned to a treatment group according to their expertise or to their preference with regard to fixation. Each patient was managed by the one of the six surgeons who was on call when the patient was seen in the emergency room.

Blinding (masking)

Item 11A

Standard CONSORT Description

Whether or not participants, those administering the interventions, and those assessing the outcomes were blinded to group assignment

Extension for Nonpharmacologic Trials

Whether or not those administering co-interventions were blinded to group assignment

Examples of Good Reporting Based on Extension

Patients were randomized [laparoscopic versus small-incision cholecystectomy] in the operating theatre and anaesthetic technique and pain-control methods were standardised. Four experienced surgeons did both types of procedure. Identical wound dressings were applied in both groups so that carers could be kept blind to the type of operation.

Item 11B

Extension for Nonpharmacologic Trials

If blinded, method of blinding and description of the similarity of interventions

Example of Good Reporting Based on Extension

Double blinding was achieved by shielding the subject's view by a vertical drape and other means (described below) and by excluding the nurse assessor from the room until the procedure and clean-up were completed ... The subject's contact with the investigator/procedurist was generally limited to the day of the procedure ... a 1-liter bag of sterile normal saline was hung at the edge of the drape within view of the subject. The knee was then draped with sterile towels, and the connecting tubing and 3-way stop-cocks were assembled and attached to an empty 1-liter waste bag and a 50-ml syringe producing a closed system for fluid delivery, aspiration and ejection. To administer the SI [sham irrigation], the 14-gauge needle was advanced to, but not through, the joint capsule via the lateral suprapatellar port. Fresh saline was drawn from the supply bag in aliquots of 40–50 mL, and 3–5 mL of saline was clysed into the subcutaneous tissue with each mimicking "exchange" before the remainder of the saline was expelled into the waste bag. Positioning of the knee and manipulation were performed as for actual TI [tidal irrigation]. After passage of 1-liter of saline through the tubing, ... the needle was removed ... All subjects and the nurse assessor remained blinded until the subjects had completed study followup.

Statistical methods

Item 12

Standard CONSORT Description

Statistical methods used to compare groups for primary outcome(s); methods for additional analyses, such as subgroup analyses and adjusted analyses

Extension for Nonpharmacologic Trials

When applicable, details of whether and how the clustering by care providers or centers was addressed

Example of Good Reporting Base on Extension (Reference)

Although the participants were individually randomized, a clustering of outcomes is potentially possible since a single therapist was treating several patients. If these clustering effects were strong, then this might alter the results. We therefore used multilevel modelling to check for any clustering effects by undertaking an analysis on the primary outcome.

(Continued)

Table 4.2 CONSORT NPT extension checklist of items for reporting trials of nonpharmacologic treatments, with examples[31] (Continued)

Results
Participant flow
Item 13
Standard CONSORT Description
Flow of participants through each stage (a diagram is strongly recommended)–specifically, for each group, report the numbers of participants randomly assigned, receiving intended treatment, completing the study protocol, and analyzed for the primary outcome; describe protocol deviations from study as planned, together with reasons
Extension for Nonpharmacologic Trials
The number of care providers or centers performing the intervention in each group and the number of patients treated by each care provider or in each center.
Examples of Good Reporting Based on Extension (Reference)
See **Figure 2**, in the CONSORT Extension for NPT Explanatory Document available at http://www.consort-statement.org/extensions/ interventions/non-pharmacologic-treatment-interventions/.
Implementation of interventions
Item: New item
Extension for Nonpharmacologic Trials
Details of the experimental treatment and comparator as they were implemented
Examples of Good Reporting Based on Extension
A single stent was implanted in 546 patients (40%), 2 stents in 487 (36%), 3 stents in 206 (15%), and 4 or more stents in 111 (8%) in both study groups (mean, 1.9 stents per patient and 1.4 stents per lesion). The mean stent diameter was 2.8 mm in both groups, and the mean length was 22.8 mm in the sirolimus–eluting stent group and 23.5 mm in the paclitaxel-eluting stent group. The maximum dilatation pressure during stent implantation was significantly lower in the paclitaxel-eluting stent group.
On average, participants attended a mean of 9.4 exercise sessions (SD, 3.2) and 10.2 sham exercise sessions (SD 3.0) of the planned 12 sessions. Participants attended a mean of 2.9 advice session (SD, 1.1) and 2.5 sham advice sessions (SD 1.1) of the planned 3 sessions. The mean duration of exercise sessions was 54.0 minutes (SD, 16.3), of which 35.6 minutes (SD, 12.6) were spent with a physiotherapist. The mean duration of sham exercise sessions was 47.0 minutes (SD, 25.0) of which 22.9 minutes (SD, 8.4) were spent with a physiotherapist. Mean durations of advice and sham advice sessions were 20.0 minutes (SD, 4.9) and 19 minutes (SD, 5.3), respectively (30).
Baseline data
Item 15
Standard CONSORT Description
Baseline demographic and clinical characteristics of each group
Extension for Nonpharmacologic Trials
When applicable, a description of care providers (case volume, qualification, expertise, etc.) and centers (volume) in each group
Example of Good Reporting Based on Extension
We dichotomized surgeon's experience in laparoscopic repair into greater than 250 repairs (experienced) and less than 250 repairs (inexperienced) ... Surgeons participating in this trial ranged in age from 27 to 70 with a median of 42 years in the laparoscopic group (55 surgeons) and from 30 to 76 with a median of 42 in the open group (77 surgeons). In the laparoscopic group, 8 surgeons were classified as experienced and 47 as inexperienced.
Discussion
Interpretation
Item 20
Standard CONSORT Description
Interpretation of the results, taking into account study hypotheses, sources of potential bias or imprecision, and the dangers associated with multiplicity of analyses and outcomes

(Continued)

Table 4.2 CONSORT NPT extension checklist of items for reporting trials of nonpharmacologic treatments, with examples[31] *(Continued)*

Extension for Nonpharmacologic Trials

In addition, take into account the choice of the comparator, lack of or partial blinding, and unequal expertise of care providers or centers in each group

Example of Good Reporting Based on Extension (Reference)

The sham acupuncture intervention in our study was designed to minimize potential physiological effects by needling superficially at points distant from the segments of "true" treatment points and by using fewer needles than in the acupuncture group. However, we cannot rule out that this intervention may have had some physiological effects. The nonspecific physiological effects of needling may include local alteration in circulation and immune function as well as neurophysiological and neurochemical responses. The question investigated in our comparison of acupuncture and sham acupuncture was not whether skin penetration matters but whether adherence to the traditional concepts of acupuncture makes a difference. For this purpose, our minimal acupuncture intervention was clearly an appropriate sham control although it might not be an inert placebo.

Our study has not entirely resolved the extent to which the effect of magnetic bracelets is specific or due to placebo. Blinding did not affect the pattern of results, but the validity of the self-reporting of blinding status could be questioned. Although the analysis of per-specification bracelets also suggests a specific effect, the result is only a trend and needs confirmation. Therefore, we cannot be certain whether our data show a specific effect of magnets, a placebo effect, or both.

First, surgeons might not be proficient in one or both treatments. The difference in malunion rates between the two treatment groups was consistent across all four study sites, indicating the difference is due to the procedure and not technical proficiency. Staff from all four centres were experienced in both techniques and, therefore, the results are probably typical of other paediatric centers.

Generalizability

Item 21

Standard CONSORT Description

Generalizability (external validity) of the trial findings

Extension for Nonpharmacologic Trial

Generalizability (external validity) of the trial findings according to the intervention, comparators, patients, and care providers and center involved in the trial

Example of Good Reporting Based on Extension

A limitation of this study is the marked degree of nonadherence to randomized treatment. The protocol stipulated that patients assigned to surgery have their surgery within 3 to 6 months after enrollment, a period thought to be appropriate in the clinical experience of the investigators. Although patients consented to this protocol, as in all clinical trials this consent could be changed at the request of the patient, and many chose to do so. This reduced the power of the intention-to-treat analysis to demonstrate a treatment effect... Another limitation is the heterogeneity of the treatment interventions. The choice of nonsurgical therapies was at the discretion of the treating physician and the patient. However with limited evidence regarding efficacy for most nonsurgical treatments for degenerative spondylolisthesis, creating a fixed protocol for nonsurgical treatment was neither clinically feasible nor generalizable.

A selection bias might have been introduced by the fact that 44 percent of the eligible patients declined to participate in the study. We believe this high rate of refusal to participate resulted from the fact that all patients knew they had a one-in-three chance of undergoing a placebo procedure. Patients who agreed to participate might have been so sure that an arthroscopic procedure would help that they were willing to take a one-in-three chance of undergoing the placebo procedure. Such patients might have had higher expectations of benefit or been more susceptible to a placebo effect than those who chose not to participate.

One surgeon performed all the procedures in this study. Consequently, his technical proficiency is critical to the generalizability of our findings. Our study surgeon is board-certified, is fellowship-trained in arthroscopy and sports medicine, and has been in practice for 10 years in an academic and medical center. He is currently the orthopedic surgeon for a national Basketball Association team and was the physician for the men's and women's U.S. Olympic basketball teams in 1996.

One limitation is the potential lack of representativeness of patients agreeing to be randomized to surgery or nonoperative care; however, the characteristics of patients agreeing to participate in SPORT [Spine Patient Outcomes Research Trial] were very similar to those in other studies (38).

Source: Boutron I, Moher D, Altman DG, Schulz KF, Ravaud P; CONSORT Group. Extending the CONSORT statement to randomized trials of nonpharmacologic treatment: explanation and elaboration. *Ann Intern Med* 2008;148(4):295–309. Reproduced with permission.
* CONSORT = Consolidated Standards of Reporting Trials.

A null hypothesis has been defined as the prediction that an observed difference is due to chance alone and not due to a systematic cause; this hypothesis is tested by statistical analysis, and accepted or rejected. Thus the aim of the study is to reject the null hypothesis.

We advise following the IMRaD format strictly. This will organize the manuscript and will facilitate the reader in understanding your trial. Oftentimes inexperienced authors are tempted to present some results and start their discussion in the Introduction section.

> **Key Concepts: Common Pitfalls Found in the Introduction Section**
> - Failure to describe the scientific problem
> - Failure to describe the study question
> - Failure to frame the null hypothesis
> - Presenting results in the introduction
> - Starting the discussion in the introduction

> **Jargon Simplified: Null Hypothesis**
> "In the hypothesis-testing framework, the starting hypothesis [that] the statistical test is designed to consider and, possibly, reject."[32]

Materials and Methods

In the Materials and Methods section, critical design aspects of a trial need to be reported. You have to report all methodological safeguards employed, clearly illustrating the internal validity of your trial. Accordingly, you will have to provide details on the method of patient allocation, randomization, treatment regimes, outcome measures utilized, and completeness of follow-up (see **Fig. 4.1**).

Allocation of patients can be done in several ways. In one method, the investigator can assign a patient to a specific treatment group. Ideally, however, it is not the investigator who makes the decision on allocating the patient to a specific treatment group. This can result in selection bias, as the investigator could wittingly or unwittingly assign a patient with a poorer prognosis to the control group. Therefore, patient allocation should be without guidance of the investigator. Ideally, patients are randomly allocated to the treatment groups. Here allocation refers to the method used to implement the random allocation sequence. The key issue is that it prevents foreknowledge of a treatment assignment and protects those who enroll participants from being influenced by this knowledge. The decision to accept or reject a participant should be made and informed consent should be obtained in ignorance of the next assignment. The methods that were used to ensure random patient allocation should be clearly described. Even if you used suboptimal randomization and allocation methods, such as hospital chart number, you need to report this to assist the readers' full understanding of your trial's merit. The CLEAR NPT checklist can serve as a guide for proper reporting[30]; try answering the questions on this checklist for your trial. Question 1 on the checklist is "*Was the generation of allocation sequences adequate?*" Here, you have to describe how you randomized your patients in order of decreasing adequacy:

1. Remote computer randomization, either Web-based or automated telephone-operated.
2. Sequentially numbered sealed opaque envelopes.
3. Coin toss.
4. Date of birth or hospital chart number.
5. Alternating allocation.

The investigator should have no clue to which treatment arm the next included patients are allocated. This leads to CLEAR NPT's next question, "*Was the treatment allocation concealed?*" Remote randomization is the preferred method of concealment and leaves little opportunity for disclosure of the next patient's treatment. The use of "alternating days" as a method of concealment, however, clearly reveals the next patient's treatment.

> **Key Concepts: Random Allocation**
> Random allocation refers to the derivation of samples by "selecting sampling units (e.g., individual patients) such that each unit has an independent and fixed (generally equal) chance of selection. Whether or not a given unit is selected is determined by chance, for example, using a table of randomly ordered numbers. Allocation of individuals to groups by chance is usually done with the aid of a table of random numbers. Not to be confused with systematic allocation (e.g., on even and odd days of the month) or allocation at the convenience or discretion of the investigator."[33]

Next, you will extensively describe the treatment regimes used for all treatment groups. This should include details about surgical technique and also details on treatment regimes other than the treatment under investigation. For example, did all patients receive the same rehabilitation protocol? Or were patients in the treatment group not allowed to bear weight? Details should be made available by answering CLEAR NPT question 3, "*Were the details of the intervention administered to each group made available?*"

Question 4 of the CLEAR NPT checklist asks whether the experience and skill of care providers was appropriate in each treatment arm. This question implies that you have to give details of participating surgeons' experience. It will be helpful to follow this guide:

- Describe the care providers' experience (number of cases treated) before the trial was initiated for each surgeon.
- Describe the learning curve for the surgeon performing the procedure in each treatment arm.
- Report the number of surgeons performing the procedure.
- Report the number of patients treated by each surgeon.
- Report important details on attending care providers (expertise).

Subsequently, the outcome measures used in your trial should be reported; more specifically, the projected primary outcome and secondary outcomes are described. The primary outcome is defined in the study protocol prior to start of the study. The sample size of the study should be based on the primary outcome. If the results of the primary outcome show a nonsignificant result, it is tempting to find positive results among the other outcomes you tested to give your study a positive conclusion. Bhandari et al. reported that in orthopaedic surgical journals only 33.3% of the trials provided an unequivocal statement of the primary outcomes, while 44.8% of the nonorthopaedic surgical journals, and 56% of the randomized trials in the general medical journals, provided a clear statement of the principal outcomes.[33] In situations where no primary outcome variable has been determined, there is a risk of doing multiple tests of significance on multiple outcomes measures. This form of *data dredging* by investigators risks forged false-positive findings. Several techniques are available to adjust for multiple comparisons, such as the Bonferroni correction.[34–36]

Key Concepts: Primary Outcome versus Secondary Outcomes

Do not be tempted to report only positive outcomes; report the primary outcome you designated in the study protocol. Clearly describe primary and secondary outcomes in the Methods section. These should be the same as originally proposed in the study protocol. In case of multiple outcomes, use a statistical correction for multiple outcomes such as the Bonferroni correction.

Key Concepts: Selecting an Outcome

The selection of an outcome instrument is complicated. Many patient-reported outcome instruments exist today. If you choose to use a validated outcome instrument, it is important that you do not add or change questions: doing so will make a new validation process necessary.[23] Many investigators do not realize this, which typically results in the use of nonvalidated outcome instruments, giving rise to nonvalidated results. We advise the selection of previous validated outcome instruments without changing their content unless you want to take the instrument through a validation process, which needs to be reported in the manuscript. Details on outcome instrument validation go beyond the scope of this chapter.

After selecting an outcome instrument it is important to decide on the minimal clinically important difference.[36,37] It may be possible to find a statistically significant difference, but statistically significant differences are not necessarily clinically relevant. For example, if the sample size of a trial is large enough, a 4-point difference on a 100-point quality of life scale can be statistically significant. However, we need to determine whether a patient will truly feel better as a result of improving 4 points on a 100-point scale.

With this in mind, it is important that you clearly indicate in the Methods section the size of change on a scale deemed clinically important.[38]

Key Concepts: Sample Size

Study power is an important aspect of your trial. Ideally the study's sample size is calculated before the start of the trial. If investigators started the trial without a-priori sample size calculation, a power analysis can be performed post hoc. If a sample size is calculated a priori, you should report this in the Methods section; in the case of post-hoc calculation, this should be reported in the Results section.

Key Concepts: Common Pitfalls in the Methods Section

- Failure to describe the methodological safeguards utilized in the trial:
  - Allocation concealment
  - Randomization
  - Blinding
  - Patients lost to follow-up
- Failure to identify the primary and secondary outcomes
- Failure to describe the intervention in the treatment group and the control group
- Failure to describe the level of experience of care providers, including learning curve and number of patients treated by each provider
- Failure to describe statistical methods in detail, including methods for correction for multiple outcomes
- Confusing statistically detectable difference and clinically relevant difference

Results

The results reported should reflect the findings of your study as proposed in its original protocol. You might be tempted to perform an additional analysis as soon as your dataset is complete. The analyses you will perform should be the one as proposed a priori in the study protocol. Failure to do this may result in data dredging and false-positive conclusions.[39]

Next, you will have to present your results in a clear and concise manner; it is very helpful to use a patient flowchart. This flow diagram should describe the numbers of patients randomized into all treatment groups, those receiving planned treatment, those finishing the study protocol, and patients analyzed for the primary end point.[40] This will facilitate readers in understanding details of the course of the trial and they can easily identify numbers lost to follow-up. Without a flowchart, understanding the whereabouts of the patients can be complicated. Surgical trials often fail to report these details, making judgment of missing patients difficult.

The use of clearly formatted tables is a must. See Chapter 15 for advice on presentation of tables.[41]

Key Concepts: Figures

Figures can convey more than words; on the other hand, if ill-prepared they can serve to confuse. In figures the horizontal (x) and vertical (y) axes should cross at zero to prevent overestimation of the treatment effect. **Figure 4.2a** shows the results of a hypothetical trial comparing different surgical approaches and blood loss. The crossing of the x-axis at the y-axis value of 370 results in a "visual" overestimation of the treatment effect. In **Fig. 4.2a**, the results look quite impressive; however, if you present the results in a correctly formatted figure, the findings are less striking (**Fig. 4.2b**).[41] Figures can be a meaningful tool in presenting the results, most certainly if you provide 95% confidence intervals (**Fig. 4.2c**). In our example this reveals overlapping 95% confidence intervals,

showing that the interventions had no significant difference in blood loss.

The Results section is the place to report protocol deviations. In the Discussion section, you can review the protocol deviations and reasons for them in greater detail. The reader should be able to appreciate the merit of your study by reading the Methods section and the Results section.

Reality Check: Limb versus Patient

Many surgical trials include bilateral fractures, and the author has two means of reporting the results: by patients or by limbs. Purpose or ignorance can result in reporting the number of extremities instead of the number of patients. This can seriously influence findings.[42] You should consider a strategy before the trial to deal with this issue. Bryant et al.[42] suggested analyzing bilateral cases as a separate group; for example, patients with bilateral osteoarthritis who have had one knee replaced and are still waiting for their other knee to be replaced. These hypothetical patients can have a lower quality of life than patients who have both knees replaced. Quality of life measurement in patients in orthopaedics can be complicated because the following options are possible: unilateral disease with unilateral replacement, bilateral disease with unilateral replacement, and bilateral disease with bilateral replacement.

Key Concepts: Common Pitfalls found in the Results Section
- Reporting analyses that are not described in the Methods section
- Data dredging
- Failure to report 95% confidence intervals
- Analyzing limbs, not patients
- Presenting results in unstructured tables
- Reporting data in vague figures
- Failure to report patients lost to follow-up: where did these patients go?
- Reporting only positive findings

Discussion

A good way to structure the discussion is to *repeat your key findings*, describe *strengths and limitations* of your study, summarize and discuss *previous literature*, and finally reach a *conclusion.* A common error is presenting new data in the Discussion section. All results should be presented in the Results section, including reasons for protocol deviations and reasons for losses to follow-up. The Discussion section can be used to clarify matters, not to present them for the first time in the article. Of course, the conclusion should be supported by the findings of your study.

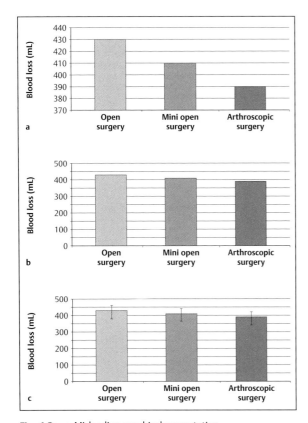

Fig. 4.2a–c Misleading graphical presentation
a A bar graph of the results of a hypothetical trial comparing different surgical approaches and blood loss. The presentation leads to visual overestimation of the treatment effect.
b A bar graph of the same results of the same hypothetical trial as in **a**, this time with the x-axis crossing the y-axis at zero. This gives true representation of the relative magnitudes of effect.
c A graph depicting the same information as **b**, this time with 95% confidence interval bars, which reveals no significant difference between the three groups.

Conclusion

After the preparation of the manuscript it is wise to ask an independent colleague to critically appraise your manuscript. This will facilitate further clarification and will help you add critical elements you may have missed. The key issue is transparency: readers should understand the merits of your study.

Suggested Reading

Altman DG, Schulz KF, Mother D, et al.; CONSORT GROUP (Consolidated Standards of Reporting Trials). The revised CONSORT statement for reporting randomized trials: explanation and elaboration. Ann Intern Med 2001;134(8):663–694

Boutron I, Moher D, Tugwell P, et al. A checklist to evaluate a report of a nonpharmacological trial (CLEAR NPT) was developed using consensus. J Clin Epidemiol 2005;58(12):1233–1240

Boutron I, Moher D, Altman DG, Schulz KF, Raved P; CONSORT Group. Extending the CONSORT statement to randomized trials of nonpharmacologic treatment: explanation and elaboration. Ann Intern Med 2008;148(4):295–309

Brand RA. Writing for Clinical Orthopaedics and Related Research. Clin Orthop Relat Res 2003; (413):1–7

CONSORT. http://www.consort-statement.org/extensions/interventions/non-pharmacologic-treatment-interventions/. Accessed September 14, 2009

Durbin CG Jr. Effective use of tables and figures in abstracts, presentations, and papers. Respir Care 2004;49(10):1233–1237

Guyatt GH, Brian Haynes R. Preparing reports for publication and responding to reviewers' comments. J Clin Epidemiol 2006; 59(9):900–906

Jüni P, Altman DG, Egger M. Systematic reviews in health care: assessing the quality of controlled clinical trials. BMJ 2001; 323(7303):42–46

Minervation. 2007. Consort: Transparent Reporting of Trials. Available at www.consort-statement.org. Accessed: December 7, 2007.

de Vet HC, Terwee CB, Ostelo RW, Beckerman H, Knol DL, Bouter LM. Minimal changes in health status questionnaires: distinction between minimally detectable change and minimally important change. Health Qual Life Outcomes 2006;4(54):54

References

1. Moher D, Cook DJ, Eastwood S, Olkin I, Rennie D, Stroup DF. Improving the quality of reports of meta-analyses of randomised controlled trials: the QUOROM statement. Quality of Reporting of Meta-analyses. Lancet 1999;354(9193):1896–1900

2. Lee CW, Chi KN. The standard of reporting of health-related quality of life in clinical cancer trials. J Clin Epidemiol 2000; 53(5):451–458

3. Estrada CA, Bloch RM, Antonacci D, et al. Reporting and concordance of methodologic criteria between abstracts and articles in diagnostic test studies. J Gen Intern Med 2000;15(3): 183–187

4. Bhandari M, Richards RR, Sprague S, Schemitsch EH. Quality in the reporting of randomized trials in surgery: is the Jadad scale reliable? Control Clin Trials 2001;22(6):687–688

5. Altman DG, Schulz KF, Moher D, et al.; CONSORT GROUP (Consolidated Standards of Reporting Trials). The revised CONSORT statement for reporting randomized trials: explanation and elaboration. Ann Intern Med 2001;134(8):663–694

6. Godlee F. Publishing study protocols: making them visible will improve registration, reporting and recruitment. BMC News and Views 2001;2:4

7. Bhandari M, Richards RR, Sprague S, Schemitsch EH. The quality of reporting of randomized trials in The Journal of Bone and Joint Surgery from 1988 through 2000. J Bone Joint Surg Am 2002;84-A(3):388–396

8. Montori VM, Bhandari M, Devereaux PJ, Manns BJ, Ghali WA, Guyatt GH. In the dark: the reporting of blinding status in randomized controlled trials. J Clin Epidemiol 2002;55(8): 787–790

9. Jokstad A, Esposito M, Coulthard P, Worthington HV. The reporting of randomized controlled trials in prosthodontics. Int J Prosthodont 2002;15(3):230–242

10. Nuovo J, Melnikow J, Chang D. Reporting number needed to treat and absolute risk reduction in randomized controlled trials. JAMA 2002;287(21):2813–2814

11. Faunce TA, Buckley NA. Of consents and CONSORTs: reporting ethics, law, and human rights in RCTs involving monitored overdose of healthy volunteers pre and post the "CONSORT" guidelines. J Toxicol Clin Toxicol 2003;41(2):93–99

12. Bossuyt PM, Reitsma JB, Bruns DE, et al.; Standards for Reporting of Diagnostic Accuracy. Towards complete and accurate reporting of studies of diagnostic accuracy: The STARD Initiative. Radiology 2003;226(1):24–28

13. Bossuyt PM, Reitsma JB, Bruns DE, et al.; Standards for Reporting of Diagnostic Accuracy. The STARD statement for reporting studies of diagnostic accuracy: explanation and elaboration. Ann Intern Med 2003;138(1):W1–12

14. Bennett JA. The Consolidated Standards of Reporting Trials (CONSORT): Guidelines for reporting randomized trials. Nurs Res 2005;54(2):128–132

15. Ethgen M, Boutron I, Baron G, Giraudeau B, Sibilia J, Ravaud P. Reporting of harm in randomized, controlled trials of nonpharmacologic treatment for rheumatic disease. Ann Intern Med 2005;143(1):20–25

16. Mills E, Wu P, Gagnier J, Heels-Ansdell D, Montori VM. An analysis of general medical and specialist journals that endorse CONSORT found that reporting was not enforced consistently. J Clin Epidemiol 2005;58(7):662–667

17. Mills EJ, Wu P, Gagnier J, Devereaux PJ. The quality of randomized trial reporting in leading medical journals since the revised CONSORT statement. Contemp Clin Trials 2005;26(4): 480–487

18. Biondi-Zoccai GG, Lotrionte M, Abbate A, et al. Compliance with QUOROM and quality of reporting of overlapping meta-analyses on the role of acetylcysteine in the prevention of contrast associated nephropathy: case study. BMJ 2006; 332(7535):202–209

19. Shea BJ, Boers M, Grimshaw JM, Hamel CD, Bouter LM. Does updating improve the methodological and reporting quality of systematic reviews? BMC Med Res Methodol 2006;6:27

20. Poolman RW, Struijs PA, Krips R, Sierevelt IN, Lutz KH, Bhandari M. Does a "Level I Evidence" rating imply high quality of reporting in orthopaedic randomised controlled trials? BMC Med Res Methodol 2006;6:44

21. Jacquier I, Boutron I, Moher D, Roy C, Ravaud P. The reporting of randomized clinical trials using a surgical intervention is in need of immediate improvement: a systematic review. Ann Surg 2006;244(5):677–683

22. Chan S, Bhandari M. The quality of reporting of orthopaedic randomized trials with use of a checklist for nonpharmacological therapies. J Bone Joint Surg Am 2007;89(9):1970–1978

23. Poolman RW, Struijs PA, Krips R, et al. Reporting of outcomes in orthopaedic randomized trials: does blinding of outcome assessors matter? J Bone Joint Surg Am 2007;89(3):550–558

24. Devereaux PJ, Choi PT, El-Dika S, et al. An observational study found that authors of randomized controlled trials frequently use concealment of randomization and blinding, despite the failure to report these methods. J Clin Epidemiol 2004; 57 (12):1232–1236

25. Jüni P, Altman DG, Egger M. Systematic reviews in health care: Assessing the quality of controlled clinical trials. BMJ 2001;323(7303):42–46

26. Brand RA. Writing for Clinical Orthopaedics and Related Research. Clin Orthop Relat Res 2003; (413):1–7

27. Guyatt GH, Brian Haynes R. Preparing reports for publication and responding to reviewers' comments. J Clin Epidemiol 2006;59(9):900–906

28. International Committee of Medical Journal Editors. Uniform requirements for manuscripts submitted to biomedical journals. N Engl J Med 1997;336(4):309–315

29. Moher D, Schulz KF, Altman DG. The CONSORT statement: revised recommendations for improving the quality of reports of parallel-group randomised trials. Lancet 2001;357(9263): 1191–1194

30. Boutron I, Moher D, Tugwell P, et al. A checklist to evaluate a report of a nonpharmacological trial (CLEAR NPT) was developed using consensus. J Clin Epidemiol 2005;58(12):1233–1240

31. Boutron I, Moher D, Altman DG, Schulz KF, Ravaud P; CONSORT Group. Extending the CONSORT statement to randomized trials of nonpharmacologic treatment: explanation and elaboration. Ann Intern Med 2008;148(4):295–309

32. Guyatt GH, Rennie D, eds. User's Guides to the Medical Literature: A Manual for Evidence-based Clinical Practice. Chicago, IL: AMA Press; 2002

33. Bhandari M, Tornetta P III, Guyatt GH. Glossary of evidence-based orthopaedic terminology. Clin Orthop Relat Res 2003;(413):158–163

34. Bland JM, Altman DG. Multiple significance tests: the Bonferroni method. BMJ 1995;310(6973):170

35. Bhandari M, Whang W, Kuo JC, Devereaux PJ, Sprague S, Tornetta P III. The risk of false-positive results in orthopaedic surgical trials. Clin Orthop Relat Res 2003; (413):63–69

36. Jaeschke R, Singer J, Guyatt GH. Measurement of health status. Ascertaining the minimal clinically important difference. Control Clin Trials 1989;10(4):407–415

37. de Vet HC, Terwee CB, Ostelo RW, Beckerman H, Knol DL, Bouter LM. Minimal changes in health status questionnaires: distinction between minimally detectable change and minimally important change. Health Qual Life Outcomes 2006;4 (54):54

38. Poolman RW, Kerkhoffs GM, Struijs PA, Bhandari M; International Evidence-Based Orthopedic Surgery Working Group. Don't be misled by the orthopedic literature: tips for critical appraisal. Acta Orthop 2007;78(2):162–171

39. Audigé L, Hanson B, Bhandari M, Schemitsch E. Interpretation of data and analysis of surgical trials. Tech Orthop 2004;19 (2):94–101

40. Minervation. 2007. Consort: Transparent Reporting of Trials. Available at www.consort-statement.org. Accessed: September 2007.

41. Durbin CG Jr. Effective use of tables and figures in abstracts, presentations, and papers. Respir Care 2004;49(10):1233–1237

42. Bryant D, Havey TC, Roberts R, Guyatt G. How many patients? How many limbs? Analysis of patients or limbs in the orthopaedic literature: a systematic review. J Bone Joint Surg Am 2006;88(1):41–45

5
Overview: What to Consider Before You Start Writing

Paul Karanicolas

Summary

This chapter will assist you in preparing to write your manuscript. There are several important steps to consider before you start writing. To begin, decide on your key message and select the most suitable journal. Next, prepare a detailed outline of what you plan to write. Finally, get organized, make time, and write.

This chapter will elaborate on the importance of each point and show you how to improve your manuscript prior to submission. By doing so, you will maximize your chances of getting your research paper published.

Introduction

You have developed an idea for a research project, performed a comprehensive literature review, written a protocol, obtained approval from the ethics review board, conducted your study, and analyzed the data. All that is left now is the seemingly simple task of preparing a written report for publication. Unfortunately, this crucial final step in the research cascade often proves the most difficult for even seasoned investigators, and can delay or prevent proper dissemination of the research findings (see Chapter 2). The amount of effort invested in the project through to this stage is immense, and preparing a polished manuscript will allow you to maximize the chances of your paper being accepted. Perhaps the biggest obstacle to preparing a research paper is the "blank screen" phenomenon (or the "blank page" phenomenon for the older generation more accustomed to typewriters). Anyone who has ever written anything has likely experienced this difficulty at some point. Although there is much to be said (after all, you will have devoted a substantial amount of time to the research project), the blank screen in front of you is simply too intimidating and often prevents you from getting started. The key to overcoming writer's block is to prepare yourself before you encounter this obstacle. In this chapter, the five essential steps that should be considered before you start writing your paper will be discussed. These suggestions will hopefully help you to write more efficiently, and maximize your chances of producing a manuscript that will be published.

Why Not Just Write?

Even if you do not have difficulties initiating your writing, it is a good idea to consider these suggestions rather than simply starting to write. Although the scientific quality of your research is important, several other factors contribute to a journal's decision to accept or reject a manuscript, including the interest to the journal's target audience, the journal's rejection rate, the presence of other recent publications on the topic, the results of your study, how well you have written the manuscript, and sheer luck.[1] If you plan accordingly, your writing can influence many of these factors by highlighting the importance of your research and presenting the readers with a clear message that is easy to follow.

> **Key Concepts: Five Things to Do *Before* You Start Writing**
> 1. Decide on your key message.
> 2. Select the most appropriate journal.
> 3. Get organized.
> 4. Prepare an outline.
> 5. Make time and write.

Decide on Your Key Message

The research you are reporting may be complex and difficult for readers to understand. When writing the manuscript, you must consider the amount of information that a reader will likely read, comprehend, and digest. Ask yourself the following question: "What is the single most important point for the reader to take away from this research?" When you have decided on your key message, you should work hard to convey that message as clearly and convincingly as possible given the results of your study.

In the ideal situation (if you have planned the study well, things have gone according to plan, and you have gotten lucky), your key message may simply be the answer to your primary research question. For example, one group of investigators asked the question, "In elderly osteoporotic patients with distal radius fractures, what is the impact of treatment with external fixation in comparison with plaster cast on stability?"[2] Since patients treated with external fixation achieved better clinical outcomes in the trial, the authors' key message was "Elderly osteoporotic patients with distal radius fractures should be treated with external fixation rather than plaster cast." If the study had ruled out an important difference between interventions, the key message might have been that the two therapies are equivalent.

In other cases, deciding on the key message you wish to portray may not be a simple feat. In one trial comparing three hip screws with two hook-pins for the fixation of femoral neck fractures, most of the outcomes did not differ significantly between the two interventions but the confidence intervals were wide, suggesting that there could be a true difference.[3] Rather than focusing on these indeterminate results, the authors' key message related to the prognostic significance of the quality of reduction in both groups. The investigators concluded that a substantial proportion of the patients in the study might have benefited from primary arthroplasty, and suggested that better prognostic tools were needed. Although this message did not arise from one of the researchers' primary objectives, it was the most clinically relevant finding from the observed results.

Even when a project does not proceed according to plan, researchers may be able to draw important conclusions (and relevant publications) if the practical or theoretical significance of the actual findings is considered carefully. For example, one group of investigators reported the difficulties they encountered in enrolling participants in a study and used the opportunity to focus on challenges encountered in randomized controlled trials of surgical interventions.[4] Virtually every study that is carefully planned and executed yields results that are worthy of publication. As a researcher, you must consider the results you have obtained in the context of existing knowledge and decide what message you feel is most important.

Once you have decided upon your key message, you must focus your energy on convincing the reader of its truth. You can accomplish this by framing each section of the manuscript (particularly the introduction and discussion) around the key message. The introduction should provide the rationale for conducting the study: Why would your message be important if it were true? The discussion section should first state the message, then elaborate on the message, then conclude with the message. Finally, the abstract should focus on the key message: conceptually, the conclusion of the abstract is the message. Staying focused in your writing will allow the audience to stay focused in their reading and effectively convey the important findings from your research.

Select the Most Appropriate Journal

Choosing a Journal

The bibliographic database Medline includes citations from over 5000 biomedical journals.[5] With so many potential journals to submit your manuscript to, how can you

possibly decide? As with many facets of medicine (and life), there is a balance of two issues to consider:
1. Where would you ideally like to see your manuscript published?
2. Where is your manuscript most likely to be accepted for publication?

One intuitively obvious factor to consider is the content area of the journal in relation to the topic you have studied. Journals can be broadly classified into three categories: general medical journals, subspecialty journals, and methodological journals.[1] General medical journals include high-profile publications such as the *Journal of the American Medical Association* and the *New England Journal of Medicine* as well as smaller national or regional journals like the *Canadian Medical Association Journal* or the *Illinois Medical Journal*. These journals accept manuscripts relating to a broad range of topics from all specialties. Manuscripts are most appropriate for these types of journals if they examine topics that are very commonly encountered, or apply specifically to practitioners from a particular region (such as economic analyses, or environmental agents only located in certain settings). In addition, to be considered for one of the highest-profile journals such as the *Journal of the American Medical Association*, the *New England Journal of Medicine*, *Lancet*, and the *British Medical Journal*, the study must be methodologically rigorous and yield clinically important results.

As a surgeon, most of the manuscripts you write will likely report on the studies you conduct in surgery and your fellow surgeons will constitute your target audience. You will therefore probably submit the majority of your manuscripts to a subspecialty journal in the field of orthopaedic surgery. Within the field of orthopaedic surgery, some journals are general (such as the *Journal of Bone and Joint Surgery*) and others are further subspecialized (such as the *Journal of Orthopaedic Trauma*). In general, as journals become more specialized, the target audience diminishes in size and the profile (and prestige) of publications in the journal similarly decreases.

> **Key Concepts: Selecting a Journal**
> Deciding which journal to submit your manuscript to is a trade-off between where you would ideally like to see your manuscript published and where your manuscript is most likely to be published.

Occasionally, you may write a manuscript with more of a methodological focus, either as an adjunct to a primary study report or in isolation. For example, while conducting a survey of orthopaedic surgeons, a group of investigators decided to examine whether the extent of flattery present in the survey's cover letter influenced the surgeons' response rate.[6] In addition to a manuscript reporting the survey's primary findings, the authors published a manuscript focused on the effectiveness of the two cover letters. Several journals focus their content on methodological questions like this one, including the *Journal of Clinical Epidemiology and Medical Care.*

There are several ways to investigate the characteristics of a journal. The first, of course, is to read a few issues of the journal to determine the topics that are typically published, the study designs, and the style of the writing. Most journals post instructions for potential authors on their Web sites; these may include descriptions of the journal's focus, different types of manuscripts that the journal accepts, and the journal's "acceptance rate" (or "rejection rate," depending on your outlook). To gain additional insight, it is wise to consult with more experienced researchers who have experience in your field of study and who ideally have submitted manuscripts to the journals you are considering, or even acted as reviewers. These individuals might be able to tell you about the specific criteria that the journals look for, the typical length of time between submission and the decision, and the likelihood that your manuscript will be accepted. In some cases, it might also be prudent to contact one of the journal's editors directly with specific questions before submission, particularly if you are unsure whether the journal might be interested in your topic of study or methodological design. Finally, several systems exist to rate the "impact" of a journal (most common is the "Impact Factor"), but these ratings do not necessarily represent a journal's ability to disseminate research findings and are potentially misleading, so they should be interpreted with caution.[7]

Most authors would ideally like to publish their work in high-impact journals. Theoretically, this maximizes the dissemination of their research and also provides the most prestige to the researchers. Ultimately the decision where to submit a manuscript involves balancing these preferences with the higher likelihood of rejection from higher-impact journals. If you are not in a rush to get your manuscript published and can accept occasional rejection, a reasonable strategy is to aim high for your paper's first submission, and resubmit to a lower-impact journal if it is rejected. Of course, authors need to be reasonable and responsible with their submissions to save time and energy for themselves and journal reviewers; clearly a case series describing 50 patients with scaphoid fractures will not be published in the *Journal of the American Medical Association.* Experienced colleagues and supervisors should be able to provide valuable guidance in this respect. Ultimately, remember that the decision to publish or reject a manuscript is highly subjective and difficult for even the most seasoned researchers to predict. This uncertainty makes the choice of target journal even more difficult for researchers.

Tailoring Your Manuscript to the Journal

An intuitive approach might be to prepare a manuscript, then decide which journal to submit it to for publication. However, to maximize the chances of acceptance to your preferred journal, a better approach is to first choose the journal you plan to submit to, and then tailor the content of the manuscript on the basis of the selected journal. The content and style of the manuscript may vary drastically depending on the journal (or category of journal) you plan to submit to.

If your manuscript will be submitted to a general medical journal or a methodology journal, you will need to provide more background information in the Introduction section for the readers to understand why the problem is significant. For example, a recent publication in the *Journal of the American Medical Association* reported the results of a trial comparing operative and nonoperative treatment for lumbar disk herniation.[8] The authors began their paper with the sentence, "Lumbar diskectomy is the most common surgical procedure performed in the United States for patients having back and leg symptoms; the vast majority of the procedures are elective." If this manuscript had been submitted to a general orthopaedic journal, or especially to a spine journal, that statement would have been self-evident and the authors could have omitted it. In contrast, the authors devote very little space in their manuscript to the technical details of the operation, which orthopaedic readers would likely be more interested in.

In summary, you should choose a target journal before you begin writing on the basis of the content of your paper, the target audience, the clinical importance of the research, and your level of patience. Once you have selected a target journal you should familiarize yourself with the journal's typical content and style, and tailor your manuscript to that journal to maximize the chances of acceptance.

Get Organized

Before you start writing, you should ensure that you have everything that you will need to allow you to focus on the task at hand without interruptions. This includes a copy of the target journal's guidelines, a list of your co-authors, a relevant literature review, a copy of the study protocol, and a report of the data analysis.

Journal Guidelines

Most journals post a list of guidelines for potential authors on their Web sites or within the printed journal. The majority of the guidelines refer to mundane issues that are relatively easy to adhere to, such as the size of margins, the reference style, and the formatting of section headers. However, some journals may also place limits on the number of words, figures, tables, references, or authors allowed. Furthermore, the content of some special sections may be restricted. You should familiarize yourself with the author guidelines for the journal you are considering, and ensure that you adhere to them as you write your manuscript. Refer to Chapter 16 for a listing of the author guidelines for some common journals.

Coauthors

Authorship can be a complex, delicate issue for the primary author to establish. Ideally, everyone's role in the project (including authorship) will be discussed at the outset of the study. Unfortunately, this usually is not the case, and it is often left to the primary author to determine who deserves credit as a coauthor and the order of authors on the manuscript. This can be especially challenging for junior researchers who have collaborated with more senior colleagues. In these circumstances you should rely heavily on the project's supervisor or senior author for guidance and assistance. Chapter 7 includes a full discussion of issues to consider in assigning authorship and suggestions for how to manage difficulties that may arise.

However you decide to assign authorship, the decisions should be made before you start writing the manuscript. The specific ordering of some of the authors may change on the basis of their contributions to the writing and editing of the manuscript, but their ultimate inclusion or exclusion should have been established before the first word is written. Once individuals are aware of their roles in the project, they will feel much more inclined to participate actively in all aspects of the study, including the interpretation of results and drafting of the manuscript.

You may choose to include some of your coauthors in the writing of the first draft, or to write the first draft yourself and involve your collaborators in the editing process. If you decide to split up the writing, you should ensure that all individuals are aware of your expectations of them, including the specific issues that they should address, an appropriate word count or page limit, and a timeline for completion. Furthermore, you should attempt to establish some guidelines regarding the paper's style; for example, whether you will be writing in the active or passive voice, or in the first or third person. If you decide to write the first draft yourself, you should still solicit as much input as possible from all of your coauthors before you begin writing, to ensure that there is general consensus regarding the key message that you will be conveying.

Protocol

Ideally, before embarking on the study you will have prepared a protocol that describes the background to the problem, the study's objectives, and its methods. The protocol provides a tremendous foundation upon which to build the manuscript. Although some modifications may be necessary to focus on your key message, often the Introduction and Methods sections of the manuscript can be drawn directly from the study protocol. Some authors even include templates for tables and figures in their study protocols; this makes the process of preparing a report even more efficient.

Before you begin writing you should gather all study documentation, including protocols, grants, and ethics board submissions that might be useful. Review these documents and reuse or modify any sections that you feel are appropriate for inclusion in the manuscript. Reading these documents might also highlight protocol violations or alterations that occurred during the study and that you should consider discussing in the manuscript.

Literature Review

Before embarking on your study, and perhaps as part of the protocol, you likely conducted a literature review relevant to the research question. You should review the studies that you found potentially relevant in the context of your study's results and your key message; your interpretation of some of the previous research may now be different. You will likely have to expand your literature search to identify research that has been published since your previous review. In addition, some topics that you did not previously consider might be important in the context of your study's findings.

For example, in the study of interventions for femoral neck fractures that was discussed previously, the investigators' initial literature review likely focused on studies comparing hip screws with hook-pins.[3] Since the authors' ultimate key message related to the importance of reduction quality as a prognostic variable, it would be important to review the literature in this area prior to writing the manuscript (in addition to updating the literature review comparing the two implants).

You should assure yourself that you are familiar with the recent literature in your field of study. You can accomplish this by reading review articles, performing broad searches of databases, and discussing topics with experienced colleagues. It can also be helpful to summarize the literature review in a point-form document (including references) that is accessible while writing the manuscript, to ensure that your discussion is accurate and contemporary.

Analysis

The results from the statistical analysis hopefully determined your key message, so you should be very familiar with the findings. However, it is important that you are comfortable with the methods used in the analysis, including the specific statistical tests performed and any secondary supportive analyses and subgroup analyses. For some studies the analysis may be simple, and you may be able to perform the testing yourself (depending on your expertise in statistics). Most of the time, it is wise to involve a statistician in the design and interpretation of the study.

See Chapter 8, "When Do You Need a Statistician?" for more information regarding this important topic. In either case, you should ensure that you have a full report of the statistical analysis readily available while you write the manuscript.

Prepare an Outline

Although the content of a manuscript will vary substantially depending on the field of study and the methodological design, the overall structure of most scientific manuscripts is essentially the same. Most research reports follow this basic structure: cover page, abstract, introduction, methods, results, and discussion. References, acknowledgments, tables, and figures follow the text of the manuscript. It can be very helpful to begin with an outline that includes a heading for each of these sections. Simply writing the headings and leaving a few lines between each for text will form a useful template for the manuscript, and will eliminate the dreaded blank screen.

Later in this book, you will find suggestions for appropriate content and structure for each of these sections. You may find it helpful to make an outline for each of these sections as well. Focusing on your key message at all times, jot down a few points that are important to cover in the introduction: Why is this problem important? The Methods and Results sections may be subdivided by inserting subheadings, such as "Participants," "Interventions," and "Analysis." Similarly, headings or point-form notes may help to arrange your thoughts for the discussion section. You should create this outline in the body of the manuscript; it can then act as a template when you start writing.

It is a good idea to involve your coauthors early and often in the process of preparing a manuscript. You may consider circulating a copy of your outline to all of your collaborators and asking for feedback or additional topics that should be covered. It is best to ensure that everyone involved in the project agrees on the key message and important points to be discussed before you start writing, so that they can be incorporated in a logical, coherent sequence.

Make Time and Write!

If you have followed the guidelines suggested in this chapter, you will have formulated the key message you wish to disseminate, selected the most appropriate journal, organized all of the necessary information you will need, and prepared an outline. Now all that is left is to begin writing the manuscript! Set aside a block of time that you can use to begin writing in a quiet location and with no interruptions. The quality of your writing will be much better if you are able to allow your thoughts to flow, rather than writing in brief segments. At a minimum, you should

plan to spend 3–4 hours during your first writing session to get a substantial start on the manuscript.

As you write the first draft of the manuscript, focus on the content of your writing rather than the grammar or style. Consider this analogous to brainstorming: allow your thoughts to flow, and write what comes to mind. Although you may later find that a substantial portion of what you have written is irrelevant or superfluous, it will be easy to edit and cut out these sections once you have considered them in the context of the whole paper. This approach is far more efficient than spending lots of time perfecting each section of the manuscript during the first draft, only to find that what you have written in the introduction does not flow with your discussion. Of course, if you take this approach, remember that one of your future revisions should focus exclusively on the grammar and style of your writing to maximize its clarity and chances of acceptance. Finally, although there is a logical sequence to the presentation of all manuscripts, you do not necessarily need to write the manuscript in that order. You may find it easier to begin by writing the Methods and Results sections, which are usually the easiest to write. The abstract should usually be the last section that you write, since it simply summarizes each section of the manuscript.

Conclusion

After putting in a substantial amount of work to see a research project through to completion, you should make every effort to write a clear, concise manuscript that maximizes its chances for publication in a high-quality journal. Preparing adequately before you start writing will make the writing process more efficient, productive, and hopefully enjoyable.

Suggested Reading

Guyatt GH, Haynes RB. Preparing reports for publication and responding to reviewers' comments. In: Haynes RB, Sackett DL, Guyatt GH, Tugwell P, eds. Clinical Epidemiology: How to Do Clinical Practice Research. 3rd ed. Philadelphia: Lippincott Williams & Wilkins; 2006:461–473

References

1. Guyatt GH, Haynes RB. Preparing reports for publication and responding to reviewers' comments. In: Haynes RB, Sackett DL, Guyatt GH, Tugwell P, eds. Clinical Epidemiology: How to Do Clinical Practice Research. 3rd ed. Philadelphia: Lippincott Williams & Wilkins; 2006:461–473
2. Moroni A, Vannini F, Faldini C, Pegreffi F, Giannini S. Cast vs external fixation: a comparative study in elderly osteoporotic distal radial fracture patients. Scand J Surg 2004;93(1):64–67
3. Lykke N, Lerud PJ, Strømsøe K, Thorngren KG. Fixation of fractures of the femoral neck. A prospective, randomised trial of

three Ullevaal hip screws versus two Hansson hook-pins. J Bone Joint Surg Br 2003;85(3):426–430

4. Kao LS, Aaron BC, Dellinger EP. Trials and tribulations: current challenges in conducting clinical trials. Arch Surg 2003;138 (1):59–62

5. National Library of Medicine. Available at: http://www.nlm. nih.gov/services/usemedline.html. Accessed December 21, 2009.

6. Leece P, Bhandari M, Sprague S, Swiontkowski MF, Schemitsch EH, Tornetta P. Does flattery work? A comparison of 2 different cover letters for an international survey of orthopedic surgeons. Can J Surg 2006;49(2):90–95

7. Chew M, Villanueva EV, Van Der Weyden MB. Life and times of the impact factor: retrospective analysis of trends for seven medical journals (1994–2005) and their Editors' views. J R Soc Med 2007;100(3):142–150

8. Weinstein JN, Tosteson TD, Lurie JD, et al. Surgical vs non-operative treatment for lumbar disk herniation: the Spine Patient Outcomes Research Trial (SPORT): a randomized trial. JAMA 2006;296(20):2441–2450

6

Ethics in Writing: Maintaining Credibility

Lyndsay Somerville, Dianne Bryant

Summary

The objective of this chapter is to increase awareness among orthopaedic investigators regarding the range of ethical issues that arise during manuscript preparation, as well as to provide tips on how to maintain credibility by writing ethically.

Introduction

The number of cases of research misconduct has risen in recent years as researchers come under increasing pressure to "publish or perish," to attain promotion and tenure.[1] Research misconduct is traditionally defined as plagiarism, fabrication, or falsification in any elements of the research process, including the reporting of research results.[2] Some experts believe that more subtle issues such as selective reporting of results or failure to report negative trials cause greater threats to the validity of research.[3,4] Other forms of misconduct include duplicate publication as well as authorship issues including honorary and ghost authorship.

Plagiarism

Scientific writing is a demanding process, requiring a great deal of time and effort from multiple individuals. The end product of this process should be a clear, concise, and accurate reflection of the ideas and intellectual contribution of the authors to the manuscript. Pressures to publish several manuscripts and the inevitable constraints ensuing from mixing clinical practice with conducting research limits the amount of time available to write manuscripts, sometimes resulting in the use of short cuts to reach a final product.

The most widely known ethical misconduct is plagiarism. Plagiarism is the replication of ideas, data, or text without permission or acknowledgment of the originator.[5] Plagiarism can be claiming another investigator's ideas as your own, or not giving credit to others' work when copying figures or words verbatim, including inappropriate referencing. This type of ethical misconduct can have severe consequences including demotion or dismissal.[6]

Jargon Simplified: Plagiarism
The replication of ideas, data, or text without permission or acknowledgment of the originator.[5]

Three forms of plagiarism are commonly encountered in the scientific literature.[6] The first is reproducing text word-for-word from someone else's work and placing it into your manuscript without giving proper credit to the original author. If you use someone else's words verbatim, you must enclose the selected text in quotation marks followed with the appropriate reference including the page number.[6]

The second type of plagiarism occurs when an author paraphrases someone else's work, but does not give credit to the originator of the idea.[6] Simply replacing words or rearranging the sentences of someone else's work is considered plagiarism if it is not properly referenced.[6]

The third type of plagiarism is recycling text, or self-plagiarism.[6] This refers to reusing parts of an article that has already been published previously by the same author. Some freedom is allotted to authors who recycle highly complex methods sections with little modification; however, it is generally only acceptable if modifying the words would alter the intended meaning.[6] The practice of self-plagiarism has not been addressed in the medical literature and no guideline on how much text (if any) can be identical between manuscripts has been offered. One form of self-plagiarism that is tolerated is reusing text from proposals such as grants or Research Ethics Board applications, or recycling of text from preliminary articles presented at conferences.[6]

Key Concepts: Common Forms of Plagiarism
- Word-for-word reproduction of others' work without giving credit to the original author
- Paraphrasing of another's work without giving credit to the originator of the idea
- Text recycling, or self-plagiarism, of articles already published by the same author

Fabrication and Falsification

According the Office of Research Integrity (ORI), fabrication occurs when investigators report false or made-up results. Falsification is a type of fabrication that includes manipulating research materials to obtain specific results, or altering or excluding data in the report in such a way that the results are not accurately represented.[7] This type of misconduct is commonly seen in the form of making up data (including reporting false methods and results) and failing to report all results.

Jargon Simplified: Fabrication and Falsification

Fabrication occurs when investigators report false or made-up results.[7]

Falsification is a type of fabrication that includes manipulating research materials to obtain specific results, or altering or excluding data in the report in such a way that the results are not accurately represented.[7]

Reality Check: Office of Research Integrity

On behalf of the Secretary of Health and Human Services the ORI (http://ori.dhhs.gov/) oversees and directs Public Health Service (PHS) research integrity activities (with the exception of the research activities of the Food and Drug Administration). Its responsibilities include developing regulations and procedures to identify and prevent research misconduct, as well as monitoring misconduct investigations and recommending actions to be taken against those who commit misconduct. It also oversees programs to educate researchers on conducting research responsibly and provides assistance for institutions regarding research misconduct.

Perhaps the most serious consequence of fabrication is its potential to affect the care of patients. If an investigator falsely reports the benefits of a treatment or underestimates the harms of a therapy, the impact on a patient may not only potentially be life threatening but may also have an impact on their psychological wellbeing.[2]

Reality Check: VIGOR Study

The *New England Journal of Medicine* printed an editorial regarding inaccurate data reported in the Vioxx Gastrointestinal Outcomes Research (VIGOR) study.[8,9] These inaccuracies raised apprehension about particular conclusions the study had made.

VIGOR was a randomized controlled trial designed to determine the number of gastrointestinal events in patients with rheumatoid arthritis treated with either rofecoxib (Vioxx) or naproxen (Naprosyn). The investigators also recorded data on the number of cardiovascular events in the two treatment groups.

The authors of the VIGOR trial failed to report three myocardial infarctions, all of which occurred in the Vioxx group. The publishing journal believed that the authors were not aware of the events early enough for them to be included in the published article. However, it was soon brought to the journal's attention that two of the authors knew about these additional events before the article was submitted. Excluding these three events rendered the analysis and subsequent conclusions invalid, reporting an underestimation of the difference in risk of myocardial infarction between the rofecoxib and naproxen groups.

Failing to report the findings of negative trials has similar consequences for patients and clinicians. Publication bias is the bias created when authors submit, or reviewers/journals accept, manuscripts for publication based on the direction of the study findings; smaller negative studies are less likely to be published. This means that the literature contains only articles that reflect a positive treatment effect, leading to an exaggerated estimate of treatment effectiveness, particularly when study results are pooled in a meta-analysis.[10] If treatment decisions are to be based on the published literature, it is imperative to prevent publication bias so that health professionals have all data available on which to make an informed decision regarding a treatment.

Jargon Simplified: Negative Trial

Trials "in which the authors have concluded that the experimental treatment is no better than control therapy."[11]

Jargon Simplified: Meta Analysis

"An overview that incorporates a quantitative strategy for combining the results of several studies into a single pooled or summary estimate."[11]

Perhaps a less serious form of ethical misconduct consists in not properly forming a-priori hypotheses about what you expect to find when conducting your research. By presenting well thought out arguments supported by the existing literature and biologic plausibility *before* conducting the analysis, then setting out to test your hypotheses by performing your research, you improve the chances that the conclusions of your research will be robust (i.e., that they will stand the test of time). If, on the other hand, you conduct your analyses based on your data (e.g., unplanned subgroup analyses) and center your interpretations on these findings, your conclusions stand a high chance of being incorrect and of misleading readers.

Jargon Simplified: A-priori Hypothesis versus Post-hoc Hypothesis

A-priori hypothesis—A hypothesis developed before data analysis.

Post-hoc hypothesis—A hypothesis developed after the analysis.

Clinical research has a defined process, including defining a research question, developing hypotheses, selecting outcomes, following an established study design, and evaluating and interpreting data. It is not unusual, however, for a wealth of data to be collected that is unrelated to the defined a-priori hypotheses and predefined outcomes. Unfortunately, it is not uncommon for investigators to search out relationships and examine subgroups not defined by the original hypotheses. Sorting through large amounts of data and picking out information based on the results of post-hoc analyses is what is known as "data mining" or "data dredging."[12,13] At times this practice can reveal new problems, and produce new hypotheses. Investigators should not emphasize these findings in their conclusions but should instead use this information to develop new research questions and direct future hypotheses. There are numerous articles that discuss the potential pitfalls of performing multiple comparisons and subgroup analyses.[14–17]

Duplicate Publication

Duplicate or redundant publication is defined as publishing an article that overlaps significantly with an article that has previously been published.[18] According to the Committee on Publication Ethics (COPE), this comprises any two or more articles published by at least some of the same authors that share the same hypothesis, data, discussion, or conclusion without properly cross-referencing the other publication.[19]

Reality Check: Committee on Publication Ethics

The major objective of COPE (http://www.publicationethics.org.uk/) is to provide support for editors who encounter violations in research and publication ethics and to make suggestions for editors on how best to deal with new incidences and issues. This committee allows editors of peer-reviewed journals to discuss important ethical issues in scientific writing, as well as to encourage those who encounter problems to seek the appropriate outlet to investigate the problem.[19]

The criteria for duplicate publication are subjective; however, several forms in the literature have been identified.[1,18,20,21] These include:

- Covert duplication, which is defined as attempting to publish a paper in two different journals concurrently
- Publishing a paper in one language and having it translated to be published in an alternate journal
- Publishing a paper in a small journal and subsequently submitting it to a larger journal without informing publishers of the previous publication
- "Salami-slicing," (also known as "least publishable units"): reporting data from the same research project in multiple manuscripts to maximize the number of papers obtained from one study[22]

Key Concepts: Criteria for Duplicate Publication

1. Submitting a paper to two different journals simultaneously.
2. Translating a paper into other languages for publication in different journals.
3. Submitting a published article to a larger journal without disclosure of past publication.
4. Dividing data from one study and reporting it in multiple publications ("salami-slicing").

In the orthopaedic literature, the duplicate publication rate has been reported to be approximately 3%, though this report did not include cases of "salami slicing."[21] A review of the surgical literature demonstrated that salami-slicing comprised 52.4% of all duplicate publications.[20]

Submitting duplicate publications wastes the time and resources of readers, reviewers, and editors and delays publication time for investigators who have submitted other works.[18,20,21] The consequences of duplicate publication are more serious if they are unknowingly included in meta-analyses, since the inclusion of duplicate data will certainly falsely inflate the precision of the estimate of the treatment effect and potentially bias the estimate itself, potentially misguiding readers.[18]

However, it is perfectly reasonable to maximize the number of publications when the quantity of information in the database justifies producing multiple publications. Further justification is afforded when there is a clear difference in the research question being asked of the data. To avoid unethical duplicate publication, investigators should submit articles serially rather than in parallel, and reference the primary and perhaps even the secondary articles. If you are republishing an article in another language, you should reference the original article at the time of submission.

Duplicate publication falsely inflates the investigator's curriculum vitae and possibly violates any copyright declaration that addresses whether their article has been submitted already or is currently under review by another journal, which authors are required to sign at the time of submission.[6,21] One way to avoid being perceived as unethical is to list in the curriculum vitae the primary publication, indent, and list duplicate publications underneath so that reviewers are aware that one project produced the list of publications.

Authorship

The increase in volume of scientific research has been accompanied by an increase in the number of authors listed on publications.[23–25] The International Committee of Medical Journal Editors (ICMJE)* has developed formal criteria to standardize the definition for authorship.[26] According to the ICMJE, authorship should be granted if an individual has met the following criteria: made substantial contributions to conceptualization and design of the study, acquired data, or analyzed and interpreted the data; drafted

---

* The International Committee of Medical Journal Editors (http://www.icmje.org/): A group of editors of medical journals who originally met to develop guidelines for formatting of manuscripts that were submitted to their journals. This group came to be known as the Vancouver group but soon expanded to a non–open membership group called the International Committee of Medical Journal Editors (ICMJE). Along with this expansion their concerns broadened to ethics related to publication in biomedical journals. This group has published the Uniform Requirements for Manuscripts Submitted to Biomedical Journals, which several journals have adopted as guidelines for authors submitting to their journal.

the manuscript or revised it critically for important intellectual content; and provided final approval of the version to be published. This committee also states that acquisition of funding, collection of data, or supervision of the research group, alone, does not justify authorship.[26]

> **Key Concepts: Requirement for Authorship**
> * Made substantial contributions to conceptualization and design of the study, collecting data, or analysis and interpretation of the data
> * Drafted the manuscript or revised it critically for important intellectual content
> * Provided final approval of the version to be published

There are two commonly encountered types of authorship that fall outside these guidelines and represent unethical practices: honorary authorship and ghost authorship. Honorary authorship, often referred to as guest or gift authorship, is defined as an author being named despite failing to meet authorship criteria.[27] Honorary authorship includes attributing authorship to clinicians who contribute patients to a research project or to an individual who obtained funding for the project but made no other contribution. A ghost author is defined as someone who has made significant contributions to the research and who meets the criteria for authorship but who is not listed as an author.[27]

> **Jargon Simplified: Honorary Authorship and Ghost Authorship**
> **Honorary authorship**—when an author is named despite not meeting authorship criteria.[27]
> **Ghost authorship**—when an individual meets the criteria for authorship, but is not listed as an author.[27]

When authorship is awarded to those who meet the criteria, they are accountable for their work and are given proper credit at the same time. The use of loose criteria for authorship reduces individual accountability for the published work, while the credit received by each author remains the same.[25] The ICMJE is currently promoting the idea of using an alternative form of authorship, whereby an individual's contributions would be detailed at the end of the article to assign appropriate credit and to maintain investigators' responsibility for their contribution.[24,26] Many journals already require such detailing of authors' responsibilities and contributions even if this information is not published.

Conclusion

It is the author's responsibility to be aware of the several forms of misconduct that exist in scientific writing. Certain types of misconduct, such as plagiarism, are familiar. However, there are many other types of misconduct that inves-

tigators are generally unaware of but which threaten the integrity of the research and have the potential to negatively affect patient care. Authors must educate themselves in the ethical conduct of research and reporting of results.

Suggested Reading

Brice J, Bligh J. Author misconduct: not just the editors' responsibility. Med Educ 2005;39(1):83–89

Committee of Publication Ethics. Guidelines on Good Publication Practice. Available at: http://www.publicationethics.org./code-conduct. Accessed December 18, 2009.

Office of Research Integrity. Available at: http://ori.dhhs.gov.proxy1.lib.uwo.ca:2048/misconduct/definition_misconduct.shtml. Accessed December 18, 2009

Roig M. Avoiding plagiarism, self-plagiarism, and other questionable writing practices: A guide to ethical writing. Available at: http://facpub.stjohns.edu/~roigm/plagiarism. Accessed December 18, 2009

Smith GD, Ebrahim S. Data dredging, bias, or confounding. BMJ 2002;325(7378):1437–1438

von Elm E, Poglia G, Walder B, Tramèr MR. Different patterns of duplicate publication: an analysis of articles used in systematic reviews. JAMA 2004;291(8):974–980

References

1. Brice J, Bligh J. Author misconduct: not just the editors' responsibility. Med Educ 2005;39(1):83–89
2. Benos DJ, Fabres J, Farmer J, et al. Ethics and scientific publication. Adv Physiol Educ 2005;29(2):59–74
3. Coultas D. Ethical considerations in the interpretation and communication of clinical trial results. Proc Am Thorac Soc 2007;4(2):194–198, discussion 198–199
4. Bevan JC. Ethical behaviour of authors in biomedical journalism. Ann R Coll Physicians Surg Can 2002;35(2):81–85
5. Fenton JE, Jones AS. Integrity in medical research and publication. Clin Otolaryngol Allied Sci 2002;27(6):436–439
6. Roig M. Avoiding plagiarism, self-plagiarism, and other questionable writing practices: A guide to ethical writing. Available at: http://facpub.stjohns.edu/~roigm/plagiarism. Accessed December 18, 2009
7. Office of Research Integrity. Available at: http://ori.dhhs.gov.proxy1.lib.uwo.ca:2048/misconduct/definition_misconduct.shtml. Accessed December 18, 2009
8. Bombardier C, Laine L, Reicin A, et al. VIGOR Study Group. Comparison of upper gastrointestinal toxicity of rofecoxib and naproxen in patients with rheumatoid arthritis. N Engl J Med 2000;343(21):1520–1528, 2 pp following 1528
9. Curfman GD, Morrissey S, Drazen JM. Expression of concern: Bombardier et al., "Comparison of upper gastrointestinal toxicity of rofecoxib and naproxen in patients with rheumatoid arthritis," N Engl J Med 2000;343:1520–8. N Engl J Med 2005;353(26):2813–2814
10. Haynes RB, Sackett DL, Guyatt GH, Tugwell P. Clinical Epidemiology: How to do Clinical Practice Research. 3rd ed. New York: Lippincott Williams & Wilkins; 2006
11. Guyatt GH, Rennie D, eds. User's Guides to the Medical Literature: A Manual for Evidence-based Clinical Practice. Chicago, IL: AMA Press; 2002
12. Riss P. From "data mining" to "salami publication"—how (not) to present data. Int Urogynecol J Pelvic Floor Dysfunct 2007;18(2):121–122

13. Smith GD, Ebrahim S. Data dredging, bias, or confounding. BMJ 2002;325(7378):1437–1438

14. Bhandari M, Devereaux PJ, Li P, et al. Misuse of baseline comparison tests and subgroup analyses in surgical trials. Clin Orthop Relat Res 2006;447(447):247–251

15. Assmann SF, Pocock SJ, Enos LE, Kasten LE. Subgroup analysis and other (mis)uses of baseline data in clinical trials. Lancet 2000;355(9209):1064–1069

16. Pocock SJ, Assmann SE, Enos LE, Kasten LE. Subgroup analysis, covariate adjustment and baseline comparisons in clinical trial reporting: current practice and problems. Stat Med 2002;21(19):2917–2930

17. Yusuf S, Wittes J, Probstfield J, Tyroler HA. Analysis and interpretation of treatment effects in subgroups of patients in randomized clinical trials. JAMA 1991;266(1):93–98

18. von Elm E, Poglia G, Walder B, Tramèr MR. Different patterns of duplicate publication: an analysis of articles used in systematic reviews. JAMA 2004;291(8):974–980

19. Committee of Publication Ethics. Guidelines on Good Publication Practice. Available at: http://www.publicationethics. org./code-conduct. Accessed December 18, 2009

20. Schein MP, Paladugu R. Redundant surgical publications: tip of the iceberg? Surgery 2001;129(6):655–661

21. Eck JC, Nachtigall D, Hodges SD, Humphreys SC. Redundant publications in the orthopedic literature. Orthopedics 2007; 30(1):60–62

22. Rogers LF. Salami slicing, shotgunning, and the ethics of authorship. AJR Am J Roentgenol 1999;173(2):265

23. Grieger MC. Authorship: an ethical dilemma of science. Sao Paulo Med J 2005;123(5):242–246

24. King CR, McGuire DB, Longman AJ, Carroll-Johnson RM. Peer review, authorship, ethics, and conflict of interest. Image J Nurs Sch 1997;29(2):163–167

25. Rennie D, Yank V, Emanuel L. When authorship fails. A proposal to make contributors accountable. JAMA 1997;278(7): 579–585

26. International Committee of Medical Journal Editors. Uniform Requirements for Manuscripts Submitted to Biomedical Journals: Writing and Editing for Biomedical Publication. Available at: http://www.icmje.org/. Accessed December 18, 2009

27. Flanagin A, Carey LA, Fontanarosa PB, et al. Prevalence of articles with honorary authors and ghost authors in peer-reviewed medical journals. JAMA 1998;280(3):222–224

7

Authorship: What You Should Know

Rad Zdero, Emil H. Schemitsch

Summary

Deciding on the authorship of scientific papers can be a complicated task. How does one determine whose names should be included in the list of authors? This chapter provides practical guidelines for authorship, including author order, number of authors, acknowledgments, and conflicts arising from authorship order and other related issues. After reading this chapter, the reader will hopefully understand that authorship is more than writing some words on a piece of paper. Rather, it implies that those listed as co-writers are "cocreators" or "codiscoverers."

Introduction

"Every bird likes to wet its beak." "Don't muzzle an ox while it is treading grain." "The laborer deserves his wages." "Give credit where credit is due." These are all pro-verbs that can be applied to the authorship of scientific papers; in other words, everyone who contributes in a significant way to a project should be recognized for their efforts by being included as a coauthor on the published paper. Responsibility should be rewarded with recognition; that is only just. But, as we shall see, the real world is sometimes more complicated than that. A host of challenges can make the authorship issue quite thorny. The aim of this chapter, therefore, is to provide the up-and-coming researcher with some key introductory insights and practical tools in dealing with the whole issue of authorship. A deeper examination can be found elsewhere.[1]

The Mysterious Case of Doctor Franklin

In 1962, James Watson, Francis Crick, and Maurice Wilkins stood together to receive the Nobel Prize in Physiology or Medicine for their proposal of a double-helix structure for DNA. However, a fourth person was missing, namely, Dr. Rosalind Franklin, a Cambridge-educated scientist whose x-ray diffraction patterns of DNA molecules proved experimentally that their structure was indeed that of a double-helix.[2,3] Without these diffraction patterns, DNA structure might have remained a mystery for years to come. Franklin, having died several years earlier in 1958 of ovarian cancer at the age of 37, was not eligible

to receive the Nobel Prize posthumously. In their Nobel Prize speeches, only Wilkins made a brief mention of Franklin.

Personality clashes and discrimination may have all contributed to the difficulties Franklin encountered in her relationships with some of her colleagues—particularly Maurice Wilkins, who had his own interests in DNA research—during her stint from 1951 to 1953 at King's College in London. It was here that her crucial photographs of diffraction patterns of DNA were taken and, without her permission, shown by Wilkins to Watson, who immediately recognized the implications. Moreover, after Crick had obtained Franklin's findings from a 1952 King's College Medical Research Council report, within 1 week he was able to begin constructing a model of DNA that was compatible with Franklin's data.

In their joint paper published as the lead article in the April 1953 issue of *Nature*, Watson and Crick make vague reference to having been "stimulated by a knowledge of the general nature of the unpublished experimental results and ideas of Dr. M. H. F. Wilkins, Dr. R. E. Franklin, and their co-workers at King's College, London." This comment, along with the fact that Franklin's own article about DNA structure in the same issue of *Nature* appeared third in a series on the topic, leaves the reader with the impression that Franklin's work was only supplemental to Watson and Crick's work when, in fact, it was absolutely central.

The mysterious case of Dr. Franklin illustrates the need for proper scientific credit being given to those to whom it belongs if scientific research is to be considered an honorable vocation. It might be a meaningful gesture, then, if the phrase "the Watson, Crick, and Franklin structure for DNA" were to begin to permeate academia today, even 50 years after the events.

What Is an "Author"?

Let us begin with an understanding of what the word "author" actually means. The word "author" comes from the Latin word "auctor," which means "source" or "origin." The dictionary defines an author as being the beginner or originator or creator of something, especially of a written work, whether fiction or nonfiction. But, in the scientific arena, as in many other fields, authorship is much more than just simply the physical act of putting pen to paper or finger to keyboard. Rather, an author of an academic article might be described as someone who is involved in one or all of the following key stages:

1. An original idea or novel application of an old idea emerges in their mind.
2. They develop and refine the idea, in greater or lesser detail.
3. They make an effort to record the idea in writing or make a record of it in some fashion.

> **Key Concepts: Authorship**
> The laborer deserves his wages!

The formal criteria of authorship developed and promulgated by the ICMJE (International Committee of Medical Journal Editors) are given and discussed in Chapter 6.

Whose Names Should Be Included?

The answer to this question is not as simple as it seems. Although, in theory, all (and only) those who contributed substantially to a project should be listed as authors, this is not always the case in practice. There are major problems regarding scientific "authorship" such as "honorary authorship" (i.e., authors are listed even though they have not really contributed significantly to the project) and "ghost authorship" (i.e., individuals are not named as authors although they contributed much to the research effort). (See Chapter 6 regarding the ethical consideration of these forms of authorship). The *Journal of the American Medical Association* published a paper investigating peer-reviewed articles in medical journals that found that approximately 19% had some evidence of "honorary authorship," while 11% showed some evidence of "ghost authorship."[4]

When it comes to including authors for your potential journal article, think of it as a train (**Fig. 7.1**). Someone is at the front driving the whole thing. Depending on how much a passenger has paid for their ticket, they will have seats in different sections of the train. And only those with legitimate tickets can get on board for the ride. Others will be kicked off.

A practical guideline for authorship, therefore, is that anyone involved significantly in one, two, or all three stages of the process described earlier should have their name included in the list of authors. Usually, it is quite obvious who the authors are. They are the people who provided visionary leadership for the project, participated in the planning and brainstorming meetings, did the literature review, gathered or provided the physical resources needed for the project, performed the experiments, built the theoretical computer models, executed the statistical and other data analyses, created the figures and tables, and actually wrote the paper with their own two hands. Otherwise, if someone is not involved significantly in any of these activities, they should not be included as authors, but perhaps they might be mentioned in the "acknowledgments" section of the article (more on this later).

Obviously, not everyone will be involved in every aspect of the project to the same degree. Each person will bring their own expertise and capability to the table. That's what teams are for, namely, shouldering the burden together. If research can be thought of as a sports "game," then some people on the "team" will be more like "players" who are physically playing the game, while others will serve more like "coaches" and "managers," developing strategies and making sure the players have all they need to win the game. The "players" might include junior members such as undergraduate summer students, graduate students, medical students, and employees, who are actually doing the hands-on work on the project. The "coaches" and "managers" might include senior members such as professors, research project coordinators, laboratory managers, and industry partners, who are providing mentoring, consultation, resources, and visionary direction for the project. This description is generally true, but it is not unusual to find senior members doing some of the actual work too, especially if the team is a small one.

What about Author Order?

It is never the water boy, towel girl, coach, trainer, or even the owner of a sports team whose name is on everyone's lips after a big win. It's always the star offensive player who scored the most points or the star defensive player who time and again prevented the opposing team from getting ahead. Even though others who are part of the sports organization made valuable contributions, without which the team might not have won, their reward is in knowing that they did their job well to make sure their team won. Theirs is a supportive role. This tends to apply to scientific authorship too.

The first author is usually the one who did most of the actual physical work on the project and who wrote most of the article. Examples of this include authors for whom the paper is a main part of their master's thesis, doctoral thesis, medical residency training, or medical fellowship requirement. Sometimes, a senior researcher or faculty member will take the lead in physically performing a project themselves, or perhaps they will write a review article or book chapter on a certain topic because of their recognized stature in the field. Although they might receive some assistance here and there from others, they will rightly be the sole or first author.

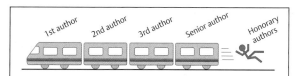

Fig. 7.1 The "authorship train."

The intermediate authors (second, third, fourth, etc.) are those who have provided some significant assistance to the first author in getting the project done. This may include any number of things, such as performing literature reviews, doing some part of the experimental work, writing a portion of the paper, performing some of the statistical analysis, giving some important feedback on certain aspects of the project, and so on.

The last author on the paper is last but not least. The last-named author is typically the most senior member of the research team for that particular project, primarily providing resources, mentoring, and consultation. They may or may not do any of the physical work on the project. They may be the supervisor of the thesis of which the article is just one part, or they may be the senior physician who is training the medical resident or fellow in the context of clinical rounds and the research project that turns into a published article.

It must be noted that the above usually applies to engineering, biology, and medicine. However, it does not necessarily apply to other fields. In some disciplines it might be the convention to list authorship based on seniority, with the most senior member of the team becoming lead author (e.g., in organic chemistry).

> **Key Concepts: Honorary and Ghost Authorship**
> "Honorary" and "ghost" authorship are no-no's!

How Many Authors?

Human beings contribute their ideas and energies best in smaller groups. Social scientists like Robin Dunbar and colleagues have discovered that human social networks typically hover around the magic "Dunbar number" of 148 people.[5,6] Yet, it has been suggested that subgroup satisfaction peaks when membership is between five and eight individuals.[7] Thus, even when larger groups have big goals, there is usually a need at times to break down the large group into smaller working units to achieve the large group's aims (examples include platoons in an army, family units in a society, provinces within a nation, and so on).

Human nature itself, therefore, holds some key insights for us in considering this question: "How many authors should be (or eventually will be) included as coauthors of your publication?" The answer to this question, though, depends on the answers to three other questions.

First, how many people significantly contributed to the project? As already discussed above, anyone who has provided pivotal ideas, key resources, or pure labor should be considered a coauthor of the paper (or at least recognized in the "acknowledgments" section). Other colleagues, friends, or family who may have made a casual and passing remark over lunch about our research aims and current activities need not be considered for authorship, even if they

caused us to reconsider certain elements of the project we happen to be working on.

Second, does the journal to which you are submitting your article have a maximum limit for the number of names? Some journals have no limits at all, which allows you to be generous to anyone who contributed to the project. This, however, can make for some unusually lengthy lists, which makes one wonder whether any author did anything really substantial at all. Other journals do have limits, which forces you to decide who really gave something valuable to the research endeavor. This can unfortunately relegate some people into the "acknowledgments" section even though the project would not have been possible without them.

Third, within which field or discipline is the project? Some fields, such as history, philosophy, and theology, lend themselves to and encourage more solitary research, with papers very often being published by only one or two authors. Other fields, such as medicine, science, and engineering, often see papers published by groups of two or more coauthors. Broadly speaking, however, authorship of academic articles typically includes no more than six or so names.

What about Authorship versus Acknowledgment?

There can be several circumstances in which you may wish to add a name, or transfer an existing author's name, to the "acknowledgments" section at the end of the article, rather than include them as one of the cowriters of the paper.

Perhaps there are several individuals who allowed you the use of some experimental equipment, provided some technical advice on one or two occasions, or even read the initial draft of the paper to give you some feedback, but were not really integral to the planning, execution, or completion of the project.

Moreover, a journal might have a maximum allowable limit for author names, forcing you to decide who should be included as an author, even among those who contributed significantly to the research effort. This, obviously, might be a subjective judgment on the part of the lead author or the rest of the team. Even so, as long as things are communicated clearly and courteously, this usually will not present a major problem for the individual.

Finally, there may be a coauthor who is unreachable (for example, they have moved and their current contact information is not attainable, they are out of the country, they have died, and so on) and is, therefore, unable to sign the copyright and conflict of interest forms that journals often require before publishing your article. In such a case, you may be able to negotiate with the journal to still include the author's name, explaining the circumstances.

What to Do When Conflicts Arise?

Do co-investigators in a research project ever disagree about authorship order and other related issues, such as intellectual property? Of course they do, especially in the fuzzy world of "teamwork." The *Canadian Medical Association Journal* published an investigation that found that over 66% of 919 "corresponding authors" (i.e., the main contact person who is in touch with the journal on behalf of all the authors of the paper) disagreed with their coauthors about the relative contributions made by members of the research team.[8]

Reasons for disagreement may include different perceptions of the relative share of contributions made by the different individuals; personal ambition fired by money, academic advancement, fame, or intellectual property rights; or just simply personality conflict. Several practical suggestions can help eliminate or minimize the conflict and its ramifications on personal relationships and the progress of research.

First, if a series of articles is being planned by the research team, you may wish to agree beforehand about rotating the assignment of lead authorship among the individuals on the team, or at least among those who are expected to do most of the actual work.

Second, if the team is composed of individuals who do not really know each other very well, are working together for the first time, or are not at the same institution, you may wish to agree to the order of authorship and the scope of work for each individual beforehand and have everyone sign a written statement to that effect.

Third, if a conflict has already begun, you may wish to agree to settle the tension within the confines of the research team itself, say, by secret ballot voting or by some conflict resolution–focused meetings or correspondence.

Fourth and finally, if the conflict is of a truly serious nature with larger ramifications personally and professionally, you may wish to agree to the decisions made by an "informal" outside arbitrator who, for example, is part of your institution or organization but who is not directly involved in your project. This might be a faculty member or staff person that you all know and trust. However, a more "formal" process may need to be involved, such as an appeal to the civil courts, the university courts, or a professional society that everyone belongs to, when issues of intellectual property, patent rights, and substantial financial reward are involved.[1]

Conclusion

Authorship, in the scientific and academic sense, is more than simply physically writing some words on a piece of paper or typing them into a computer. Rather, it implies that the persons listed as cowriters are, in fact, "cocreators" or "codiscoverers." Along with this come some of the challenges of assigning authorship to an article for publication when conflicts and other unforeseen circumstances arise. All this in the name of progress!

Suggested Reading

Biagioli M, Galison P, eds. Scientific Authorship: Credit and Intellectual Property in Science. New York: Routledge; 2002

References

1. Biagioli M, Galison P, eds. Scientific Authorship: Credit and Intellectual Property in Science. New York: Routledge; 2002
2. Maddox B. Rosalind Franklin: The Dark Lady of DNA. New York: Harper Perennial; 2003
3. Elkin LO. Rosalind Franklin and the Double Helix. Phys Today 2003;56(3):42–48
4. Flanagin A, Carey LA, Fontanarosa PB, et al. Prevalence of articles with honorary authors and ghost authors in peer-reviewed medical journals. JAMA 1998;280(3):222–224
5. Dunbar RIM. Coevolution of neocortical size, group size and language in humans. Behav Brain Sci 1993;16(4):681–735
6. Hill RA, Dunbar RIM. Social network size in humans. Hum Nat 2003;14(1):53–72
7. Allen C. Life with alacrity: the Dunbar number as a limit to group sizes. Available at: http://www.lifewithalacrity.com/2004/03/the_dunbar_numb.html. Accessed December 18, 2009.
8. Ilakovac V, Fister K, Marusic M, Marusic A. Reliability of disclosure forms of authors' contributions. CMAJ 2007;176(1):41–46

8

When Do You Need a Statistician? More than Just Number Crunchers

Jason W. Busse

Measure twice and cut once
— Proverb

Summary

Statisticians can assist surgical researchers in more than simply the analysis of data; through input and involvement in designing the research question, selecting the study design, and offering suggestions on the implementation, statisticians are a great resource. This chapter will explore the role of a statistician; specifically, when to seek out statistical expertise, typical roles of a statistician, and how this input can assist in your research.

Introduction

As surgeons become involved in increasingly complex studies, there is a commensurate need to access statistical expertise to ensure optimal design, conduct, and interpretation of research efforts. Too often, clinicians approach statisticians after a trial has already begun or after data has been collected, and after valuable opportunities for statistical input have been lost. Statisticians cannot rescue a poorly designed study after the trial has begun.

> **Key Concepts: Most Common Problems in Study Proposals When a Statistician Is Not Involved**
> - Outcomes are not clearly defined.
> - There is not an analysis plan for secondary aims of the study.
> - Sample size calculation is too simplistic or absent.
> - Assumptions of statistical methods are not appropriate.

Statistics is the science of learning from data through methods of data collection, graphics, organization, and inference. It is the art and science of summarizing data, ideally in a form that can be easily understood by those who are not statisticians. Clinical investigations usually involve collecting a lot of data, which requires synthesis to arrive at a conclusion:
- Did the new treatment work?
- Are the two groups being compared the same or different?
- Is the new method more precise than the old method?

While you may consult a statistician at any time during a project, the best time is typically at the beginning. In general, statisticians are pleased to offer assistance in clinical research, though most (if not all) will balk at:
1. Being contacted several days before a grant/protocol/proposal is due.
2. Rewriting inappropriate statistical sections.
3. Analyzing data that has arisen from a poorly designed trial.

Designing a proper study question to address an area of clinical uncertainty is the first step in any research initiative, and one way to focus your research is to use the **PICO** approach.

> **Key Concepts: PICO Approach**
>
> | **P**eople, patients, or population | Whom are you asking the question about? |
> | --- | --- |
> | **I**ntervention | What intervention are you interested in? |
> | **C**ontrol or comparison | What are you comparing the intervention with? |
> | **O**utcome | What outcome are you interested in measuring? |

While clinicians are often best positioned to provide insight into the appropriate choice of patients and the intervention, consultation with a statistician may offer valuable insight into the choice of control or comparison groups and the selection of outcome measures. For example, most granting agencies will require that the treatment effect in a clinical trial is measured by both a disease-specific and a general health-related quality of life measure.

> **Key Concepts: Reasons to Consult a Statistician**
> - They are trained formally in study design options.
> - They can provide unbiased input on research questions.
> - Their involvement adds credibility to your grant application.
> - They will provide input on sample size/power considerations.
> - They can advise on interim data monitoring.

- They can assist in end point selection:
  - Subjective versus objective
  - Measurement issues.
- They can help in management of missing or incomplete data.

Every research question can be addressed by mean of multiple designs, from those with minimal safeguards against bias (case report or case series) to those with considerable safeguards (randomized controlled trials or systematic reviews). Each study design has merits and drawbacks and many, if not most, surgical questions cannot be answered with randomized controlled trials.[1] Observational studies, surveys, or case–control studies may in fact be the best choice for a given research question. The choice of the appropriate research design is an important issue for any research question and, if there is uncertainty, consultation with a statistician can provide critical insight into this decision.

Once a research question has been properly designed and the appropriate study design has been chosen, there remains the critical issue of conduct. A basic question is: "How large does my study sample have to be to provide meaningful results?" Sample size calculations are as much an art as they are a science and they are influenced by the likely effect and associated precision of an intervention (often derived from a systematic review of the literature), the choice of outcome measure(s), and the magnitude of effect required to be considered clinically significant (often provided by clinicians' input). Without clinical input, a sample size calculation may lead to a trial that is powered to detect statistically significant but clinically unimportant results. Without statistical input, a sample size calculation may be either under-powered or over-powered to answer the research question.

Most studies require collection of data, and this process must be accountable to both safeguards against bias and the ultimate analysis. Data collection should ideally be by someone who is blinded to the research question for case-control studies, to treatment allocation for randomized controlled trials. Furthermore, there are important considerations about the type of data collected; a statistician can provide valuable input in this process. Subjective data (e.g., pain) may be more vulnerable to interpretative bias than more objective end points (e.g., infection), and may therefore influence the strength of inferences following from the analysis. At the same time, clinical input into the choice of study end points is critical, as statistical significance does not equate to clinical significance.

While it is often desirable to work collaboratively with a statistician to devise a primary end point for a given study, there is sometimes merit in composing a composite end point (an end point that is made up of two or more outcomes). Consider an extreme example in which the experimental treatment increases the death rate. If the researchers composed a composite end point that included death, they would avoid the spurious attribution of benefit on a given outcome when its reduction resulted from the increased occurrence of death in the treatment group. However, the design of a composite end point, even when appropriate, is often complex[2] and should be informed by consultation with a statistician.

Jargon Simplified: Composite End Point
One that is composed of two or more outcomes.

In any study, one of the chief mandates should be to limit missing data and loss to follow-up. However, almost all clinical trials are, to some degree, affected by this issue. Patients who are lost to follow-up often have different prognoses from those who are not lost; the former group may be lost because they had an adverse outcome, or because they were doing well and so did not return to the clinic to be assessed. A simple way in which to manage this problem is to exclude any missing data from the analysis altogether. However, this strategy is vulnerable to considerable criticism. A statistician can assist by designing sensitivity analyses to explore the impact of the missing data in a more rigorous manner.

Key Concepts: Loss to Follow-Up
Missing data and loss to follow-up should be avoided wherever possible in a study, but the majority of clinical trials are still affected by this issue. The primary problem with loss to follow-up is that the prognoses for patients lost to follow-up may differ from those who continue in the study.

Once you have decided that your study could benefit from input by a statistician, there remains the question of whether to involve a statistician as a collaborator or as a consultant. This decision should be based on the complexity of your study, your research experience, and your available resources. In terms of qualifications, look to access an individual with a Masters degree or a PhD in statistics or a statistics-related field. While it can be beneficial to hire a statistician who specializes in an area relevant to a specific problem you are having, this should not necessarily be your chief criterion. A consultant whose background is narrowly focused may miss broader issues.

Reality Check: Choosing Between Collaborating versus Consulting with a Statistician
- A collaborator
  - Is an active co-investigator.
  - Is brought in early in planning.
  - Helps develop aims and design.
  - Continues to input throughout trial planning and while the study continues.
- A consultant
  - Is inactive as a co-investigator.
  - Is often not brought in until either:

- You need a sample size calculation, or
- The trial has been criticized/rejected due to lack of statistical input, or
- You have finally collected all of the data and don't know what to do next.
  – Is only involved sparsely for planning or for analysis.

Many surgical research questions benefit greatly from both clinical and statistical input. A statistician can be more than just a resource for data analysis after a trial is complete. Whether engaged as a collaborator or as a consultant, a statistician can provide valuable input into the design, implementation, and analysis of surgical research.

Suggested Reading

Guyatt G, Rennie D. User's Guides to the Literature. A Manual for Evidence-based Clinical Practice. Chicago, IL: AMA Press; 2002

References

1. Solomon MJ, McLeod RS. Should we be performing more randomized controlled trials evaluating surgical operations? Surgery 1995;118(3):459–467
2. Ferreira-González I, Busse JW, Heels-Ansdell D, et al. Problems with use of composite end points in cardiovascular trials: systematic review of randomised controlled trials. BMJ 2007;334(7597):786–792

9

The Structured Abstract

Ole Brink, Lars C. Borris

Summary

This chapter provides instructions on creating an effectively written and formatted abstract. Although there is no gold standard of abstract writing, many journals provide authors with specific instructions on how to formulate an abstract. The abstract is one of the most important components of an article and it often determines whether or not the remainder of the article will be read.

Introduction

The abstract is a very important part of the scientific article and it can be compared with a menu card. The reader is the hungry customer who reads the menu card outside the restaurant before entering to order a meal. If the menu card is not interesting enough, the customer finds another restaurant; similarly, the reader finds another article to read. Thus, the abstract should sharpen the readers' appetite to convince them that it is worthwhile to read the complete article. When the abstract is boring, unintelligible, meaningless, or badly structured, readers will continue surfing on Medline/PubMed until they find something more inviting.

Since 1665 when the first scientific journal was started, the number of journals has been steadily increasing.[1] Today more than 5000 scientific journals are indexed in Medline, and worldwide ca. 600 000 articles are indexed each year.[2] In 2008, almost 800 million searches were performed in Medline. Thus, it is obvious that there is great competition to attract the reader's attention and it is for this reason that it is important to write an interesting abstract.

When the first scientific papers appeared, they were primarily in letter format and mostly descriptive. During the 20th century the articles became more structured, but it was not until the late 1960s that an abstract was added to the articles.[3] Among the first scientific journals to demand an abstract were the *Journal of the American Medical Association* and the *Canadian Medical Association Journal*; and later came *Lancet* and the *British Medical Journal*.[3] Currently, almost all scientific journals demand an abstract in their instructions for authors. While the articles have become very structured in accordance with the so-called IMRaD (Introduction, Methods, Results, and Discussion) format, there is no uniformity in the presentation of the abstracts.[1] When the abstract formats used in different orthopaedic journals are compared, it can be concluded that there is no "gold standard." By no means do all journals demand a structured abstract, but of those that do the format is in accordance with the IMRaD format or the eight-headed structure.[4] The latter was recommended in 1987 by an ad-hoc working group established by R. Bryan Haynes from McMaster University in Canada together with 358 prominent scientists from 18 countries.[3] The group recommended the structured abstract because it permits the reader to more accurately and more quickly judge a paper's validity and findings, improves search retrievals, and facilitates peer review. Haynes later optimized the recommendation as summarized below.[5] A comparison between the IMRaD format and Haynes's eight-headed structure is also presented below, and it appears that there are many points of resemblance. The eight-headed structure has its strengths when used in abstracts for clinical studies and particularly interventional studies. For other studies modifications may be needed.

> **Jargon Simplified: IMRaD Format**
> A structured format for articles that includes sections for Introduction, Methods, Results, and Discussion.

> **Key Concepts: Top 14 Orthopaedic Journals' Web Site Instructions for Authors Concerning Abstract Format**
> See **Table 9.1**.

> **Key Concepts: Suggested Structure for Abstracts of Original and Review Articles**
> See **Table 9.2**.

> **Key Concepts: Comparison of the IMRaD Format and the Eight-Headed Format in Structured Abstracts**
> See **Table 9.3**.

Writing Your Abstract

When you begin writing an abstract, it important that you follow the instructions for authors specific to the particular journal to which the paper will be submitted to be considered for publication, as these instructions may differ markedly from journal to journal (see Chapter 16). More and more journals require a structured abstract, but some do not. It is always recommended to write a structured abstract because of the many advantages of that format.

Table 9.1 Top 14 orthopaedic journals' Web site instructions for authors concerning abstract format (journals are ranked according to impact factor)

Rank	Journal	Type of abstract and specific requirement	Maximum length
1	*Osteoarthritis & Cartilage*	Structured: eight-headed format for original articles	250 words
2	*Journal of Orthopaedic Research*	Structured: purpose, methods, results, and conclusion	200 words
3	*Orthopedic Clinics of North America*	Nonstructured synopsis	Five sentences
4	*Journal of Bone and Joint Surgery*	Structured: methods, results, conclusions, and level of evidence	325 words
5	*Spine*	Structured: study design, objective, summary of background data, methods, results, and conclusions	300 words
6	*Clinical Orthopaedics & Related Research*	No specific requirements	200 words
7	*Gait & Posture*	No specific requirements	250 words
8	*European Spine Journal*	No specific requirements but must include main problem, methods, results and conclusions	?
9	*Journal of Arthroplasty*	No specific requirements	125 words
10	*Journal of the American Academy of Orthopaedic Surgeons*	No specific requirements	150 words
11	*Journal of Bone and Joint Surgery (Br)*	No specific requirements	150 words
12	*Clinical Journal of Sport Medicine*	Structured: eight-headed format for original articles	250 words
13	*Journal of Orthopaedic Trauma*	Structured: eight-headed format for original articles	250 words
14	*Arthroscopy*	Structured: purpose, methods, results, conclusions, level of evidence	300 words

Table 9.2 Suggested structure for abstracts of original and review articles

Original Articles

1	*Objective*	The exact question(s) addressed by the article
2	*Design*	The basic design of the study
3	*Setting*	Location and level of clinical care
4	*Patients or participants*	The manner of selection and number of patients or participants who entered and completed the study
5	*Interventions*	The exact treatment or intervention
6	*Main outcome measures*	The primary study outcome
7	*Results*	The key findings
8	*Conclusions*	Key conclusions including direct clinical applications

Review Articles

1	*Purpose*	The primary objective of the review article
2	*Data sources*	A succinct summary of data sources
3	*Study selection*	The number of studies selected for review and how they were selected
4	*Data extraction*	Rules for abstracting data and how they were applied
5	*Results of data synthesis*	The methods of data synthesis and key results
6	*Conclusions*	Key conclusions, including potential applications and research needs

Table 9.3 Comparison of the IMRaD format and the eight-headed format in structured abstracts

IMRaD format	Eight-heading format
1. Introduction	1. Objective
2. Methods	2. Design
	3. Setting
	4. Patients or participants
	5. Interventions
	6. Main outcome measures
3. Results	7. Results
4. Discussion	8. Conclusions

The word count typically varies between 150 and 300 words. Before you begin to write your abstract, the entire article should have been finalized, including the conclusions. Consider what is important and what is less important for inclusion in the abstract and make an outline. The abstract should not state anything that is not written in the article and the conclusions should be consistent with the findings of the study. The abstract should not include references, tables, or figures because these items cannot be handled by certain databases such as Medline.

> **Key Concepts: What Not to Include in an Abstract**
> • Any information not presented in the article
> • Conclusions that are inconsistent with the study findings
> • References
> • Tables and figures

We now show how to write an abstract using the eight-headed structure.[5]

Objective

State the purpose or questions as the study addresses. If a null hypothesis (H_0) was tested, it should be stated here.

Design

Describe the basic design of the study and the observational period. Haynes distinguished between following study designs[4]:
• Intervention studies (e.g., randomized trials)
• Studies for screening and diagnostic tests
• Studies of prognosis (e.g., cohort studies)
• Studies of causation (e.g., randomized controlled trial, cohort, case–control, survey)
• Description of the clinical features of medical disorders (survey, case series)
• Health-economic studies (cost–effectiveness, cost–utility, cost–benefit)

Be precise and brief when describing the design. Give specific details such as randomization, blinding, crossover, or whether placebo controls have been used.

Setting

Setting refers to the location and level of clinical care. Describe whether the setting is in primary or tertiary care and whether it is in private practice or institutional (e.g., hospitals). Describe the kind of hospital. Information about the setting will help reader generalize the outcome from the study to their own settings.

Patients/Participants

Explain the selection procedure and entry criteria of the study. The selection procedure can be described as random sample, population-based sample, referred sample, consecutive sample, volunteer sample, or convenience sample. Indicate what kind of disease/disorder the sample includes. The number of patients, their sex, age, and other characteristics if necessary must be described. In case of matching, explain how it was performed.

Intervention (or Assessment of Risk Factors)

Here, the exact treatment has to be explained including the type of method and the duration of administration. For observational studies, the independent variables should be clearly outlined.

Main Outcome Measure

The main outcome measure refers to the primary outcome measures from the study, as planned *before* data collection began. If the paper does not include the planned outcomes, then this must be explicitly stated. If the hypothesis used in the paper was formulated during or after data collection, then this has to be stated in this part of the abstract.

Results

In this the part of the abstract the main results from the study are presented. It is important here to be selective and brief in the presentation because it is not possible to display all findings. In the event that more than one patient group was involved in the study, refer to the specific groups using identifiers (e.g., group A or group B) to keep the word count low. Show absolute numbers and percentages, *P*-values, coefficients, ratios, and confidence intervals.

Conclusions

The main conclusion(s) of the study must be included here. Together with the title, the conclusion is the most important part of the abstract. Many readers will focus first on the title and thereafter on the conclusion(s). It is therefore important that they are both informative. The conclusion should be short, simple, and easily comprehended.

"Conclusions logically connect the title, study methods and results all together and deliver the take home message."[6] Be careful not to draw conclusions that cannot be supported by the data presented in the paper. When you conclude on your findings, avoid speculation and wide generalization.

The eight-headed format has its strength in clinical articles and in particular in interventional studies. In other types of studies it might be necessary to make some modifications to the abstract. In observational studies, exemplified by a cohort study, where the aim of the study is to expose potential risk factors of a disease, "none" or "not applied" might be written in the section of intervention.[4] In observational studies of more exploratory type it could also be difficult to describe main outcome measures, and a modification of the abstract might be necessary.[5]

Conclusion

What we have set out here is just a proposal for setting up a menu for a structured abstract. In general, to write an informative abstract it is essential to be familiar with every aspect of a study in terms of design, statistical methods main findings, and conclusions. Only then can the author(s) deliver a clear message to the reader. Bon appétit!

References

1. Sollaci LB, Pereira MG. The introduction, methods, results, and discussion (IMRAD) structure: a fifty-year survey. J Med Libr Assoc 2004;92(3):364–367
2. US National Library of Medicine, National Institutes of Health. Available at: http://www.nlm.nih.gov/pubs/factsheets/nlm.html. Accessed December 31, 2009
3. Ad Hoc Working Group for Critical Appraisal of the Medical Literature. A proposal for more informative abstracts of clinical articles. Ann Intern Med 1987;106(4):598–604
4. Nakayama T, Hirai N, Yamazaki S, Naito M. Adoption of structured abstracts by general medical journals and format for a structured abstract. J Med Libr Assoc 2005;93(2):237–242
5. Haynes RB, Mulrow CD, Huth EJ, Altman DG, Gardner MJ. More informative abstracts revisited. Ann Intern Med 1990;113(1):69–76
6. Alexandrov AV, Hennerici MG. Writing good abstracts. Cerebrovasc Dis 2007;23(4):256–259

10

Writing an Introduction

Emil H. Schemitsch, Rad Zdero

Summary

This chapter provides practical instructions on creating an interesting and informative Introduction section for scientific journal articles. The introduction should provide the reader with general information on the topic being addressed, the specific problem that the researchers are hoping to resolve, and the researchers' investigative plan. We discuss several tips for writing an effective Introduction and provide the reader with examples of a well-written and a poorly written Introduction.

Introduction

Browsing the scientific literature will reveal that journals have differing formats and expectations regarding the quality and quantity of writing found in the articles they publish. However, there is a certain general template for such writing that is almost universal and which is expected by editors, reviewers, and readers of scientific manuscripts. The purpose of this chapter is to provide the researcher with some practical guidelines for creating both an interesting and an informative Introduction section for the typical scientific journal article they hope to submit to a journal for publication.

What Is the Aim of an Introduction Section?

The main goal of an Introduction section is to give the reader a broad overview, a "birds-eye view," if you will, of the problem that will be addressed in the investigation. This is important for several reasons.

First, some readers may not be specialists in the field or may not be acquainted at all with the topic and thus will need some basic introductory knowledge to be able to understand both the science and the significance of the study. Among others, these might include science or engineering undergraduate students involved in researching their thesis project, medical students who are trying to identify which specialty to pursue, and researchers and scientists in other fields of expertise, for whom the paper offers information that is crucial to their own work.

Second, some readers, though also specializing in the field, are perhaps new and inexperienced surgeons and researchers for whom the scientific literature provides a source of ongoing education and training for their own endeavors. In many respects, scientists and researchers who publish their findings are teachers and mentors for their peers and even for the next generation, whether they realize it or not.

The main thing to remember is that even though readers may indeed be educated and intelligent, they will still need to be informed on the topic at hand.

> **Key Concepts: Assumptions about Readers**
> Always assume that readers are intelligent, but never presume that readers are informed.

What Is the Content of an Introduction Section?

An effective Introduction is like a conical funnel that has three main segments: an initial wide mouth that receives a large volume of fluid, a V-shaped portion that focuses the fluid, and a narrow hole out of which the fluid exits (**Fig. 10.1**).

General Information

The initial mouth of the Introduction funnel is open and wide and hence encompasses general information. In other words, this segment answers the question: "What background information is needed?" These remarks put forward the broad context of the surgical technique, orthopaedic device, biomechanical parameter, or population group in which resides a specific problem that is to be addressed later. All statements should be supported from the literature as much as possible by at least three to five bibliographical references, though there are some clinical practices and knowledge that are so widely accepted and familiar that thorough referencing may not be necessary. This segment should comprise approximately one-quarter of the Introduction and be contained in one paragraph of about 25 to 100 words.

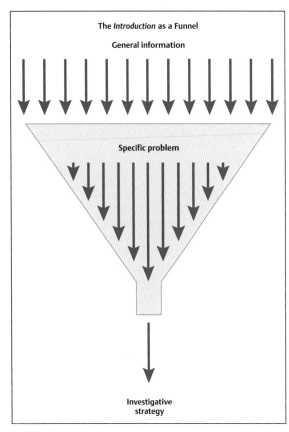

Fig. 10.1 An illustration of the metaphor that likens the Introduction section to a funnel.

Specific Problem

The V-shaped segment of the Introduction funnel narrows the content and raises the specific problem. In other words, this segment answers the question: "What is the problem?" The goal here is to expand in some detail on the area in the literature that has an unresolved issue or that has a gap in knowledge. This must be clearly communicated as being the main motivation for the study. This is, in effect, the literature review portion of the article in which all the main papers previously published that are directly related to the study are cited. These papers, not uncommonly between 10 and 20 in number, are the ones that form the core background reading for the study. After reading this segment, the reader should be convinced of the need for the investigation and understand its potential significance to patients, clinicians, and/or researchers and its impact on the field in general terms. This segment should cover approximately one-half of the Introduction and will contain one or several paragraphs totaling about 100 to 500 words.

Investigative Strategy

The narrowest part of the Introduction funnel is the exit hole; it should provide several concise statements about the study's investigative strategy. In other words, this segment answers the question: "How is the study going to practically address the problem?" It is here that the reader is told in brief about the method that will be used, the measurements that will be taken, the comparisons that will be made, and, if appropriate, the results that might be expected (i.e., the hypothesis). In essence, this is a focused summary statement of what the study is about. From this portion, the reader should be confident that the study that will now be presented will be feasible, appropriate, focused, and systematic. No referencing to previous studies should be done here. This segment should amount to approximately one-quarter of the Introduction and will be contained in one paragraph of about 25 to 100 words.

Tips and Tricks for an Effective Introduction Section

Know the Journal

Every journal has its own specific formatting rules. Researchers are therefore encouraged to refer to the author's instructions of the journal to which they are submitting their article so as to be in full conformity with expectations for the Introduction. To get an idea of these expectations, an excellent habit is to read several papers that have recently been published in the journal to which a paper will be submitted.

Keep the Focus

It is best to ensure that all statements are directly related to the study without getting side-tracked by interesting but tangential ideas that are beyond the scope of the investigation. These may be legitimate and pressing subjects for future investigations, but they should not be presented here. It must be kept in mind that the goal is to provide only the information and ideas that will help the reader properly understand the study being reported.

Divulge the Data

Whenever possible, any statements that are made regarding trends or findings from prior studies should be accompanied by actual numbers, whether it be in the form of percentages, proportions, or absolute values. This gives the reader a better appreciation of your remarks. For example, it is more informative to communicate to the reader that a study showed that "10% of femoral shaft fractures achieved full union" than that "a minority of femoral shaft fractures achieved full union."

Recognize the References

As far as possible, provide bibliographic references for all statements, whether comments refer to trends, results, trademarks, or techniques. The reader may be interested in seeking out some of them for their own purposes. Moreover, it is usually expected that a review of the literature will include papers from at least the past 5 to 10 years, unless the problem that is to be investigated has only recently been made known to the scientific community or has never been considered before.

Write Lists

Sometimes inexperienced writers tend to ramble by putting too many ideas into one paragraph without making any distinction between individual points. Thus, to present information in a way that is reader-friendly, it is sometimes helpful to provide the material in a listlike sequence. This makes things clearer because it breaks down the ideas in small digestible bits. For example, if several important points need to be made in the same paragraph or several successive paragraphs, writers should consider distinguishing them by starting a new sentence for each point with the words "Firstly...," "Secondly...," or alternatively, "Moreover....," "Furthermore...," and so on.

Maintain the Formality

It is common to keep a formal tone in the writings that appear in scientific journals. It is optimal, therefore, to write in the third person (although some journals permit writing in the first person) and to focus any critique of a paper on its content, rather than to use personal pronouns for oneself and to appear to be personally attacking a particular author. For example, it is better to write that "The techniques developed by Smith et al. are brought into question by recent results...," rather than "We believe that Smith et al. did a poor job in developing their methodology because of recent results..." Furthermore, word contractions (e.g., "didn't," "weren't," etc.) should never be used, while idioms and jargon (e.g., "gold standard," "benchmark tests," "sawbones," etc.) should be used rarely and only if they are well-known terms within the particular scientific community that is most likely to read the manuscript.

Count the Words

A perusal of published articles in the surgical, orthopaedic, and biomechanical literature shows a wide range of word counts for Introduction sections, being anywhere between 250 and 750 words. This is usually adequate to provide enough detail to the reader without becoming too cumbersome.

Just Say No

Several things should generally be avoided in the Introduction section. First, figures and tables rarely appear in an Introduction section, unless absolutely necessary and only if permitted by the journal's format. These items are almost universally reserved for the Methods, Results, and Discussion sections of an article. Second, to avoid repetitiveness, writers should take care not to comment prematurely on the details of their methodology or present any of their results at this point. Third, never use subtitles, since the relatively short length of an Introduction section does not warrant such a breakdown of the material for reader-friendliness. Finally, never directly quote the text of nonscientific popular writings since this will not be accepted by either the reviewers or the editor of the journal. It is uncommon though acceptable to quote from scientific papers, but this should be avoided unless there is a specific reason why this must be done.

> **Key Concepts: Tips for Writing an Effective Introduction**
> - Know the journal: Become familiar with the format and quality of the target journal either before or while writing an article.
> - Keep the focus.
> - Divulge the data.
> - Recognize the references.
> - Write lists.
> - Maintain the formality.
> - Count the words.
> - Just say no to figures, tables, results, subtitles, and quotations from nonscientific works.

Examples of Good and Bad Introductions

> **Reality Check: A Good Introduction**
> The following excerpt is taken from a published paper by Lever et al.[1] The details of the bibliographical references given in square brackets in the text below are not provided, but their numbering as it appears in the original text is shown.

Introduction

Restoration of shoulder function is the ultimate goal when managing proximal humerus fractures. Regardless of the fracture configuration as described by Neer [1], management may pose significant challenges [2]. Quality of bone stock that may compromise stable fixation, and the predisposition of the glenohumeral joint to become stiff without early motion, are two conflicting problems.

Proximal humeral fractures are often challenging to deal with surgically, because the indications and techniques are controversial [2]. The results are frequently fraught with complications, with no "gold standard" having been established in the literature, necessitating a tailor-made approach for each patient [3]. However, minimally displaced or undisplaced fractures of the surgical neck can be treated non-operatively with good functional outcomes [3–5]. Displaced unstable fractures, though, will achieve better results with operative care, because they are prone to develop nonunions if managed nonoperatively. Other indications for operative management of these injuries include open fractures, injuries associated with vascular compromise, fracture-dislocations, floating shoulders, bilateral upper-extremity fractures, and polytrauma [6–9].

The choice of the implant to be used for open reduction and internal fixation of proximal humerus fractures depends on many factors. Fracture configuration, humeral head vascularity, quality of bone stock, overall geometry, and experience of the operating surgeon all must be taken into consideration [10]. A number of studies have examined the biomechanical properties of various methods of fixation of proximal humerus fractures, such as K-wires, T-plates, angled plates, cloverleaf plates, locked plates, intramedullary nails, tension band wires, and primary prostheses [11–24]. Plate fixation has shown superior biomechanical properties in nonosteopenic bone and comparable qualities in osteopenic bone [11]. Even so, to the authors' knowledge, truss-like plating structures for use in surgical repair of humeral fractures have not been assessed biomechanically in the literature, despite their known stabilizing properties in other fields.

The purpose of this study was to define the mechanical stability of five plate-fixation systems, including a new plating technique, for treatment of surgical neck fractures of the humerus. It was expected that plate constructs with truss-like structures would provide optimal mechanical stability in comparison to other fixation techniques, because of the inherent stabilizing characteristics of trusses.

Reality Check: A Bad Introduction

The text of the good version of the Introduction presented above has been altered to provide the example of a suboptimal version below. Readers are encouraged to circle or make a list of the poor aspects of the following passage as they read along.

Introduction

Restoration of shoulder function is the ultimate goal when managing proximal humerus fractures. Regardless of the fracture configuration as described by Neer [1], management may pose significant challenges [2]. Quality of bone stock that may compromise stable fixation, and the predisposition of the glenohumeral joint to become stiff without early motion, are two conflicting problems.

Proximal humeral fractures are often challenging to deal with surgically. That's because the indications and techniques are controversial [2]. The results are frequently fraught with complications, with no "gold standard" having been established in the literature, necessitating a tailor-made approach for each patient [3]. However, minimally displaced or undisplaced fractures of the surgical neck can be treated non-operatively with good functional outcomes [3–5]. Displaced unstable fractures, though, will achieve better results with operative care, because they are prone to develop nonunions if managed nonoperatively, among other indications for operative management [6–9].

The choice of the implant to be used for open reduction and internal fixation of proximal humerus fractures depends on many factors. Fracture configuration, humeral head vascularity, quality of bone stock, overall geometry, and experience of the operating surgeon all must be taken into consideration [10]. Several studies have examined the biomechanical properties of various methods of fixation of proximal humerus fractures [11–13]. Plate fixation has shown superior biomechanical properties in nonosteopenic bone and comparable qualities in osteopenic bone. Even so, to the authors' knowledge, researchers haven't either recognized or made any effort at all to biomechanically assess truss-like plating structures for use in surgical repair of humeral fractures in the literature, despite their known stabilizing properties in other fields. Our study, on the other hand, showed that the truss-like construct A had a stiffness which was statistically greater than the other constructs we'd tested ($P < 0.05$).

The purpose of this study was to define the mechanical stability of five plate-fixation systems, including a new plating technique, for treatment of surgical neck fractures of the humerus.

Comparing the Good and Bad Introductions

The content of the two Introduction sections examined above is nearly identical and both have the three main segments necessary to properly instruct the reader, namely, general information (the first paragraph), specific problem (the second and third paragraphs), and investigative strategy (the last paragraph). However, there are subtle and not-so-subtle differences that would make the first one acceptable by the editor of a scientific journal and the second one unacceptable.

The good introduction adequately references its statements using 24 references in total, maintains a formal tone throughout, twice uses itemized lists to provide details regarding papers it is citing, explains the nature of the knowledge gap in the literature that provides the motivation for the study, and gives a hypothesis statement.

The bad introduction, on the other hand, provides far fewer references to papers that did similar biomechanical work previously, uses word contractions several times, makes vague statements about previous studies without giving details, personally criticizes prior researchers for not doing an adequate job in the field, prematurely provides the results of the study's findings, does not offer a hypothesis statement, and makes reference to "construct A" without defining it properly.

Conclusion

This chapter has attempted to give researchers practical tools and guidelines for writing an informative Introduction section for scientific journal articles they intend to submit to a journal for potential publication. The reader should now appreciate that there is a certain template for an Introduction section in scientific journal articles that is expected by editors, reviewers, and readers alike and that should be followed in order generate an effective scientific paper.

References

1. Lever JP, Aksenov SA, Zdero R, Ahn H, McKee MD, Schemitsch EH. Biomechanical analysis of plate osteosynthesis systems for proximal humerus fractures. J Orthop Trauma 2008;22 (1):23–29

11

Writing a Methods Section

Emil H. Schemitsch, Rad Zdero

Summary

This chapter provides instructions on creating an effectively written and formatted Methods section for scientific journal articles. The Methods section is an important component of the scientific paper, as it allows a reader to appreciate exactly how the study was conducted. Through practical tools and guidelines, we give surgical researchers specific instructions and recommendations on how to formulate a Methods section.

Introduction

Inspection of the scientific literature shows that there are differing formats and expectations regarding the quality and quantity of writing found in journal articles. Nonetheless, there is a general template for scientific writing that is almost universal and which is expected by editors, reviewers, and readers of scientific manuscripts. The purpose of this chapter is to provide the researcher with a practical guide for generating an interesting and informative Methods section for the typical scientific journal article.

What Is the Aim of a Methods Section?

The overall objective of a Methods section is to provide the reader with an accurate description of all the techniques, materials, instrumentation, specimens, population groups, and other resources that were utilized to undertake the investigation. There are several key reasons why this is important.

First, a methodology section allows other researchers in the field to verify the quality of the study. By provision of enough step-by-step detail, readers should be enabled to completely replicate the investigation and [it is hoped] generate the same results in their own laboratory, field setting, or clinical context.

Second, a methodology section provides the specialist in the field with information on the latest technique, material, or device. Arming other practitioners with such data may allow for immediate application and implementation of these items, which can hasten patient progress, improve clinical practice, and enhance research output.

Third, a methodology section facilitates ongoing training and education for many readers. An awareness of new materials, methods, and instrumentation will allow inexperienced surgeons and researchers, undergraduate students, graduate students, medical students, and orthopaedic residents to grow in their own skill and understanding. This can supplement other training opportunities, such as workshops at conferences, in-house training modules, and scholastic practicums, which are often time-consuming and expensive.

> **Key Concepts: Scope of the Methods Section**
> The Methods section should allow readers to completely replicate the study in their own laboratory or context.

What Is the Content of a Methods Section?

A Methods section is the heart of the entire journal article because it describes what tasks were actually performed during the course of the investigation. Everything else in the paper, in effect, is merely commentary that describes the motivation for what was done (the Introduction), the tangible outcome of what was done (the Results), or the philosophical significance and practical application of what was done (the Discussion). A Methods section can be composed in a variety of ways depending on the nature of the study and the formatting expectations of the journal. However, just as with a racing car, there are four "wheels" or components that appear in nearly every Methods section of an orthopaedic research paper. All four wheels are necessary for the car to move forward. These components typically appear in the sequential order given below, namely, description, preparation, testing, and analysis. Each of these main segments should be distinguished where possible by its own suitably specific subtitle.

Description

This initial segment describes all the information on the main raw material that was used for the study. In other words, it answers the question: "What target group was utilized or modeled?" This may include living populations, cadaveric specimens, synthetic materials, or computer models. It is here that all the relevant data are given where available and appropriate.

For living population studies, facts should be provided about the number of persons, age, sex, anatomic feature of interest, general health status, exclusion/inclusion criteria, study model (retrospective or prospective), date for start and end of study, as well as any other information relating to the patients included in the study.

For cadaveric specimen studies, information should be given regarding number of specimens, age, sex, anatomic feature of interest, cause of death, examination method for pathology, exclusion/inclusion criteria, storage requirements, tissue stripping, as well as any other information relating to the cadaveric specimens included in the study.

For synthetic material studies, attention should be drawn to the number of specimens, geometric dimensions, material properties, human anatomic features that are being replicated, reasons for their use as a surrogate for human tissue, manufacturer, as well as any other information relating to the synthetic materials used in the study.

For computer modeling studies, it is appropriate in this segment to limit oneself to simply describing the particular human anatomic feature or synthetic material that will be the basis for the development of the model and the reasons why this is necessary for the study.

Preparation

This segment provides the reader with details of the process involved in preparing the target group for assessment and evaluation. In other words, it answers the question: "How was the target group properly prepared for testing?"

For living population studies, this might involve reporting details about patient training, patient questionnaires, surgical interventions, prophylactic treatments, database extraction, the subgrouping of specific study groups for later statistical comparison, as well as any other information relating to living populations included in the study.

For cadaveric specimen and synthetic material studies, this segment should provide details about specimen modifications, surgical interventions, manufacture of specialized tools or devices, the subgrouping of specific study groups for later statistical comparison, as well as any other information relating to the cadaveric specimen and synthetic materials included in the study.

For computer modeling studies, details should comprise the material property values used, element shape, number of elements and nodes, commercial software package used, as well as any other information relating to the computer models used in the study.

Testing

This segment explains the exact nature of the tests or evaluation tools employed and the manner in which the data were collected and stored. In other words, it answers the question: "How were the target groups tested and the outcome data collected?"

For living population studies, this may include providing the reader with the patient questionnaire used (presented in a figure), detailing the parameters about how this questionnaire was administered (patient-administered, surgeon-administered, frequency, time limits, test conditions, etc.), delineating how outcome measures were obtained during or after surgery, reporting on the techniques used to extract data from radiographs or clinical examinations, as well as any other information relating to the living populations included in the study.

For cadaveric specimen and synthetic material studies, information might include the test machines used, the parameters applied and/or evaluated (force, torque, velocity, density, rate, volume, mass, concentration, frequency, etc.), the frequency of data collection, the number of data collected, signal filtering, calculation of secondary outcome measures from the primary outcome measures that were actually collected, as well as any other information on the cadaveric specimens and synthetic materials used in the study.

For computer modeling studies, this segment should involve reporting the type and value of the input parameters used (force, torque, concentration, etc.), "trigger" criteria used to determine whether a solution was reached, the computational run-time required to obtain a complete solution, as well as any other information relating to the computer models used in the study.

Analysis

This segment gives information about any statistical analysis that was performed on the outcome measures. In other words, it answers the question: "How were the data analyzed to detect statistical differences between study groups?" This segment is necessary when the authors can draw conclusions about differences between specific study groups and make proposals to the reader that one technique or device is superior to another for use in a clinical or research setting. Several items should be listed here, namely, the type of analysis performed (one-way ANOVA, Student *t*-test, etc.), the *P*-value chosen as the criterion for statistical difference, the particular post-hoc method used for specific pairwise comparisons between study groups, as well as any other items relating to the statistical analysis that was performed on the outcome measures. Because of the variety of methods available for statistical analysis, it is quite easy to make some fundamental errors by applying the wrong statistical tools for the study at hand. Thus, it is recommended that adequate statistical training be obtained by someone on the research team who will then perform the analysis, or that a statistician be consulted to determine the most appropriate approach. However, such a statistical analysis is not always needed or appropriate for an article, as in the case of the reporting of individual surgical case studies, computer modeling using fi-nite-element analysis, or biomechanical characterization of a novel prototype implant device or material for which there is no comparable comparison either in the literature or commercially.

A Word on Mixed-Mode Studies

In mixed-mode studies, however, a combination of several different types of "target groups" (i.e., living populations, cadaveric specimens, synthetic materials, and computer models) will appear in the same investigation for the purposes of validation. In this case, the Methods section will sometimes be more reader-friendly if each of these "target groups" is dealt with separately by having its own subsection within which is followed the pattern described above, namely, description, preparation, testing, and analysis. The writers have to use their own judgment in this regard.

Key Concepts: The "4-Wheel" Methods Section
See **Fig. 11.1**.

Tips and Tricks for an Effective Methods Section

Know the Journal

Reading several recently published articles from the journal to which one wishes to submit an article will give the writer an excellent idea about the format and quality of the Methods sections typical of the journal and increase the chances of acceptance of the paper for publication.

Be Aware of Synonyms

A writer should be aware that a Methods section is some-times called "Materials and Methods," "Methods and Ma-terials," or "Methodology," depending on the preference of the particular journal. These terms and phrases are all identical in meaning and should not lead to confusion when writing a journal paper.

Use Visual Aids

The importance of visual aids (in the form of photographs, drawings, flowcharts, etc.) cannot be overstated since they will greatly help the reader understand exactly what was done in the study. The old popular adage that "a picture is worth a thousand words" holds true even for the scientific researcher of today. It is also important that these figures be properly labeled (using letters, numbers, arrows, circles, etc.) to identify any specific features of interest that were particularly important during testing or data collection and then explained clearly in the figure caption. Such labeling, of course, should not be done when it would lead to unnecessary clutter or when the feature of interest is pictured in such a way as to be obvious even to the non-specialist.

Key Concepts: Importance of Figures
A picture is still worth a thousand words for today's researcher.

Use Subtitles

Use subtitles to break down the information into manage-able segments. This gives the reader an "at-a-glance" over-view of what the study was about. There are no rigid rules to be followed in this regard, since this will depend on the nature of the study. For example, a biomechanics paper dealing with orthopaedic trauma of the femur might have a Methods section with the following subtitles: Fe-moral Specimen Description, Femoral Fracture Fixation Technique, Mechanical Testing, and Statistical Data Analy-sis. Similarly, a clinical paper dealing with the success of a particular surgical technique might have a Methods sec-tion with the following subtitles: Patient Group Demo-graphics and Injury Mode, Surgical Repair Technique, Clin-ical Outcome Measures, and Statistical Data Analysis.

Appeal to Precedent

It is important to make reference to similar prior studies regarding specific materials, test methods, test para-meters, or boundary conditions that are used in the study. This will give assurance to the reviewer, editor, and reader that something completely inappropriate is not being pro-posed. This, of course, may not always be possible in the case of a novel methodology that has never been consid-ered by previous researchers, and it may not always be ne-cessary in the case of a well-established "gold standard" method or material that is almost universally utilized in the field. For example, when necessary, it is far better to

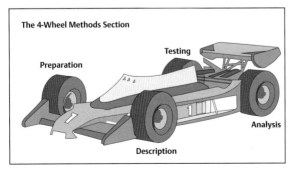

Fig. 11.1 A "4-wheel" methods section.

state that "the femurs were axially loaded at a rate of 5 mm/min based on a prior similar study by Smith et al." than to simply report that "the femurs were axially loaded at a rate of 5 mm/min."

Divulge the Details

Nothing is more irksome to the researcher than reading a paper that does not provide enough detail about what was done. Recall that one of the purposes of a Methods section is to allow a reader to be able to exactly replicate the study in their own laboratory or clinical context. Therefore, brand names, geometric dimensions, material composition, numerical values for test parameters, as well as other methodological details, should be given generously. For example, it is far better to report that "the distal ends of the repaired humeral fractures were potted in square-tube steel chambers (100 mm × 100 mm × 50 mm high) using commercially available cement (Fast Flow Concrete), rigidly mounted at the distal end using an industrial vice, and the proximal end externally loaded torsionally at 1 deg/s until failure" than to merely state that "the repaired humeral fractures were potted in cement-filled chambers, rigidly fixed distally, and the proximal end externally loaded torsionally until failure."

> **Key Concepts: Importance of Details**
> A good Methods section always has three things: details, details, and more details.

The Art of Science

There is an aspect of doing research and writing research papers, including Methods sections, that cannot be conveyed to someone in step-by-step instructions. Ironically, there is an aspect to all scientific endeavors that, rather than being an exact science, is in fact a creative "art." One must use one's own judgment as to constructing effective sentences, the appropriateness of using certain figures, the amount of detailing required to allow the reader to replicate the study in their own context, and so on. Truth be told, editors, reviewers, writers, and readers all often use their intuition, rather than any objective criteria as such, to distinguish between high- and low-quality scientific papers. This means that, although there are general templates that should be followed for Methods sections, there is room within those parameters to be creative. Remember that there is an art to science.

> **Key Concepts: The Art of Science**
> There is an art to science.

Just Say No

Several habits should be avoided in the Methods section. First, to avoid redundancy, writers should not prematurely present any results or discuss the philosophical implications of the techniques or materials at this point. Second, never directly quote the text of nonscientific popular writings since this will not be acceptable to the typical journal. It is uncommon but acceptable to quote from scientific papers, but this should be avoided unless there is a specific reason why this must be done. Third, do not use acronyms, abbreviations, or short forms without explaining in full what they mean the very first time they appear in the manuscript, unless they are widely recognized by people in the field. (The journal may also require a listing of abbreviations used in the paper, but they should nevertheless be given in full at the point of first use in the text.) Finally, the Methods section should be complete, meaning that all methodological elements of the study are fully described without revisiting any aspects with additional details in the Results or Discussion sections.

> **Key Concepts: Tips for Writing an Effective Methods Section**
> - Know the journal.
> - Be aware of synonymous titles for the section.
> - Use visual aids.
> - Use subtitles.
> - Appeal to precedent.
> - Divulge the details.
> - Practice the art of science.
> - Just say no to "bad habits."

Examples of Good and Bad Methods Sections

Reality Check: A Good Methods Section
The following excerpt is taken verbatim from Lever et al.[1] Details of the bibliographical references in square brackets in the text below are not provided, but their numbering as it appears in the original text is shown. For the sake of clarity, the original figure citations have been changed to correspond to the figure numbering in this book.

Methods
Specimen Preparation
Twenty-nine cadaveric humeri were harvested. All soft tissues were removed. The specimens were wrapped and immediately frozen at −20 °C. All humeri were radiographed prior to inclusion in the study and were reviewed by two investigators independently. Any humeri with osteolytic lesions, osteoarthritis, significant osteopenia, or previous fracture were excluded. Three

specimens had advanced osteoarthritis, and one specimen had a healed proximal humerus fracture; thus, these specimens were excluded. A total of 25 humeri were available for the study.

Each specimen was thawed at room temperature before testing. All humeri were osteotomized transversely at 230 mm distal to the most superior aspect of the humeral head. The humeral shafts were then potted with methylmethacrylate in steel tubes (50-mm diameter × 100-mm length), so that the humeri were flush with the bottom of the tubes.

In each humerus, a standardized transverse surgical neck osteotomy was created 10 mm distal to the inferomedial margin of the articular surface of the humeral head. The osteotomy was provisionally stabilized with bone-reduction forceps prior to definitive fixation. All plate-fixation devices [**Fig. 11.2**] were positioned posterior to the bicipital groove, 10 mm distal to the tip of the greater tuberosity, on the lateral aspect of the humerus.

Implant Configurations

The 25 humeri were randomly assigned to one of five methods of fracture fixation [**Fig. 11.2**].

Construct A was an AO, 4.5 mm, narrow, low contact dynamic compression (LCDC), eight-hole plate (Synthes, Paoli, PA). This plate was adopted for use in the humerus and was inserted to create a truss-type construct [25]. The plate was contoured manually into a modified "blade plate," with a 90-degree angle situated between the third and fourth screw holes from the proximal end. A 70-mm long, 4.5-mm cortical "triangulation" screw was inserted distal to the fracture line and angled via freehand fluoroscopic guidance to engage the most medial hole in the transverse part of the plate within the humeral head. Two additional 6.5-mm cancellous screws were placed into the humeral head for additional fixation. The shaft was secured with standard 4.5-mm cortical screws and AO/ASIF techniques.

Construct B was an AO, 3.5 mm, LCDC, 10-hole plate (Synthes, Paoli, PA). This small fragment plate was contoured and also inserted as above to create a truss-type construct. A 70-mm-long, 3.5-mm cortical screw was inserted distal to the fracture site and was angled superiorly into the humeral head to act as a "triangulation" screw. Fixation was supplemented proximally with two cancellous screws of 4.0-mm diameter directed into the humeral head. The shaft was secured with standard 3.5-mm cortical screws and AO/ASIF techniques.

Construct C was an AO, five-hole, proximal humeral blade plate (Synthes, Paoli, PA). This is a 4.5-mm dynamic compression (DC) plate to which a pediatric size blade plate has been added to the proximal end and angled at 90 degrees. The 40-mm-long blade was inserted using the pediatric blade plate instruments. Proximal fixation was enhanced with the insertion of a single 6.5-mm, fully-threaded cancellous screw, which was angled superiorly into the humeral head, but which did not pass through the horizontal part of the plate and, thus, did not act as a truss support. The plate was secured to the shaft using 4.5-mm cortical screws and standard AO/ASIF techniques.

Construct D was an AO, five-hole, T-plate (Synthes, Paoli, PA). This plate was secured proximally, using three 6.5-mm-diameter cancellous screws in the T-region of the plate. The plate was secured to the shaft distally, using 4.5-mm cortical screws inserted in standard fashion.

Construct E was an AO, five-hole, cloverleaf plate (Synthes, Paoli, PA). This device was modified and inserted according to the method described by Esser [26], with the anterior and superior flanges removed. Five cancellous screws of 4.0-mm diameter were inserted into the humeral head, and 3.5-mm cortical screws were used to secure the plate to the shaft.

Mechanical Testing

Biomechanical testing was performed on an Instron 8501 servohydraulic testing machine (Instron, Canton, MA). Two testing modes were used—namely, bending and axial compression [**Fig. 11.3**]. A testing apparatus similar to a design described previously in the literature was used [11].

To simulate a "cortical contact" model, specimens were tested before any surgical neck osteotomy and fixation. Initially, each intact specimen was nondestructively tested to serve as an internal control. The stiffness results of the intact humeri tests were used to rank all 25 specimens in order from strongest to weakest, so that they could be equally distributed and assigned to one of the five study groups in rank-order fashion. The deforming forces were then applied to assess the biomechanical stiffness of the constructs. The potted specimens were mounted and secured into a custom jig that could be adapted to orient the humeral shaft in varying degrees of abduction and forward flexion. Direct axial compression of 100 N was applied to the superior aspect of the humeral head to produce shear loading on the construct. Fixed to the plunger of the mechanical tester was a steel block with a hollowed cup that simulated the shoulder joint and acted as the indenter. The humeri were tested at 20 degrees of abduction and 20 degrees of forward flexion. The testing apparatus was then adapted to apply anterior-to-posterior forces and lateral-to-medial forces of 100 N, perpendicular to the shaft. With the humerus positioned at 90 degrees of flexion, forces were applied on the lesser tuberosity, in a posterior direction. With the humerus positioned at 90 degrees of abduction, forces were applied on the center of the greater tuberosity, in a medial direction. Fixed to the plunger of the mechanical tester was a flat plate, which acted as the indenter. The choice of 100 N ensured that all tests were kept within linear elastic limits of the specimens to prevent the onset of any permanent da-

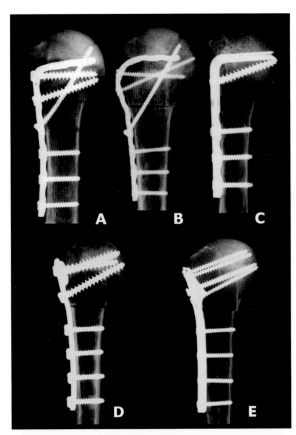

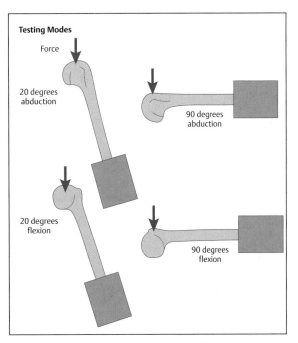

Fig. 11.3 Biomechanical test set-up. Bending and axial compression tests were performed on all specimens. To simulate a "cortical contact" model, specimens were tested before any surgical neck osteotomy and fixation. For "no-cortical-contact" (or gap) testing, a humeral model was created with a 5-mm bone gap to represent bony comminution and loss of cortical contact.

Fig. 11.2 Specimens were randomized into five different study arms. Construct A is an eight-hole, LCDC plate contoured into a blade supported by one, 70-mm-long, 4.5-mm-diameter cortical screw, which acts as a truss. Construct B, is a 10-hole LCDC plate arrangement identical to construct A, but using one, 70-mm long, 3.5-mm-diameter cortical screw as a truss. Construct C, is a five-hole DC blade plate with one 6.5-mm-diameter cancellous screw that does not pass through the horizontal part of the plate and, thus, does not act like a truss. Construct D, is a five-hole T-plate supported by three 6.5-mm-diameter cancellous screws. Construct E, is a five-hole cloverleaf plate supported by five 4-mm-diameter cancellous screws.

mage, thus allowing for the completion of all experiments. The existence of a small, nonlinear toe region may have been attributable to slack being taken up in the system during initial loading of the specimens. Otherwise, the rest of the load–displacement behavior was linear.

Finally, a "no-cortical-contact" (or gap) model was created to represent bony comminution and loss of cortical contact. All 25 of the previous implants were loosened, and 5 mm of bone was resected on the distal side of the surgical neck osteotomy site. The implants were then, again, rigidly fixed and tested, using the same protocol described above.

Data Analysis

Load–displacement curves were obtained for each specimen, and the slopes were calculated, which represented the biomechanical stiffness of the constructs. Normalized stiffness values were then computed by dividing the stiffness of repaired specimens by the stiffness of their corresponding intact specimens. One-way analyses of variance (ANOVA) were employed to determine any differences between plate systems for pooled groupings within cortical contact and no-cortical-contact models. If $P > 0.05$, then the ANOVA P-value is reported as not being statistically significant. However, any pooled ANOVA that showed $P < 0.05$ were then further assessed post hoc, using unpaired Student's t tests for multiple pairwise comparisons to determine which pairwise comparison showed the statistical difference. For these cases, the Student's t test P-value is reported.

Reality Check: A Bad Methods Section

The text of the good version of the Methods section presented above has been altered to provide the suboptimal version below. The figures are not reproduced below, but it is to be assumed that the same figures were created for this version also. Readers are encouraged to circle or make a list of the poor aspects of the following passage as they read along.

Methods

Specimen Preparation

Twenty-nine cadaveric humeri were harvested. All soft tissues were removed. The specimens were wrapped and immediately frozen. All humeri were radiographed prior to inclusion in the study and reviewed by two investigators independently. A total of 25 humeri were available for the study because of previous pathology in four of the specimens.

Each specimen was thawed at room temperature prior to testing. All humeri were osteotomized transversely at 230 mm distal to the most superior aspect of the humeral head. The humeral shafts were then potted with methylmethacrylate in steel tubes, so that the humeri were flush with the bottom of the tubes.

In each humerus, a standardized transverse surgical neck osteotomy was created 10 mm distal to the inferomedial margin of the articular surface of the humeral head. The osteotomy was provisionally stabilized with bone-reduction forceps prior to definitive fixation. All plate fixation devices [**Fig. 11.2**] were positioned posterior to the bicipital groove, 10 mm distal to the tip of the greater tuberosity, on the lateral aspect of the humerus.

Implant Configurations

The 25 humeri were randomly assigned to one of five methods of fracture fixation [**Fig. 11.2**].

Construct A was an AO, 4.5 mm, narrow, LCDC, eight-hole plate. This plate was adopted for use in the humerus and was inserted to create a truss-type construct. The plate was contoured manually into a modified "blade plate," with a 90-degree angle situated between the third and fourth screw holes from the proximal end. A 4.5 mm cortical "triangulation" screw was inserted distal to the fracture line and angled via freehand fluoroscopic guidance to engage the most medial hole in the transverse part of the plate within the humeral head. Two additional 6.5-mm cancellous screws were placed into the humeral head for additional fixation. The shaft was secured with standard 4.5-mm cortical screws and AO/ASIF techniques.

Construct B was an AO, 3.5 mm, LCDC, 10-hole plate. This small fragment plate was contoured and also inserted as above to create a truss-type construct. A 70-mm-long, 3.5-mm cortical screw was inserted distal to the fracture site and angled superiorly into the humeral head to act as a "triangulation" screw. Fixation was supplemented proximally with two cancellous screws of 4.0-mm diameter directed into the humeral head. The shaft was secured with standard 3.5-mm cortical screws and AO/ASIF techniques.

Construct C was an AO, five-hole, proximal humeral blade plate (Synthes, Paoli, PA). This is a 4.5-mm DC plate to which a pediatric size blade plate has been added to the proximal end and angled at 90 degrees. The blade was inserted using the pediatric blade plate instruments. Proximal fixation was enhanced with the insertion of a single 6.5-mm, fully-threaded cancellous screw, angled superiorly into the humeral head, but which did not pass through the horizontal part of the plate and, thus, did not act as a truss support. The plate was secured to the shaft using 4.5-mm cortical screws and standard AO/ASIF techniques.

Construct D was an AO, five-hole, T-plate. This plate was secured proximally, using three 6.5-mm-diameter cancellous screws in the T-region of the plate. The plate was secured to the shaft distally, using 4.5-mm cortical screws inserted in standard fashion.

Construct E was an AO, five-hole, cloverleaf plate (Synthes, Paoli, PA). This device was modified and inserted according to previous studies with the anterior and superior flanges removed. Five cancellous screws of 4.0-mm diameter were inserted into the humeral head, while 3.5-mm cortical screws were used to secure the plate to the shaft.

Mechanical Testing

Biomechanical testing was performed on an Instron 8501 servohydraulic testing machine (Instron, Canton, MA). Two testing modes were used—namely, bending and axial compression (Fig. 2) [**Fig. 11.3**].

To simulate a "cortical contact" model, specimens were tested before any surgical neck osteotomy and fixation. Initially, each intact specimen was nondestructively tested to serve as an internal control. The stiffness results of the intact humeri tests were used to rank all 25 specimens in order from strongest to weakest, so that they could be equally distributed and assigned to one of the five study groups in rank-order fashion. The deforming forces were then applied to assess the biomechanical stiffness of the constructs. The potted specimens were mounted and secured into a custom jig that could be adapted to orient the humeral shaft in varying degrees of abduction and forward flexion. Direct axial compression of 100 N was applied to the superior aspect of the humeral head to produce shear loading on the construct. Fixed to the plunger of the mechanical tester was a steel block with a hollowed cup that simulated the shoulder joint and acted as the indenter. The humeri were tested at 20 degrees of abduction and 20 degrees of forward flexion. The testing apparatus was then adapted to apply anterior-to-posterior forces and lateral-to-medial forces of 100 N, perpendicular to the shaft. With the humerus positioned at 90 degrees of flexion, forces were applied on the lesser tuberosity, in a posterior direction. With the humerus positioned at 90 degrees of abduction, forces were applied on the center of the greater tuberosity, in a medial direction. Fixed to the plunger of the mechanical tester was a flat plate, which acted as the indenter.

Finally, a "no-cortical-contact" (or gap) model was created to represent bony comminution and loss of cortical contact. All 25 of the previous implants were loosened, and 5 mm of bone was resected on the distal side of the surgical neck osteotomy site. The implants were then, again, rigidly fixed and tested, using the same protocol described above.

Data Analysis

Load–displacement curves were obtained for each specimen, and the slopes were calculated, which represented the biomechanical stiffness of the constructs. Normalized stiffness values were then computed by dividing the stiffness of repaired specimens by the stiffness of their corresponding intact specimens. One-way ANOVA were employed to determine any differences between plate systems for pooled groupings within cortical contact and no-cortical-contact models. If $P > 0.05$, then the ANOVA P-value is reported as not being statistically significant. However, any pooled ANOVA that showed $P < 0.05$ were then further assessed post hoc, using unpaired Student's t tests for multiple pairwise comparisons to determine which pairwise comparison showed the statistical difference. For these cases, the Student's t test P-value is reported.

Comparing the Good and Bad Methods Sections

The content of both Methods sections above is much the same, since both have the four segments of description (Specimen Preparation), preparation (Implant Configurations), testing (Mechanical Testing), and analysis (Data Analysis). Nevertheless, there are differences in the amount of detailing that would make the first one acceptable by the editor of a scientific journal, while the second one would need to be improved.

The good Methods section provides precedent from the literature in several places to justify its approach, always explains abbreviations upon first appearance unless widely known to the typical readership, and provides much detail regarding all parameters, techniques, and materials used.

The bad Methods section does not provide the following items: details about the inclusion/exclusion criteria for the specimens, precedent from the literature in several places where it could have done so, dimensions and test parameter values in several places, names of manufacturers for some of the devices used, and reasons for using a 100 N load during tests. It also does not provide any explanation for the abbreviations, merely assuming that the reader is familiar with all of them, which may not be the case.

Conclusion

This chapter provides for researchers some practical tools and guidelines for writing a successful Methods section for scientific articles that they wish to submit to a journal. It is hoped that the reader has learned that there is a certain template for a scientific journal article that the author is expected to adhere to by editors, reviewers, and readers alike. This expectation should be considered when writing so as to generate an effective scientific journal paper. Even so, it must be remembered that there is an art to scientific writing that can only come with experience.

References

1. Lever JP, Aksenov SA, Zdero R, Ahn H, McKee MD, Schemitsch EH. Biomechanical analysis of plate osteosynthesis systems for proximal humerus fractures. J Orthop Trauma 2008;22 (1):23–29

12

Results: Basics of Analysis

Paul Karanicolas

Summary

The purpose of this chapter is to provide you with skills to write a clear Results section in your manuscript. It provides you with a general framework and outlines common pitfalls in writing the Results section. This will assist you in conveying the message you feel is important to your readers.

Introduction

The Results section is the crux of the research report: after describing the rationale and methodology employed, this is your opportunity to inform the reader of the actual study findings. This chapter discusses several issues to be considered while writing a Results section; these pointers will ensure that your key message is being delivered to your intended readers. To start, read the two examples of Results sections in the Reality Check below. As you read, decide for yourself which style you prefer, and try to identify the specific aspects that attract you to the preferred sample.

Reality Check: Two examples of Results Sections One Good and One Not So Good—Can You Tell the Difference?
(The figures, tables, and bibliographical references mentioned in the examples are not provided, but their numbering appears as it would in the published text.)

Example A
Patients were randomized to receive internal fixation (IF) or hemiarthroplasty (HA). There was no difference between groups in terms of mortality (17.0% versus 17.5%), pain score (1.22 versus 1.41), mobility score (5.71 versus 5.92), or loss of flexion (4.8 versus 4.2 degrees) when we compared them with t-tests (p = NS) (Table I). The HA group had less shortening at one year (8.6 versus 17.0 mm, $p < 0.05$). Since the clinical outcomes were similar, this difference is not very important.
The HA group consisted of 112 patients, 40% male, with a mean age of 72.4, mean mobility score of 6.3, and mean ASA score of 1.7. The IF group consisted of 126 patients, 30% male, with a mean age of 72.2, mean mobility score of 6.3, and mean ASA score of 1.7 (Table 2) (1) ...

Example B
Over the period of study 881 patients with an intracapsular fracture were admitted. Figure 1 shows the number of patients who were excluded and the reasons for this. Table I gives the details of the 255 patients randomized; the groups were similar in terms of baseline characteristics. For these patients, 39 deviations from the trial protocol occurred in 26 patients as listed in Figure 1.
The primary outcome was mortality for which there was no statistically significant difference between the groups (Fig. 2, p = 0.112). There was a tendency for an improved survival after internal fixation in those aged 90 years and over (Figs. 3 to 5) and in those with a lower mobility score (Table II). Table III gives details of pain and functional assessment of the survivors.
Fourteen patients in the hemiarthroplasty group required secondary procedures, 17 reoperations in total. Seven were revised to total hip replacement (THR) for loosening. One of these THRs dislocated twice and had a later acetabular cup support. One fracture below the implant was plated and two patients with sepsis were treated by a Girdlestone excision arthroplasty (1) ...

General Framework for the Results Section

Hopefully, after reading the two Results sections given above you will have come to the conclusion that example B is much easier to read and comprehend than example A. This chapter will focus on the differences between these two examples, to help you write a clear and concise Results section that conveys the important points that your paper addresses.

Perhaps the most obvious difference between the two examples is the general structure of the Results section. In example A, the writer is eager to display the most important results (the primary outcome), and therefore fills the first paragraph with several numbers and statistical comparisons. This writing lacks a logical progression of ideas and leaves the reader confused. The second example is framed around a clear flow of thoughts, which makes it much easier for the reader to follow.

The specific structure of the Results section depends on the nature of the study design. Clearly a randomized controlled trial will present different results from a systematic review. However, the principles of how to frame the section and the important elements that need to be included are constant. Remember that tables and figures are much easier for readers to interpret than a series of numbers. The purpose of the Results section is to introduce the tables and figures, highlight the most important findings, and describe results that cannot be displayed in a graphical or tabular format. Thus, the best Results sections are succinct, and include very few numerical values.

Readers might find the following framework helpful for most study designs (randomized controlled trials, cohort studies, and case–control studies): When writing the Results section, begin by discussing baseline characteristics, patient follow-up, and protocol violations or deviations. Next, discuss the primary outcome, followed by secondary outcomes, and subgroup analyses, if relevant. Finally, include any other important observations.

Jargon Simplified: Primary and Secondary Outcome

Primary outcome—"Specific key measurement(s) or observation(s) used to measure the effect of experimental variables in a study, or for observational studies, to describe patterns of diseases or traits or associations with exposures, risk factors or treatment."[2]

Secondary outcome—"Other key measures that will be used to evaluate the intervention(s) or, for observational studies, that are a focus of the study."[2]

Key Concepts: General Framework for the Results Section

1. Baseline characteristics, follow-up, protocol violations.
2. Primary outcome.
3. Secondary outcomes and subgroup analyses, if appropriate.
4. Other observations.

Baseline Characteristics, Follow-Up, Protocol Violations

When interpreting the results from a study, readers must place the observed outcomes in the context of the patients and procedures involved in the trial. Researchers can assist the reader in this process by beginning the Results section with a description of the participants enrolled in the study and any losses to follow-up or deviations from the protocol. The CONSORT statement, a set of guidelines that describe how to report a randomized controlled trial (see Chapter 3), suggests including a figure that displays the number of patients screened, eligible, enrolled, lost to follow-up, and ultimately analyzed in the trial (**Fig. 12.1**).[3] This type of figure transmits a tremendous amount of information to the reader that would otherwise require several paragraphs of explanation. Instead, a simple statement referring the reader to this figure (similar to that in example B) is sufficient. Researchers can easily produce a similar

figure for cohort, case–control, and other types of study design.

Jargon Simplified: CONSORT

"Stands for Consolidated Standards of Reporting Trials, encompasses various initiatives developed by the CONSORT Group to alleviate the problems arising from inadequate reporting of randomized controlled trials (RCTs)."[4]

A table (usually Table 1 in the manuscript) is the simplest way to describe the baseline characteristics of the participants. Again, a brief statement referring the reader to the table is all that is needed in the Results section of the manuscript. If the groups differed substantially in one or more characteristics, it might be helpful to highlight these areas in the text.

The beginning of the Results section is also a good place to describe the median length of follow-up and any protocol deviations that occurred (such as participants excluded after randomization, or participants who received an intervention that they were not randomized to). These details will help the reader to place the observed outcomes in the context of the trial. They may be included in the first figure or described separately in the first or second paragraph of the text.

Primary Outcome

The results of the primary outcome analysis are central to your message, and should therefore be prominently emphasized in the Results section. Normally this can best be accomplished with a statement describing the primary findings and a referral to the appropriate figure or table. It is not necessary to inundate the reader with numerical values and statistical comparisons. However, you should state whether or not there was a significant difference between the groups, including the exact *P*-value or confidence interval for the treatment effect.

Secondary Outcomes and Subgroup Analyses, if Appropriate

You should report the results of any secondary outcomes and subgroup analyses that you chose to conduct after the primary outcome. Again, this can usually best be accomplished by referring the reader to one or more tables or figures and highlighting interesting results in the text. Although it is preferable to avoid numerical values in the text, the exact results for all outcomes and subgroup analyses (including all *P*-values) should be available to the reader somewhere in the manuscript, either in tabular, graphical, or text form.

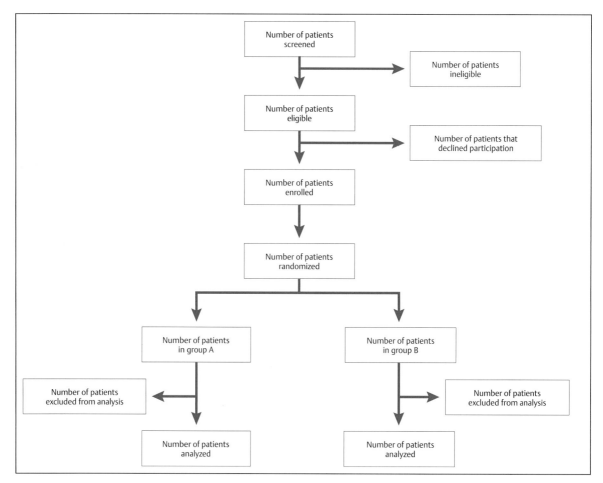

Fig. 12.1 The participants enrolled in a trial, illustrating of the number of patients screened, eligible, enrolled, lost to follow-up, and ultimately analyzed. (From: Altman DG, Schulz KF, Moher D et al. The revised CONSORT statement for reporting randomized trials: explanation and elaboration. *Ann Intern Med* 2001;134(8):663–694. Reprinted with permission.)

Other Observations

The Results section should end with other interesting observations that are not appropriate for one of the other sections, and might not be appropriate to place in a table or figure. Often this involves a discussion of specific complications, such as in example B.

Researchers should avoid including too much information in this section: it is not important for readers to know the specific details of every complication that occurred in the trial. Rather, you should include a discussion of common themes that are important in the overall interpretation of the study.

Key Concepts: Common Pitfalls to Avoid in the Results Section

1. Describing methods.
2. Presenting selective or partial results.
3. Improper presentation of *P*-values.
4. Duplicating results from tables or figures.
5. Making inferences or conclusions.

Common Pitfalls to Avoid

By simply organizing your Results section into a logical progression and limiting the use of numerical values, you are more likely to be successful in conveying the key messages from your study. This section describes some pitfalls commonly seen in published reports of trials and provides suggestions for how to avoid them. All of the pitfalls described here are present in our example A. Go back to that specific example now and see if you can spot the common pitfalls before reading on.

Describing Methods

It may seem intuitively obvious that methods belong in the Methods section, and results belong in the Results section. Unfortunately, even seasoned investigators sometimes ignore this simple concept when preparing their manuscripts. Two statements in example A illustrate this principle: the first sentence ("Patients were randomized…") and the second sentence ("…when we compared them with *t*-tests"). These phrases clearly refer to the methods of allocation and analysis, and would be far more appropriate in those sections. It may seem innocuous to include a few statements like this in the Results section, but there are several reasons not to do so. Words are at a premium when preparing research papers, limited by the journals' guidelines (often) and the readers' attention spans (always). What is saved in one area can be spent in another, so you should avoid duplication. Also, as discussed earlier, the Results section is critical to conveying your key messages; you do not want to distract the reader with unnecessary comments about the methodology. Refer to Chapter 11 for a full discussion of how to frame your Methods section and the important elements to include.

Presenting Selective or Partial Results

Although it is important to frame the results to emphasize your key message, your intention should not be to mislead the reader. Presenting selective or partial results can be very misleading, may be unethical, or may simply suggest bad research practice. Not surprisingly, the key to avoiding this without overburdening the reader with piles of statistics is to present your results in tables or figures. It is entirely appropriate to highlight interesting findings in the text of the Results section so long as the remainder of the results are available elsewhere. Researchers should be especially careful in presenting (and readers cautious in interpreting) the results of subgroup analyses.[5] It is critical that all subgroup analyses are planned ahead of time and that all results are presented, not just the analyses that yielded significant results.

Improper Presentation of *P*-Values

Researchers, journal editors, and clinicians have come to depend on statistical *P*-values to indicate a "positive" finding. Although completely arbitrary, the generally accepted threshold of statistical significance is a *P*-value of less than 0.05. A threshold for significance is needed by clinicians to infer whether differences observed in a study are likely due to chance (a type I error) or whether they are indicative of a true underlying difference between the groups. Unfortunately, the acceptance of this arbitrary threshold has had a negative consequence: some authors now report the statistical results as "$P < 0.05$," "$P > 0.05$," or "P = NS (nonsignificant)."

Reporting the results of statistical tests in a dichotomous (yes or no) fashion such as this discards potentially useful information and may be misleading. Although we accept *P*-values less than 0.05 as suggestive of a true difference between groups, remember that this is not an absolute criterion: a *P*-value of 0.05 simply indicates that there would be a 5% chance of observing the results in the study if the two groups were actually equal. Similarly, a *P*-value of 0.001 indicates that the difference seen between groups could be simply due to chance 0.1% of the time. From a reader's perspective, we should be much more confident that a true difference between groups exists in a study with a *P*-value of 0.001 rather than a study with a *P*-value of 0.049. Lumping these results together into a statement such as "$P < 0.05$" is irrational and simplistic.

It is also important to remember that a *P*-value greater than 0.05 does not indicate (or even suggest) that there is no true difference between groups. It simply indicates the extent to which any difference between groups observed in the study is potentially due to chance. A "nonsignificant" result in a study could be due to an insufficient sample size, chance (sample size calculations typically allow for "negative" results 10–20% of the time when true differences exist), bias, or finally, equivalence between the groups. To minimize the chances of misleading readers, always report the exact *P*-value (to three decimal places) and interpret the results in the Discussion section.

An alternative approach to reporting the precision of an estimate without *P*-values, known as estimation, is becoming more popular among health researchers.[6,7] This approach involves creating a confidence interval (usually 95%) around the estimate of treatment effect (most commonly a relative risk [RR], odds ratio [OR], or risk difference [RD]). Readers may consider the confidence interval to represent the plausible range of the treatment effect based on the study's data. They can then interpret the upper and lower limits of the confidence interval as the "best-case" and "worst-case" scenarios. If the lower limit of the confidence interval excludes the null value (1.0 for the RR and OR, 0.0 for the RD), they can conclude that there is likely a true difference between groups. When applied in this manner, the conclusions are exactly equivalent to the standard technique of hypothesis testing using a threshold of $P = 0.05$. The advantage of the estimation technique is that it provides additional information: the upper and lower limits of the confidence intervals, which readers may interpret as the best- and worst-case scenarios given the data from the trial.

In summary, you must present your results with some measure of the precision: either *P*-values or confidence intervals (or both, although this is somewhat redundant). Either way, you should report exact values rather than simplifying them to "significant" or "nonsignificant."

Duplicating Results from Tables or Figures

Tables and figures can convey large volumes of information much more effectively than can written descriptions (refer to Chapter 13 for a detailed treatment). Many researchers feel the need to duplicate this presentation of results by describing the key findings in the text. Remember, the Results section is intended to introduce the tables and figures, highlight the important findings, and describe any results that cannot be depicted in tabular or graphical format. Note that "highlight" is not synonymous with "duplicate." If results are presented in a table or figure, do not repeat the numerical values in the text of the paper. Simply state the important finding, for example, "mortality was lower in group A than in group B," and reference the table or figure.

Making Inferences or Conclusions

The last pitfall is similar to the first one. The Results section is the appropriate place to present your results in a simple, factual, and objective manner. You should avoid making inferences, conclusions, diatribes, or any other statements that involve interpreting the results. These comments belong in the Discussion section (refer to Chapter 14 for suggestions on how to frame the Discussion section), which is typically the longest section in the paper to allow for these types of remarks. Presenting your results in an unbiased manner allows the reader to reach his or her own conclusions before you discuss your interpretations.

While writing the Results section, you may inadvertently insert some comments that would be more appropriately placed in the Discussion section. As an illustration, example A above includes the statement, "Since the clinical outcomes were similar, this difference is not very important." This comment does not present results; the results had already been alluded to (the clinical outcomes were similar). The importance of a difference is open to interpretation, and requires a judgment based on values and beliefs. To identify inappropriate statements like this, it is suggested that you read over your Results section, specifically searching for comments that could involve values, interpretations, or conclusions, and remove or relocate them.

Conclusion

The Results section of a manuscript is an important component in which to deliver your message. You must avoid the temptation to fill this section of the paper with details and numerical values that could detract from the key points. The most elegant and effective Results sections simply introduce the tables and figures, highlight the key points, and describe findings that are inappropriate for a tabular or graphic format.

Suggested Reading

Altman DG, Schulz KF, Moher D, et al.; CONSORT GROUP (Consolidated Standards of Reporting Trials). The revised CONSORT statement for reporting randomized trials: explanation and elaboration. Ann Intern Med 2001;134(8):663–694

Durbin CG Jr. Effective use of tables and figures in abstracts, presentations, and papers. Respir Care 2004;49(10):1233–1237

References

1. Parker MJ, Khan RJK, Crawford J, Pryor GA. Hemiarthroplasty versus internal fixation for displaced intracapsular hip fractures in the elderly. A randomised trial of 455 patients. J Bone Joint Surg Br 2002;84(8):1150–1155
2. Clinical Trial Data Element Definitions. Available at: http://prsinfo.clinicaltrials.gov/definitions.html. Accessed December 21, 2009.
3. Altman DG, Schulz KF, Moher D, et al.; CONSORT GROUP (Consolidated Standards of Reporting Trials). The revised CONSORT statement for reporting randomized trials: explanation and elaboration. Ann Intern Med 2001;134(8):663–694
4. CONSORT. Available at: http://www.consort-statement.org. Accessed December 21, 2009.
5. Oxman AD, Guyatt GH. A consumer's guide to subgroup analyses. Ann Intern Med 1992;116(1):78–84
6. Montori VM, Kleinbart J, Newman TB, et al.; Evidence-Based Medicine Teaching Tips Working Group. Tips for learners of evidence-based medicine: 2. Measures of precision (confidence intervals). CMAJ 2004;171(6):611–615
7. Simon R. Confidence intervals for reporting results of clinical trials. Ann Intern Med 1986;105(3):429–435

13

Results: Tables, Figures, and Appendices

Jacquelyn Marsh, Dianne Bryant

Summary

The objective of this chapter is to provide a detailed overview of the types of information that one might present in tables, figures, and appendices, as well as guidelines and tips on how to present this information effectively when preparing a manuscript.

Introduction

In preparing a manuscript, you should consider other methods than text that can present information more concisely than text. Tables and figures are used to display data and to provide a visual representation of the important results of a study. Tables present information such as patient characteristics, and exact numerical values that cannot be effectively presented in a figure. A figure is any illustration other than a table, such as a chart, graph, photograph, or drawing. Both tables and figures can present certain information more clearly and in less space than the same information would require in the text.[1]

Appendices are used to present supplementary material that was not included in the main body of the report. The appendix allows the author to provide readers with detailed information that could otherwise be distracting to read in the main body of the article. Items that may appear in an appendix include tables or figures that are not essential to the main message of the manuscript, questionnaires, surveys, or other research instruments used in a study.[1] Increasingly, journals allow such information to be supplied as supplementary online material accessible via the Web.

Tables

Tables are an effective way to present a large amount of data in a small amount of space. Tables should be used to display crucial data that are directly related to the content of the article.[2] The text should not duplicate all of the information included in the table; rather the text should highlight the information that is most important.[1]

Be careful not to make tables too complex. A table should be arranged in an orderly display of columns and rows, so that the data are easily comparable.[3] (Always make full use of the table formatting features of your word-processing software to generate a proper cell structure; do not submit tables made to "look right" by use of the tab function or by typing repeated spaces to obtain visual alignment.) In some cases, it may be more useful to break one large table into separate smaller tables. It is important to be selective, however, in choosing how many tables to include in the paper; a large number of tables compared with text will make it more difficult for the reader to follow your manuscript.

In general, the first table in a manuscript presents the demographic characteristics of the study participants. This table allows the reader to review the characteristics of the subjects in your study and begin to judge whether your sample was representative of the population they are inquiring about. This table is especially important to clinicians who will use this information to determine whether the results of your study are likely to be generalizable to their patients. Data in this sort of table should present characteristics that are thought to be potential confounders and should be divided by treatment groups if the study contains more than one group.

When reporting the results of a study in the form of a table, it is a good idea to present both the numerator and the denominator unless your dataset is complete. If the dataset is complete, then include the number of patients in your sample by group in the column header. It is much more informative to include the mean (if reporting a continuous variable), or the incidence rate (if reporting a dichotomous variable), by group as well as reporting the treatment effect (mean difference, relative risk [RR], odds ratio [OR], etc.) and *P*-value. One might also decide to report the outcomes at each time point to inform the reader of the magnitude of change observed within each group over time, though this is less often done.

Jargon Simplified: Continuous Variable, Dichotomous Variable, and Incidence Rate

- **Continuous variable**—"A variable that can theoretically take any value and in practice can take a large number of values with small differences between them ."[4]
- **Dichotomous variable** —"A variable that can take one of two values, such as pregnant or not pregnant, dead or alive, having suffered a stroke or not having suffered a stroke ."[4]
- **Incidence rate**—"Number of new cases of disease occurring during a specified period of time; expressed as a percentage of the number of people at risk."[4]

- **Incidence rate** – The number of new events over a specified time interval.

Key Concepts: General Guidelines for Creating a Table
1. Always use the word-processor's table facility; do not manually align information using tabs or spaces or re-set margins.
2. Provide a title that identifies the specific purpose of the table.
3. Use footnotes to define items that have been abbreviated or require further explanation.
4. Provide the unit of measurement for each variable. The units can appear after the descriptor or after the value. Be consistent in which method you use. Most style guides specify the placement of the unit after the descriptor (most often in the column heading or leftmost column). Only when a column has values with different units is it usual to give the units after each value in a table.
5. For each result, specify the type of measure (mean, median, incidence, etc.) and provide a measure of dispersion (e.g., standard deviation, standard error, interquartile range).
6. Align all values in each column along the decimal point (using the word processor's decimal tab feature, not by spacing to achieve alignment), and have the same number of decimal places in all values for one variable
7. Avoid spurious precision when presenting your results—use rounding rules to reduce the number of decimal places.
8. For each result, specify the summary measure (mean difference, RR, OR, etc.) and provide a measure of precision around the estimate (e.g., 95% confidence interval). This will help the reader to interpret your results: *P*-values do not provide this information.

Table 13.1 **Patient characteristics by treatment group**

Characteristic	ACL double[a] N = 146	ACL single[b] N = 148
Age (years)[c]	25.7 ± 9.0	25.1 ± 8.8
Sex (male)	91 (62.3%)	86 (58.1%)
Weight (lb)[c]	161.4 ± 5.6	158.9 ± 6.1
Height (inches)[c]	69.0 ± 3.6	67.5 ± 2.1
Annual income		
<$20 000	7 (4.7%)	5 (4.7%)
$20 000 to $40 000	28 (19.2%)	29 (4.7%)
$40 000 to $60 000	68 (46.6%)	73 (4.7%)
$60 000 to $80 000	25 (17.1%)	21 (4.7%)
>$80 000	18 (12.3%)	20 (4.7%)

[a] Anterior cruciate ligament double-bundle reconstruction.
[b] Anterior cruciate ligament single-bundle reconstruction.
[c] Presented as mean and standard deviation.

Reality Check: An Example of a Table Reporting Patient Characteristics
See **Table 13.1**.

Reality Check: An Example of a Table Reporting Results Using a Dichotomous Metric
See **Table 13.2**.

Table 13.2 **Outcomes of hip fracture patients by treatment group**

Outcomes	HA[a] N = 101	THA[b] N = 102	RR (95% CI)[c]	P-value
Non-union	19 (18.8%)	17 (16.7%)	0.89 (0.50 to 1.59)	0.69
Revision	15 (14.8%)	10 (9.8%)	0.67 (0.32 to 1.40)	0.29
Infection	5 (5.0%)	7 (6.9%)	1.35 (0.47 to 3.92)	0.58

[a] Hemi-arthroplasty.
[b] Total hip arthroplasty.
[c] Relative risk with 95% confidence interval.

Reality Check: An Example of a Table Reporting Results Using a Continuous Metric
See **Table 13.3**.

Table 13.3 **Outcomes of patients with osteoarthritis of the hip following joint resurfacing or total joint replacement**

Outcome (mean ± SD)	Resurfacing N = 101	Replacement N = 102	Mean Difference (95% CI)[a]	p-value
Pain VAS[b] (mm)	9.8 ± 2.1	9.2 ± 1.9	0.6 (0.0 to 1.2)	0.03
ROM[c] (degrees)				
Abduction	41.8 ± 4.1	38.7 ± 4.2	3.1 (1.0 to 5.1)	0.003
Flexion	111.1 ± 9.6	99.5 ± 9.4	11.6 (9.0 to 14.2)	<0.001
External rotation	21.3 ± 7.6	21.0 ± 8.1	0.3 (−1.9 to 2.5)	0.79
Quality of life	49.7 ± 10.2	50.1 ± 10.5	−0.4 (−3.3 to 2.5)	0.78

[a] Relative risk with 95% confidence interval.
[b] VAS, visual analog scale.
[c] ROM, range of movement.

Key Concepts: Tables
A table can be useful to put large amounts of data into a small space, but be sure to not make tables too complex. You may wish to split up a large table into smaller tables, but be mindful of how many tables in total you generate because it may reduce the readability of your manuscript.

Figures

A figure may be a chart, graph, photograph, drawing, or any type of illustration other than a table.[1] Figures should include only the essential facts, without unnecessary detail, and should also be easy to read and understand. Although figures are an effective way to illustrate interactions and general comparisons, they are not meant to be as precise as tables.[5,6] Figures provide a quick glance at the overall pattern of results and are an effective way to present and clarify the data. Like tables, however, figures should not simply be a repetition of data reported in the text; rather the text should highlight the important information from the figure.

Commonly included figures are photographs to illustrate tests, apparatus, procedures, results of imaging, and so on. These types of figures provide excellent visual appeal. However, reproduction during publication can alter the contrast and detail in photographs. It is therefore important to provide the journal with an image with sharp contrast and clear prints. If possible, provide the photograph in black and white, as many journals will not publish in color and those that do often charge a fee to do so. Further, the transformation from a color photograph to black and white may produce an inaccurate image.[3] It may be beneficial to add arrows to identify important features of the photograph if they are difficult to decipher. For more specific instructions on submitting photographs, consult the journal or publisher.

When reporting the results of a clinical trial (randomized trial or prospective cohort), one figure that is extremely useful, and may even be required by the journal, is called a patient flow chart. This type of figure identifies the number of patients initially screened for the study, the number of patients who were excluded and why, and how many patients entered, withdrew, or completed the study.[7] **Figure 3.1** presented in Chapter 3 displays an example of a patient flow chart for a randomized clinical trial.[8]

> **Key Concepts: Figures**
> Figures should be a simple and easy to understand way to present data or comparisons, with less precision than a table. When submitting a manuscript, provide the journal with a black and white copy of the image, or a high-quality, high-contrast color image as reproduction can alter the contrast and details of the image.

Graphs

Graphs can display complex relationships that may not be easily described in the text such as time series data or correlations between variables.[9] An efficient graph represents the overall pattern of results while providing the necessary

detail to show the relevance of the data. Data should be presented in a way that relates to clinical understanding, and include both the date points and related indicator of variance (e.g., standard error, standard deviation, 95% confidence intervals) around that data point.[10,11]

> **Jargon Simplified: Time Series Data**
> "Typically used in observational studies, time series design monitors the occurrence of outcomes or endpoints over a number of cycles and determines if the pattern changes coincident with an intervention or event."[4]

Use a graph when the essential purpose is to illustrate a general relationship among the various groups or a specific trend within the data.[8,12] Use a table when it is essential that the numerical values of the data be presented exactly. In other words, when you want the reader to focus on the pattern of the results, a graph is preferred. However, if it is essential that the reader know the exact numerical values, then a table is more effective.[1]

The graph should be easy to interpret so that the reader is able to understand the significance, the cause, and the implications of the data plotted on the graph.[9] It is therefore important to use the appropriate type of graph to display the data being reported. The most common types of graphs are the bar graph, pie chart, line graph, scatter plot, and histogram.[6,13]

> **Key Concepts: Examples of the Use of Each Type of Graph**
>
> | **Categorical variables** | |
> |---|---|
> | Bar graph | Uses bars to represent nominal categories. The axis must include zero. |
> | Pie chart | Shows percentages and proportions. There should be no more than five segments. |
> | **Continuous variables** | |
> | Line graph | Shows the relation between two quantitative variables with a continuous line. |
> | Scatter plot | Shows how strongly two variables are correlated using individual data points. |
> | Histogram | Shows a single frequency distribution. A form of bar graph used with interval or ratio-scaled variables. |

Although graphs are one of the best ways to display data, there are several common mistakes that can be made. One common error is in selecting the axes for the graph. Avoid truncating, enlarging, or compressing the axes in ways that can make the graph misleading. Inappropriate scaling can give the graph a deceptive appearance, such as inflating the difference between two groups, making the difference seem significant when in fact it is not.[7,8] See also Chapter 4 for some examples of incorrect and misleading graphical presentation of data.

Key Concepts: Mistakes to Avoid When Using Graphs
Truncating, enlarging, or compressing the axes can make a graph misleading.
Inappropriate scaling can erroneously appear to inflate the difference between two groups, suggesting a significant difference when none exists. (See **Fig. 4.2** and **Fig. 13.4**.)

Another frequently committed error is connecting discrete points; for example, representing repeated measurements of an individual patient over time with a continuous line. A continuous line implies certainty of that patient's results at any given time. A similar error is extending a regression line beyond the observed data points included on the graph. This suggests that conclusions can be drawn for values for which no evidence exists. Thus, extrapolation beyond the data can lead the reader to false conclusions.[7,9]

Reality Check: A Bar Graph
See **Fig. 13.1**.

Reality Check: A Scatter Plot with Regression Line and 95% Confidence Intervals around the Regression Line
See **Fig. 13.2**.

Reality Check: A Histogram
See **Fig. 13.3**.

Reality Check: Good and Poor Line Graphs
See **Fig. 13.4**.

Key Concepts: General Guidelines for Creating a Graph
1. Select the most appropriate type of graph according to the type of data you are presenting (nominal, ordered, interval, ratio).
2. Provide a title that identifies the specific purpose of the graph.
3. Label each axis and provide the unit of measurement.
4. Use appropriate scaling for each axis. Improper scaling can give a misleading appearance, making the difference between groups seem larger.
5. Provide a legend to define the symbols used on the graph.
6. Use symbols rather than colors to differentiate between groups as some journals will only print in black and white or will charge you a fee to reproduce your graph in color.

Key Concepts: Use of Graphs
A graph is used to illustrate complex relationships or general trends, so that readers can appreciate the pattern of results, rather than specific numerical data. When producing a graph, avoid these common mistakes:
1. Manipulating your axes in a way that is misleading.
2. Connecting discrete data points.
3. Extending the regression line beyond the observed data.

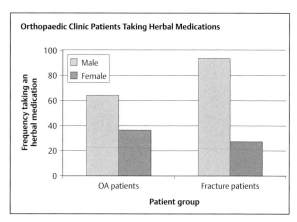

Fig. 13.1 Example of a bar graph. (Orthopaedic clinic patients with either a fracture, or osteoarthritis who were taking one or more herbal medications.)

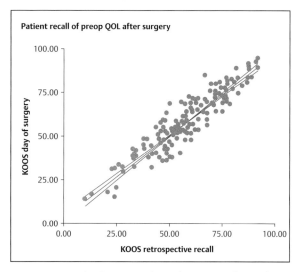

Fig. 13.2 Example of a scatter plot with regression line and 95% confidence intervals around the regression line. (Patients' recalled rating of quality of life compared with actual rating for the Knee Injury and Osteoarthritis Outcome Score [KOOS].)

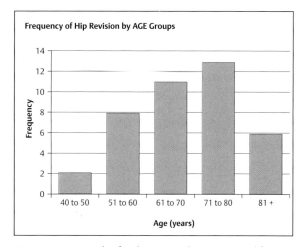

Fig. 13.3 An example of an histogram showing age and frequency of patients who required revision hip surgery.

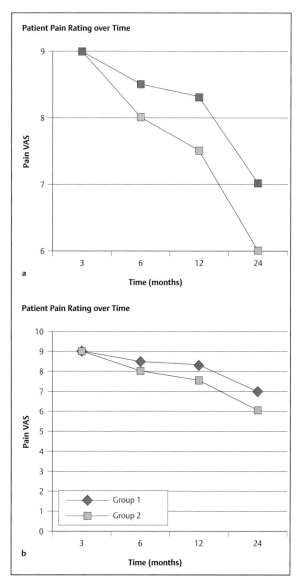

Fig. 13.4a, b a An example of a poorly presented line graph of patient pain rating over time with inappropriate scaling of the vertical axis.
b Same results as in **a**, but this time with an appropriately scaled vertical axis.

Appendices

The purpose of an appendix is to include supporting material that is not an essential part of the text itself.[3] It allows the author to provide readers with detailed information that could otherwise be distracting in the main body of the text. Increasingly, journals are providing opportunities for authors to present supplementary material that is accessible to readers online only, which reduces the number of printed pages. An appendix should be included only if it helps the reader to understand, evaluate, or replicate the

study. Examples of materials appropriate for appendices include questionnaires, surveys, or other research instruments used to collect data, rare or inaccessible text, additional analyses, tables, figures, or raw data on which analysis was performed.[1]

If the paper includes more than one appendix, each one should appear on a separate page at the end of the manuscript, and be labeled with a capital letter in the order in which they appear in the text (Appendix A, Appendix B, etc.). Each appendix must have a title.

An appendix may also contain tables, figures, and graphs. As in the main text, each appendix table or figure should be numbered, along with the same label letter as the appendix (e.g., Table A1). Any tables or figures appearing in an appendix must also be cited according to the same rules that apply to the main text. If the appendix includes a test or questionnaire, written permission must be obtained from the copyright holder for that instrument, and full credit should be given to the copyright holder in the article.[1]

Key Concepts: What Can Be Included in an Appendix?
- Questionnaires, surveys, or other research instruments used to collect data
- Rare or inaccessible text
- Additional analyses, tables, figures, or raw data on which analysis was performed

Key Concepts: Purpose of Appendices
The purpose of an appendix is to provide additional information to the reader that may otherwise be distracting in the text. All appendices need to be titled, and if you include multiple appendices, ensure that they are all on separate pages and labeled with a capital letter in the order in which they appear in the text. Figures and tables should also be labeled according to the appendix in which they appear. Finally, ensure that written permission is obtained from the copyright holder for any applicable information you choose to include in the appendix.

Conclusion

Tables, figures, and graphs are an essential component of the presentation of results. They help to organize and summarize data, and allow the reader to easily interpret results of the research findings.[1] These items should enhance rather than confuse the reader's understanding of the research. Accordingly, include them only if they helps to convey the meaning of the results more clearly or in less space than would description in the text.[6] In constructing a table, figure, or graph, carefully define what needs to be communicated and determine whether text, a table, or a graphic representation is the best way to convey this information.[13] Include any supplementary materials in an appendix, at the end of the manuscript. Overall, when used ap-

propriately, these tools can enhance your paper and clarify your research results to the reader.

Suggested Reading

American Psychological Association. Publication Manual of the American Psychological Association, 4th ed. Washington, DC: American Psychological Association;1994

Iverson C, Flanagin A, Fontanarosa PB, et al. American Medical Association Manual of Style: A Guide for Authors and Editors. 9th ed. Hagerstown, MD: Lippincott Williams & Wilkins;1997

Runyon RP, Haber A, Pittenger DJ, Coleman KA. Fundamentals of Behavioral Statistics. 8th ed. McGraw-Hill Companies, Inc. United States 1996

References

1. American Psychological Association. Publication Manual of the American Psychological Association. 4th ed. Washington, DC: American Psychological Association; 1994

2. Iverson C, Flanagin A, Fontanarosa PB, et al. American Medical Association Manual of Style: A Guide for Authors and Editors. 9th ed. Hagerstown, MD: Lippincott Williams & Wilkins; 1997

3. Huth EJ. Style Manual Committee, Council of Biology Editors. Scientific Style and Format: The CBE Manual for Authors, Editors, and Publishers. 6th ed. New York: Cambridge University Press; 1994

4. Guyatt GH, Rennie D, eds. User's Guides to the Medical Literature: A Manual for Evidence-based Clinical Practice. Chicago, IL: AMA Press; 2001

5. Runyon RP, Haber A, Pittenger DJ, Coleman KA. Fundamentals of Behavioral Statistics. 8th ed. United States: McGraw-Hill Companies, Inc.; 1996

6. Lwanga SK, Tye C-Y, Ayeni O. Teaching Health Statistics—Lesson and Seminar Outlines. 2nd ed. Geneva: World Health Organization; 1999

7. Durbin CG Jr. Effective use of tables and figures in abstracts, presentations, and papers. Respir Care 2004;49(10):1233–1237

8. Altman DG, Schulz KF, Moher D, et al.; CONSORT GROUP (Consolidated Standards of Reporting Trials). The revised CONSORT statement for reporting randomized trials: explanation and elaboration. Ann Intern Med 2001;134(8):663–694

9. Bowen RW. Graph It! How to Make, Read, and Interpret Graphs. Boston, MA: Prentice-Hall; 1992

10. Riffenburgh RH. Statistics in Medicine. 2nd ed. New York, NY: Academic Press;1999

11. Hurlburt RT. Comprehending Behavioral Statistics. Belmont, CA: Wadsworth Inc.; 1994

12. Norman GR, Streiner DL. Biostatistics: The Bare Essentials. 2nd ed. Hamilton, ON: BC Decker Inc.; 2000

13. Schriger DL, Cooper RJ. Achieving graphical excellence: suggestions and methods for creating high-quality visual displays of experimental data. Ann Emerg Med 2001; 37(1): 75–87

14

How to Frame a Discussion

Kyle Jeray, Stephanie Tanner

Summary

The purpose of this chapter is to provide you with an approach to writing the Discussion section in your manuscript. The Discussion section should be divided into three parts: opening (introduction), middle (body), and end (conclusion). This chapter outlines what specifically you should include and what you should avoid in each of these three parts of the Discussion section.

Introduction

When writing a manuscript, authors must ask "Why should the reader care about this manuscript?" The authors must answer this question particularly well if they are planning on writing a research paper with worthwhile clinical implications to make an impact on the scientific community. The Discussion section is the place where the authors have the opportunity to discuss the clinical implications supported by the data of the study. If the Discussion section is not presented in an organized and complete manner, the manuscript will probably be rejected. So the Discussion section is, arguably, the most important part of the manuscript. This section's function, in a nutshell, is to explain the results, to discuss other related literature as it pertains to the content of the research paper, to examine the strengths and weaknesses, and most importantly to answer the question raised in the introduction. Unfortunately, this function is often lost or never achieved in the Discussion. Consequently, the Discussion is commonly cited as the weakest part of the paper. This is because the Discussion often becomes the author's attempt to convince the reader of their specific interpretation and/or speculation of the information; and further, the author's attempt to make unsupported conclusions in an effort to sell the work and demonstrate its importance.

The framing of the discussion section is extremely important. An organized structure will guide the reader throughout the discussion and will prevent the reader from being mislead, although some writers may initially find uniform structuring difficult and even restrictive (1). However, by framing the discussion, the author will have a clear path to present the manuscript topics and will avoid confusing the reader. The Discussion section, similar to an abstract or a manuscript, should have an introduction (a statement or short paragraph of the principal finding or

answer to the primary research question raised in the Introduction section of the manuscript), followed by the body, and then a conclusion. The aim of this chapter is to help you write an effectively structured Discussion section, to make writing it an easier task, and lastly to improve your chances of successful publication.

Key Concepts: Outline for Framing the Discussion

Opening: The Introduction
- State the answer (principal finding) to the question raised in the Introduction section (purpose statement).

Middle: The Body
- Support your findings using your results.
- Cite other papers' results as indicated for support.
- Establish the novelty or uniqueness of the paper.
- Explain how the findings fit or conflict with other published papers on the topic.
- Defend your findings—why are the answers different from previous published findings?
- Discuss the strengths, weaknesses, and limitations of your study—compare and contrast with other similar studies.
- Discuss any unexpected results that either do not support your findings or lead to other unexpected or surprising answers.

End: The Conclusion
- Restate the answer to the question and indicate the meaning or importance of the study: are there important applications, recommendations, implications, or speculations arising from the study?
- Consider future needs or possibilities for research and unanswered questions.
- End with a strong, clear, evidence-supported conclusion.

Framing the Opening to the Discussion

In the framework of a Discussion section, the first sentence or, at most, the first short paragraph should either accept or reject the null hypothesis and clearly state that the information provided by your paper is indeed contributing new information to scientific research (Example 1 in Reality

Check). This statement should answer the question raised in the Introduction section. Thus, be sure to use the same key words from the study question/hypothesis in the discussion. Also be sure to identify the studied population. Often the writer may choose to restate the question/null hypothesis (approximately one sentence in length) before providing the answer (Example 2).

Alternatively, the author may provide a very short context (one sentence or at most two) prior to answering the question (Example 3).

Reality Check: Framing the Opening to the Discussion

Example 1: Addressing the Question in the First Sentence
The pain-control infusion pump provided no additional pain relief to the patient as evidenced by the lack of decrease in narcotic use and no difference in the patient perception of pain between the control and treatment groups following iliac crest bone graft harvesting. The results failed to prove the hypothesis in this setting.

Example 2: Restatement of the Question
The purpose of this study was to determine whether a continuous infusion of 0.5% bupivacaine into the iliac crest harvest site provides pain relief that is superior to the relief that is provided by the use of systemic narcotic pain medication alone in patients undergoing reconstructive orthopedic trauma procedures. The use of a pain-control infusion pump provided no additional pain relief to the patient, as evidenced by the lack of decrease in narcotic use and no difference in the patient perception of pain between the control and treatment groups.

Example 3: Adding a Context Sentence or Two Then Stating the Answer
The most frequent complication from autologous iliac crest bone grafting is donor site pain. In an effort to minimize this complication, continuous infusion of local anesthetic using pain pumps have been employed in clinical practice. This randomized, double-blind study, however, showed that the pain-control infusion pump provided no additional pain relief to the patient, as evidenced by the lack of decrease in narcotic use and no difference in the patient perception of pain between the control and treatment groups.

However, you should avoid starting the discussion with a history lesson. Also, avoid starting the discussion with a regurgitation of the results. After the question is answered, you should support your answer(s) by stating the relevant results in the body of the discussion. Finally, avoid adding information of secondary importance at the beginning of the Discussion section. That information should be in the body of the discussion. Remember also to start your discus-

sion with your most important message to capture the readers' attention.

Key Concepts: Pitfalls in Opening a Discussion
- Avoid starting the discussion with a history lesson.
- Avoid starting the discussion with a regurgitation of the results.
- Avoid adding secondary information in the beginning of the discussion.

Key Concepts: Opening your Discussion
Remember to begin your discussion with your most important point so as to capture the readers' attention.

Framing the Body of the Discussion

After the introduction, the next part of the Discussion section is the body. Keeping the information organized is essential here to ensure clarity. The purpose is to weave together a story and maintain the reader's attention. This is the time to clearly support the answer stated by the results. This should not be the time to repeat all the results mentioned in the Results section; rather you should liberally reference important tables and state judiciously the relevant results from the paper. Avoid going off on tangents. Begin with discussing the most important answers or topics and proceed to the answers with lesser importance. The exception to this rule is if you have a scientific reason for logical placement of the order of discussion topics. An example might be a procedural paper in which the logical order is important to the overall continuity of the discussion.

To maintain the interest of the reader, topic sentences beginning each paragraph should tell the overall story of the paragraph. As the writer proceeds, additional paragraphs should link with the topic using transitional sentences. Typically, specific subheadings in the Discussion section are discouraged. In Discussion sections there are almost always topics that need to be discussed that are not easily transitioned with a topic sentence that relates to the study directly. In such a case, rather than creating a new paragraph that does not seem to fit, you should use a transition sentence within the body of the previous paragraph. However, this can be very difficult to achieve. Here wordiness and length can become the writer's enemy. The goal is to be as clear and concise as possible. According to reviewers, wordiness and verbiage are the most common writing problems. Additionally, redundancy, poor grammar, unnecessary complexity, and poor flow of ideas are other common writing pitfalls noted by reviewers.[2] Remember again not to go off on tangents but to keep the discussion relevant to your results. The best technique for avoiding these typical mistakes made by authors is simply to review the discussion after it has been written.

The goal of the content in the body is to support your answer or findings. Remember that the answer is not the same as the results, but an interpretation of the results. Therefore, you need to convince the reader that the information is new, valid, and relevant. Although the results themselves may do this, typically this is not enough and the Discussion section is the place to further elaborate and support the answer to the reader.

You should establish that the fact that the research being reported brings unique information to the scientific community. A manuscript that lacks originality is often predictable, and a manuscript that offers trivial results is often destined for rejection by journals. The most common criticism from reviewers is that papers often bring nothing new.[1] Typically, whenever a paper involves novel research, this fact is mentioned in the Introduction, but it should be reemphasized here in the body of the Discussion section. This can be done by adequately explaining how your study is different from other reported studies, but do not overemphasize or underemphasize the importance of these differences. Also be cautious of claiming priority by using phrases such as "the first study" or "the only report." If you are claiming priority, modesty requires the use of phrases such as "To our knowledge, this is the first report…." This is better than saying "This is the first report …" because it is always possible that someone somewhere has done research that is very similar to yours.

You should explain your results and findings, rather than simply allowing readers to draw their own conclusions. The reader wants to know how your findings fit in with the existing current knowledge. This involves mentioning other studies and findings in the literature and whether these agree or disagree with your current study. If the findings differ dramatically, then you must explain possible reasons for this. Appraise your research and discuss/compare, with brevity, important papers that are relevant to your topic. Avoid a summary of each paper, but evaluate the paper as if you were a reviewer, by looking at the methodology, findings, and conclusions. Often this may illustrate why the findings differ or are similar. But be careful to avoid sweeping critical statements. Avoid tangential and irrelevant lengthy discussion. This may be the hardest to do at this point in the discussion.

Your findings have to be defended. Explain why your answer adds value to the current literature. Again, you are trying to create a narrative to convince the reader and reviewer. By explaining the rationale for the specific study design and examining all the variables and their dependencies, you will strengthen your credibility. While defending your answer it is helpful and almost a must, to discuss conflicting papers as noted above. Do not offer opinions that are not supported by the results in the paper. This will lessen your credibility and weaken the paper. It is very difficult to defend gross speculation. However, there may be alternative explanations or interpretations for the results. They can be and should be discussed. Some of the results within a paper may be conflicting with the conclusion. If this occurs, it is necessary to explain as best as you can why some of your results do not support your conclusions. Often this will lead to an author identifying the strengths and weaknesses of their study.

You should discuss the limitations and strengths of the study. Usually, most if not all of the strengths have been covered, but the limitations of the methods, weaknesses of the study design, and validity of assumptions have not been addressed. An explanation of each is suggested, if it was not addressed in an earlier part of the discussion, and should be included in the body of the discussion. Questions to address include: "What were the problems of the study? Is the power analysis justifiable? Is the sample size adequate? Was there selection bias or respondent bias? Was the follow-up of appropriate length? Did the authors consider or control for confounding factors?" In discussing the limitations, the author may even point out what the results do not mean. This helps the reader avoid reaching unjustified conclusions and adds credibility to the authors.

It is not uncommon in studies for unexpected findings or results to occur. They may be very minor or trivial and not warrant any discussion. They may also be interesting and even more exciting than the original question. In this case, you would need a description of its significance in the first sentence or paragraph of the discussion. Remember to be honest and indicate that the finding was unexpected and/or surprising. Be modest and describe your findings with balance throughout the paper. If you are unsure about addressing unusual findings, remember that reviewers will rate you poorly for the omission.

Reality Check: Pitfalls in Writing the Body of a Discussion—What to Avoid
- Avoid sweeping critical statements/gross speculation.
- Avoid going off on tangents.
- Avoid lengthy or wordy discussion (when in doubt, shorten!).
- Avoid redundancy.
- Avoid poor grammar.
- Avoid unnecessary complexity (keep it simple).
- Avoid poor flow of ideas.

Key Concepts: Tips for an Effective Discussion
- Support your findings.
- Keep it clear and concise.
- Reference your results often.
- Establish newness.
- Defend your results:
  1. Discuss alternative explanations.
  2. Address strengths and weaknesses.
  3. Address unexpected findings.

Framing the End of the Discussion

The end of a manuscript is often indicated by another section titled "Conclusions." Otherwise it is the last paragraph in the Discussion section of the paper and usually starts with "In conclusion…" or "In summary…." The conclusion of the discussion should end with a restatement of the answer to the question and, if applicable, state the applications, recommendations, implications, or speculations of the study. If your conclusion is more of an implication or speculation, avoid words like "must" or "will" and soften it with "may," "might," or "probably." Unwarranted conclusions, the absence of any real conclusions, or most commonly unsupported conclusions are major reasons why manuscripts are rejected.

Reality Check: Framing the Conclusion in the Discussions

Example 4: Bad Concluding Sentence
Pain pumps are ineffective devices to provide postoperative pain relief.

Example 5: Good Concluding Sentence
In conclusion, the results of this small, unstratified study indicate that the continuous infusion of bupivacaine at iliac crest bone-graft donor sites is not an effective pain-control measure in hospitalized patients receiving systemic narcotic medication.

Example 4 demonstrates a bad concluding sentence. The statement is too general and is not supported by the data. The authors are making a huge speculation to generalize results to all pain pumps. It is not enough to have correct conclusions—the conclusions must be consistent with the results reported in the paper. To avoid this pitfall, conclusions can be improved by narrowing the statement or making the recommendations less general, as demonstrated in Example 5.

Finally, although it is important to address what questions have not been answered and what further work is needed, dealing with this in the conclusion only weakens the paper. These questions can be addressed in the body of the discussion. As the author, you want to drive home the most important findings and leave the reader with that thought. The best papers are those that end with strongly supported conclusions that effectively answer the all-important question "Why should the reader care about this manuscript?"

Reality Check: Pitfalls in Concluding a Discussion—What to Avoid
- Avoid unwarranted conclusions.
- Avoid unsupported conclusions.
- Avoid absence of a conclusion (all studies must have some valid point).
- Avoid ending the paper with what further work is needed.

Key Concepts: Conclusion of your Discussion
- Restate the answers to the questions.
- Discuss application or implication and/or recommendations based on results.
- End the paper with a strong, evidence-supported clear conclusion.

Conclusion

The Discussion section can be subdivided into three parts: the opening, the body, and the end. Within each segment of the discussion, there is specific information that the author should include and some that should be omitted or removed. By following the suggestions provided in this chapter, and avoiding the common pitfalls listed, you will find writing a clear and concise discussion a less daunting task.

Suggested Reading

Byrne DW. Publishing Your Medical Research Paper: What They Don't Teach in Medical School. Baltimore, MD: Williams & Wilkins; 1998
Docherty M, Smith R. The case for structuring the discussion of scientific papers. BMJ 1999;318(7193):1224–1225

References

1. Docherty M, Smith R. The case for structuring the discussion of scientific papers. BMJ 1999;318(7193):1224–1225
2. Byrne DW. Publishing Your Medical Research Paper: What They Don't Teach in Medical School. Baltimore, MD: Williams & Wilkins;1998

15

Referencing and Acknowledgments

Richard Gould, Bradley Petrisor

Summary

Referencing and references within a manuscript form arguably one of the most important parts of the work, but one that may be overlooked. Without clear and accurate referencing throughout a scientific paper, combined with a methodically presented references section, any paper could appear to be nothing more than assertion or opinion. This chapter addresses issues of choosing references, referencing style, and technique. After reading the information presented below, any author should feel comfortable in preparing their references prior to submission for publication.

Introduction

Taken at the simplest level, appropriate referencing acknowledges the work of others. It is essential to reference any quotation, thought, or idea that another person has described at an earlier time. It is also important to give credit to others who have worked in the same field, and whose work is linked to the current paper. A definition of plagiarism can be found in the Jargon Simplified box below. Plagiarizing another's work is highly frowned upon in the scientific community and even the suggestion of it can result in irreparable damage to one's career. Accurate referencing protects the author from such accusations.

> **Jargon Simplified: Plagiarism**
> **Plagiarism**—"The replication of ideas, data or text without permission or acknowledgement" of the originator.[1] "The act or an instance of plagiarizing." (*The Concise Oxford Dictionary*, 8th edition)
> **Plagiarize**—"Take and use (the thoughts, writings, inventions, etc. of another person) as one's own." (*The Concise Oxford Dictionary*, 8th edition)

From a different viewpoint, references act as the foundation of a scientific article. A scientific article is written to communicate research results to those in the scientific community. In general, a story is written around the research question. The important components of this story are to first explore the research done previously that has led to the research question, and then to explain how the results obtained in the paper relate to the results found in other published literature.

References are woven into the paper to explain to the reader why the research question was asked in the first place and, subsequently, what the present results add to the greater knowledge of the scientific community. The references can be used to explain a gap in current understanding or an unexplained phenomenon that led to the commissioning of the study. When the results of the paper are discussed, referencing to other publications can help build a body of evidence that support the findings of the study, or even to cast doubt on results that have been obtained previously. A well-compiled and concise reference list will also show depth of understanding of the subject matter, and will be viewed favorably when the paper is to be reviewed by journal editors.[2]

Finally, a comprehensive reference section provides enthusiastic readers with plenty of opportunities to explore the subject further, which will increase their own knowledge. This is, after all, the purpose of scientific research.

How to Reference

The referencing process can be broken into two major components. First, the references must be selected. This section of the process requires a thorough search of published materials to find the best available resources. Inappropriate selection of references may lead to the inclusion of sources that are of poor quality, have recently been discredited, or have known author bias. Without the investment of time in the selection process, one or more key articles may be missed, which could affect the conclusions of the paper and possibly reduce the validity of the study.

Once all the resources are gathered, they must be presented in a methodical and logical manner. This will enable the reader to follow the author's explanations. It will also allow those who wish to do so to verify information presented. If the paper reaches a conclusion that is thought to be controversial, it is highly likely that a detailed check into the sources stated will be undertaken if the conclusions are to be accepted in the wider community.

The following sections will look at each of these components separately, and highlight important points, and pitfalls, not to be overlooked.

Reference Selection

In general, references should be selected so that any reader will be able to find them quickly and easily. The most common sources for references are peer-reviewed journals, which fulfill this requirement. Peer-reviewed journals can be accessed easily through online tools (such as the PubMed search engine), and most allow the full-text article to be retrieved electronically. Electronic retrieval normally requires a subscription fee to the journal in question, though most institutions will have access to a large collection of electronic journals through their library. Peer-reviewed articles are more likely to be of a high standard and to have less bias, and may add substantial weight to an argument. The arguments for the use of peer-reviewed journal articles are strong, and these articles should be treated as the preferred source when available. The strength of peer-reviewed papers is so clear that it could be argued that they should be the only source of reference.[3] Indeed, most peer-reviewed papers themselves will only use other papers of the same standard in their reference list.

When the information cannot be obtained from a journal paper, alternative sources must be found. Other types of references include book chapter citations, narrative summary reviews, meeting abstracts as well as Internet citations. These references have inherent problems that must be appreciated before they are included as a resource.

Book chapters and narrative reviews often reflect author opinion and experience and are mostly not peer-reviewed, which leaves them heavily open to author bias. A book chapter is also not likely to reflect the most recent advances or changes reported in the literature, because of the inherent delay in the publication process. Book chapters are useful for explaining concepts that are clearly known or understood. References to them are most commonly seen at the beginning of a paper in the introduction and explanation of a study. This information may not be available in recent journals, but is widely agreed upon among the scientific community in question. When selecting a book from which to reference, choose one that is highly respected in its field and focused on the specific area being discussed.

Meeting abstracts are also sometimes cited. It may be considered that these references provide potentially the most up-to-date information available if the meeting is very recent and if they represent works in progress or preliminary studies.[4] If the meeting abstract is older, every effort should be made to locate the subsequent peer-reviewed publication. This may prove difficult, however, as many studies that appear in abstract form at meetings never make it to full publication (see Chapter 2).[4–6] A meeting abstract that is several years old has less value as a reference. If the abstract discusses the current progress of a study, or preliminary results, then care should be taken not to extrapolate this information further than is stated

in the source. Meeting abstracts are often not indexed by journal search engines, and may not be available publicly. This can make them difficult for a reader to locate, which is contrary to the general principle of providing a reference.

Internet references are, of course, a relatively new method of providing sources. The primary shortcoming of an Internet reference stems from the dynamic and ever-changing appearance of the Internet itself. Even a relatively short delay between submission and publication of a paper may be long enough for an Internet reference to move from the web page address given. In a worse-case scenario, it could disappear all together. Indeed, one study suggested that between 15% and 18% of Internet references were not accessible as given, and further searching was needed to locate them.[7] An Internet reference is therefore considered as the least reliable source for information, although it can be used to comment on social beliefs or opinions on a subject, or to report on current affairs. If an Internet reference must be used because no other alternative source exists, then efforts should be made to locate a "perma-link" for the article, that is, a web address that will remain constant. This feature will generally only be found on the much larger web sites, such as news reporting agencies (CNN, BBC, etc.) and government-run web sites.

The discussion above clearly supports the use of peer-reviewed journal articles. Although there are still additional considerations before the article should be included as a reference, peer-reviewed journals are the "gold standard" for citation material.

It may seem too obvious to even state, but it is essential that the article should be read and understood by the author prior to its inclusion in a paper. It may be surprising how often this is not the case. Work by Simkin and Roychowdhury suggests that as few as 20% of authors actually read the article from which the citation is based.[8] This practice has been dubbed by some as a form of "low-key misconduct," which could potentially harm the author.[9] Perhaps more importantly, not reading the article has the potential to "propagate misconceptions" about the true findings of a study.[9] Authors themselves should also be aware so as not to fall victim to someone else's misconception. Whenever possible, all efforts should be made to locate the original study that produced the data—rather than citing an article that lists the study as a reference—to ensure that the conclusions of the original authors are clear.

Another potential problem that exists with referencing is the concept of "self-citation." Self-citation refers to an author using his or her own previously published papers heavily in the reference list. While it may be important, or even necessary, to cite oneself, especially if there are few other investigators writing on a particular topic, some have suggested that repeated self-citation may falsely validate one group's thoughts and conclusions and may "artificially inflate an article's importance," perhaps deliberately to gain personal advantage.[10] This concept is also closely related to journal self-citation in which citations from one particular journal are cited above others. Again, potential problems with this practice are be that it creates an inflated "impact factor" of a particular journal.[10] The impact factor of a journal is used as the measure to assess the importance of a given journal[11] and is calculated as a ratio of citations over one year and publications from two years. This impact factor can therefore be altered if a high number of citations from one journal are recorded

Given the ideas outlined above, the arguments for using peer-reviewed articles are clear. A peer-reviewed article with an unbiased view that provides clear background and rational for conducting the study is the superior source for information.

Key Concepts: References

- Articles taken from peer-reviewed journals provide the best reference material. These should be selected as references whenever possible.
- Books will not be up-to-date on recent developments and may have author bias.
- Internet sources are not constant, and may change, move, or disappear. They should not be used unless it is unavoidable.

Technical Aspects

Once the references have been collected, the focus moves to incorporating the references in the written work. The reference should be cited as soon as is reasonably possible after the material or quotation has been used. Most commonly, this will be at the end of the sentence in question. If the sentence is long and complex, and draws information from many sources, it is acceptable to place the citation part-way through the sentence. This makes it clear to the reader which source provided the information quoted.

Citations are usually formatted in one of two ways: citing the authors name with the year of publication (author–date system, referred to as the Harvard system[12]), or by citing numbered references by number; the "Vancouver system"[13] is the most formalized numbered reference system, as will be discussed below, and is widely adopted. Both citation formats have their own strengths and weaknesses.

Harvard ("Name–Date") System

The Harvard system cites the author's name and year of publication within the text. The reference section then lists all the references alphabetically by first-author name. The strength of the Harvard system is its flexibility. When writing a paper, the order of whole sections of text can be changed without a thought of changes required to the reference section. A drawback of the format is that it greatly expands the size of the finished article. When many sources need to be cited regularly, the addition of the authors' names and

years of publication can reduce readability. If the paper will contain many statistics and numbers, then the presence of additional dates may make the paper unattractive to read.[12]

Reality Check: Harvard Style

Harvard-Style Citation
Patellar resurfacing during knee arthroplasty was shown to reduce anterior knee pain (Waters and Bentley, 2003).

Harvard-Style Reference
Waters TS, Bentley G. (2003) Patellar resurfacing in total knee arthroplasty. A prospective, randomized study. *J Bone Joint Surg Am* 85-A(2):212–217.

Vancouver ("Numbered") System

The Vancouver system was developed from a consensus meeting held in 1978 by a group which became the International Committee of Medical Journal Editors (ICMJE); it has subsequently been adopted by the US National Library of Medicine, and so is becoming increasingly common in scientific literature.[13] The associated web page gives advice on how to reference different types of material, including legal documents and audiovisual material. It is a valuable resource when writing a paper (see Suggested Reading). The formal Vancouver system proper is strictly defined in terms of the order and format of the various elements of the reference in the reference list. The detailed punctuation between the elements is also precisely prescribed; as well as being unambiguous visually, this facilitates "automatic" parsing of the elements of a reference by referencing software of the type discussed below. It is common for "Vancouver" to refer to any numbered referencing system, but one should be aware whether the formal Vancouver style is meant or some variant of numbered referencing. Apart from the stylistic differences, the advantages and difficulties associated with the practical use of any numbered system with sequential citation are common to all such systems.

The Vancouver system uses a numerical citation in the text to refer to the reference. The reference list is numbered in order of text citation. Some feel that the Vancouver system allows the text to flow more easily as the citation is less obtrusive (particularly if the citation is superscripted) and potentially makes it easier to look up the citation in the reference list.[14] The primary practical disadvantage of the Vancouver system for the author is that should a new reference be added to the text, all other references must be renumbered to ensure that the numbering is consistent with the order of citation. A complex scientific manuscript may undergo many major revisions of the text that would greatly change the order in which the references were cited. Large papers often use numerous references, which can make maintaining the accuracy of the citations very difficult. The difficulty in handling complex referencing has been obviated, however, with development of powerful computer-based referencing software, which has the ability to automatically maintain the numbering system as changes are made. Referencing software is discussed later in this chapter.

The US National Library of Medicine also produces an annual list of the accepted abbreviations for scientific journal titles. Abbreviating titles is common practice in the Vancouver format, but accepted abbreviations (as returned by PubMed or used in Index Medicus) should be used to ensure compatibility.

> **Reality Check: Vancouver Style**
>
> **Vancouver Style Citation**
> Patellar resurfacing during knee arthroplasty was shown to reduce anterior knee pain.[1]
>
> **Vancouver Style Reference:**
> 1. Waters TS, Bentley G. Patellar resurfacing in total knee arthroplasty. A prospective, randomized study. *J Bone Joint Surg Am* 2003 Feb;85-A(2):212–217.

Both of the reference formats listed above would be acceptable for a scientific article. The choice between the two is partly based on the author's preference, but an important consideration before the selection of the citation format is chosen is the style of referencing preferred by the journal to which the paper is to be submitted. Most journals will provide guidelines for authors that stipulate the format of the citations, and further guidance can be obtained by reading papers already published by the journal. It is incumbent on the author to conform to the particular style pertaining to the journal while at the same time providing accurate referencing. This may seem straightforward, but it has been noted by multiple groups that accurate referencing may in fact be a common problem. Studies of referencing suggest that errors are frequent and can occur in as many as 20–56% of references cited.[15-17] Many of these occur in the authorship details, and while some may be considered typographical in nature, such errors makes it potentially very difficult to find the citations; and as already mentioned, may propagate errors throughout the scientific literature.

> **Key Concepts: Accuracy of References**
> * It is imperative that references are provided timely in the text in conjunction with the thought or quotation they are representing.
> * References should be provided accurately, consistently, and in the appropriate journal style, both within the text and in the reference list.

Further Technical Considerations

Both the Harvard and numbered formats can have subtle variations that are preferred by different journals. It is important that these differences are appreciated and incorporated in your manuscript.

In the Harvard system, one common source of confusion is how to cope with papers that have many authors. The recommendation for citation is to list just the first author (who is the primary author for the paper) and then use "et al." to substitute for the other authors names when there are three or more authors.[12] This keeps the citation to a manageable size. It is also quite common for authors to have published more than one paper on a similar topic in the same year, which could lead to two identical name–date citations referring to different articles. In these cases, the citation should include a letter as a suffix: for example, (Jones, 2001a). The letter should indicate the chronological order of publication. The first publication of an author is "a," the second "b," and so on. Clearly, no suffix is required if it is the only one of the author's publications cited for that year.

The precise ordering of the references in the list, within the overall requirement to alphabetical by the first author's name, may differ between journals. Some will be strictly alphabetized letter by letter; others will group single-author, then two-author references, and list those with three or more ("et al." in the text) chronologically; some list references chronologically within the alphabetization by first-author's name. Unless the journal's instructions for authors specify this in detail, it is not likely to be important in the submission or acceptance process and is a detail that will be dealt with by journal editorial staff during preparation of the paper for publication. Some journals use a numbered system of citation but order the reference list alphabetically, so that the citations in the text do not occur sequentially.

For the Vancouver system, or any numbered system, a computer program is recommended to maintain the order of the citations. If no program is used, then it is best to wait until the paper is finalized before completing the references. It may be helpful to temporarily name the references as you cite them during preparation of the paper and only convert the citations into the number format as a final step. The simple use of a word-processing program's "end note" facility can make it much easier to cope with automatic renumbering of references and citations as additions or deletions are made.

The box below shows examples in Vancouver format for other commonly referenced materials.

Referencing a Book
1. Brinker MR, editor. Review of Orthopedic Trauma. Philadelphia: Saunders; 2001.

Referencing a Web Page
2. Pledge to cut orthopaedic wait. British Broadcasting Corporation. Available from: http://news.bbc.co.uk/1/ hi/wales/3895223.stm. Accessed July 15, 2004.

Referencing Software

Referencing software provides an easy tool for obtaining, organizing, and incorporating references into a research publication. Such packages are very useful when a large number of references is expected; for example, it is not uncommon for papers to cite well over fifty references. They are also very useful when multiple authors are writing a paper as they allow for the sharing of resource references via databases. Through the use of these programs, authors have the ability to search Internet databases such as PubMed for journal articles and incorporate them into a reference database. Other reference types such as book chapters or nonindexed sources can also be entered manually and saved. The effect is to compile a large database containing all the references that will be used in the article. The database stores the required information from each source so that it is able to generate an accurate citation in the reference list.

Some software can be incorporated into word processing programs so that the reference database can be accessed and references cited into the article as it is being written. The software will also keep track of the order of citations and automatically correct for changes. Many programs also allow the author to choose a bibliography type according to a specific journal. This allows a pre-formatted reference list to be produced that is consistent with the style required by the journal to which the paper will be submitted. These programs can greatly reduce the time that is spent on the detailed technical aspects of both entering and editing citations, plus the time-consuming process of formatting the reference list to conform to the journal guidelines. All journals will have different requirements about small details related to the style of the reference. These differences may include changes to punctuation or typeface for different parts of the reference, and would be time-consuming to implement manually if the reference list is very long.

Not everyone, however, feels that the use of automated referencing programs is useful, with the suggestion that they lack the requisite detail needed for some journals, and also that they can unnecessarily duplicate references.[14] It is important to proof-read any changes that the referencing software has made, and in some cases to refine a reference listing if it seems clumsy. The primary purpose of these programs is to manage the references, and finer points of style or grammar will be beyond their capabilities. In spite of these limitations, automated referencing software can implement immediate bibliographic changes during revisions and provides a convenient way to collate the resources located when preparing a paper. These programs also allow easy re-formatting of the references to comply with different journal requirements, which is very useful if the paper is being submitted to a second journal for whatever reason.

Key Concepts: Referencing Software
- Referencing software can be an important tool to aid the preparation of a paper, but be aware of the limitations of the particular program being used.
- Always proof-read any computer-generated changes to your work.

Acknowledgments

There are potentially many people who may help in the preparation of a manuscript in preparation for publication. The ICMJE has stipulated that any contributors to a manuscript not meeting the criteria for authorship should be listed and included in an acknowledgments section.[13] Chapters 6 and 7 consider the issues of authorship more fully.

Key Concepts: Criteria for Authorship
"Authorship credit should be based on: (1) substantial contributions to conception and design, or acquisition of data, or analysis and interpretation of data; (2) drafting the article or revising it critically for important intellectual content; and (3) final approval of the version to be published. Authors should meet conditions 1, 2, and 3."
(International Committee of Medical Journal Editors web site [http://www.icmje.org])

Common examples of people who are acknowledged include those who prepared the manuscript, such as typists and proof-readers, those who provided technical support to the study, such as statisticians or computer engineers, and those who provided resources or materials free of charge.

There is no fixed format for acknowledgments, though you should confirm this with the journal to which you plan to submit. Common acknowledgments include phrases such as "The authors would like to thank …" or "We wish to acknowledge the role of …," or similar phrases that express gratitude for the contribution that was rendered.

Conclusion

References are a vital component to a scientific manuscript. They help the authors "tell the story" by helping us to understand the rationale for the study as well as how the results fit in to the greater body of literature. Accordingly, accurate referencing of peer-reviewed journals in the style outlined by the journal of interest is vital to the success of any scientific article

Suggested Reading

International Committee of Medical Journal Editors Uniform Requirements for Manuscripts Submitted to Biomedical Journals: Sample References. Available at: http://www.nlm.nih.gov/bsd/uniform_requirements.html. Accessed April 24, 2009

United States National Library of Medicine. List of Serials Indexed for Online Users. Available at: http://www.nlm.nih.gov/tsd/serials/terms_cond.html. Accessed April 24, 2009

References

1. Fenton JE, Jones AS. Integrity in medical research and publication. Clin Otolaryngol Allied Sci 2002;27(6):436–439
2. Glick M. You are what you cite: the role of references in scientific publishing. J Am Dent Assoc 2007 Jan;138(1):12, 14
3. Foote M. Why references: giving credit and growing the field. Chest 2007;132(1):344–346
4. Bhandari M, Devereaux PJ, Guyatt GH, et al. An observational study of orthopaedic abstracts and subsequent full-text publications. J Bone Joint Surg Am 2002;84-A(4):615–621
5. Callaham ML, Wears RL, Weber EJ, Barton C, Young G. Positive-outcome bias and other limitations in the outcome of research abstracts submitted to a scientific meeting. JAMA 1998;280(3):254–257
6. Weber EJ, Callaham ML, Wears RL, Barton C, Young G. Unpublished research from a medical specialty meeting: why investigators fail to publish. JAMA 1998;280(3):257–259
7. Falagas ME, Karveli EA, Tritsaroli VI. The risk of using the Internet as reference resource: a comparative study. Int J Med Inform 2008;77(4):280–286
8. Simkin MV, Roychowdhury VP. Read before you cite! Complex Systems. 2003;14(3):269–274
9. Ball P. Paper trail reveals references go unread by citing authors. Nature 2002;420(6916):594
10. Gami AS, Montori VM, Wilczynski NL, Haynes RB. Author self-citation in the diabetes literature. CMAJ 2004;170(13):1925–1927, discussion 1929–1930
11. Callaham M, Wears RL, Weber E. Journal prestige, publication bias, and other characteristics associated with citation of published studies in peer-reviewed journals. JAMA 2002;287(21):2847–2850
12. Harvard Style. Style Manual for Authors, Editors and Printers. 6th ed. Sydney: John Wiley & Sons; 2002
13. International Committee of Medical Journal Editors. Uniform Requirements for Manuscripts Submitted to Biomedical Journals: Writing and Editing for Biomedical Publication. Available at: http://www.icmje.org. Accessed August 10, 2009
14. Foote SB, Wholey D, Halpern R. Rules for medical markets: the impact of medicare contractors on coverage policies. Health Serv Res 2006;41(3 Pt 1):721–742
15. Gosling CM, Cameron M, Gibbons PF. Referencing and quotation accuracy in four manual therapy journals. Man Ther 2004;9(1):36–40
16. Putterman C, Lossos IS. Author, verify your references! Or, the accuracy of references in Israeli medical journals. Isr J Med Sci 1991;27(2):109–112
17. Buchan JC, Norris J, Kuper H. Accuracy of referencing in the ophthalmic literature. Am J Ophthalmol 2005;140(6):1146–1148

16
Author Instructions

George Mathew, Sheila Sprague

Summary

Most peer-reviewed journals require a quality paper to be clear, concise, and accurately written, and to adhere meticulously to the journal's stated editorial policy, to be deemed worthy of publishing. Each journal may have specific requirements for authors to follow in order for it to consider their research for publishing. Such instructions are assessable at the journal's Web site and it is crucial that these directions are followed. This chapter will review the common instructions and recommendations for authors who intend to submit articles for publication to quality orthopaedic journals such as the *Journal of Bone and Joint Surgery*, *Clinical Orthopaedics and Related Research*, *Journal of Orthopaedic Trauma*, and *Orthopaedic Clinics of North America*. The principles presented in this chapter are relevant to all scientific journals.

Beginning Steps

Unlike in the past when papers had to be submitted through mail, most journals now use online systems for manuscript submissions. If you are a first-time user of the journal's Web site, you will be required to register so that manuscripts can be submitted electronically.

Jargon Simplified: Editorial Manager
Editorial Manager is an online manuscript submission and peer-review Web site. Many orthopaedic journals including the *Journal of Bone and Joint Surgery*, *Journal of Orthopaedic Trauma*, and *Clinical Orthopaedics and Related Research* use the Editorial Manager to receive and track manuscript submissions from authors.[1]

After registering and logging in with the user ID and password that you are allocated via e-mail, you should click the link for submitting a new manuscript and follow the instructions at the top of each page. Take note of the technical requirements that each journal system may have and ensure that your submission complies with them.

Key Concepts: Editorial Manager Requirements
- Manuscript must be in document format, not PDF format.
- There should be no figures in the manuscript text; figures should be separate from the text file.
- Figures should not be formatted using a word processor (such Microsoft Word) but with a recognized image file format (acceptable file formats will be indicated).
- For other recommended specifications, visit http://www.editorialmanager.com/homepage/faq11.html

Each journal will have different requirements for manuscript submissions. The following will discuss the commonly seen specifications in quality orthopaedic journals.

Manuscript

Title Page

The title page is often a primary requirement for a professional paper. Journals will require the title of the manuscript and the authors' names in the order in which they should appear along with their mailing address, telephone number, fax number, and e-mail address to be on the title page. Some journals may limit the number of characters that may be used in a title. For example, *Clinical Orthopaedics and Related Research* limits the title to no more than 80 characters including spaces. The title page will be unblinded (i.e., the authors' names will appear) and some may require sources of support (e.g., pharmaceutical, industry) to be included.[2] Ensure that the spelling, order, and affiliation of each author are correct as the author will be responsible for any misspelled names published.

Key Concepts: Title Page
Common elements to be included:
- Title of manuscript (with or without character limit)
- All authors' names in the appropriate order and spelled correctly, along with their affiliation, mailing address, telephone number, fax number, and e-mail address
- Sources of support

Some journals will require the rest of manuscript to be blinded. That is, your manuscript must not contain the authors' names or initials or the institution associated with the study.[2] Others may give you the option for an open or blinded review. Page headers may contain the manuscript title but not the authors' names. This blinding policy is usually very strict; if not followed, the manuscript will most likely be returned to the corresponding author. Your manuscript should also have an abbreviated running title, which is likely to be limited in the number of characters. Other components of the manuscript may be subject to strict guidelines that authors must follow. Refer to Chapter 17 for more details on cover pages and title pages.

Cover Letter and Acknowledgment

A cover letter may or may not be mandatory depending on the journal you choose. The contents of a cover letter should state that all coauthors have approved and reviewed the manuscript and that the work has not been published or submitted elsewhere. Authors may also have to declare any potential conflicts of interests (e.g., commercial). Acknowledgments, if included, should be listed on the unblinded title page and not in the text of the manuscript.

Abstract

An abstract will almost always have a word limit of around 200 to 300 words. The abstract should give a summary of the paper as a whole, and often journals will indicate specific headings that they want in an abstract. Refer to Chapters 9 and 20 for additional details on preparing a good abstract.

> **Reality Check: Abstract Requirements**
>
> ### The Journal of Bone and Joint Surgery[3]
> - 325 words or under
> - Headings: Background, Methods, Results, Conclusions, Level of Evidence or Clinical Relevance
>
> ### Journal of Orthopaedic Trauma[2]
> - 250 words or under
> - Headings: Objectives, Design, Setting, Patients/Participants, Intervention, Main Outcome Measurements, Results and Conclusions
>
> ### Clinical Orthopaedics and Related Research[4]
> - 200 words or under
> - No heading requirements, but should state the study's main conclusions and clinical relevance
>
> ### The Orthopedic Clinics of North America[5]
> - No specific abstract requirements

Body

As with the abstract, journals may also require the body of the manuscript to be organized into main headings.

> **Reality Check: Body Requirements**
>
> ### The Journal of Bone and Joint Surgery[3]
> - Headings: Introduction, Materials and Methods, Statistical Methods, Results, Discussion
>
> ### Journal of Orthopaedic Trauma[2]
> - Headings: Introduction, Patients and Methods (Materials and Methods for basic science articles), Results, Discussion
>
> ### Clinical Orthopaedics and Related Research[4]
> - Headings: Introduction, Materials and Methods, Results, Discussion, Acknowledgments, References, Tables, Legends
>
> ### The Orthopedic Clinics of North America[5]
> - Consistent headings

As well as for the headings, there are other formatting specifications that different journals may have. Font type and size, margin size, double-spacing, and indentation of paragraphs are examples of formatting details to obey if you want your work published in any specific journal.

Illustrations

Journals often have very specific guidelines regarding illustrations and figures. Virtually all journals will require your illustrations and figures to be attached as separate files when you are submitting your paper electronically. When submitting to a journal, you need to be aware of its requirements for file format (i.e. TIFF, JPEG), sizing, and resolution, the font to be used in the artwork, and figure legends, as most journals have very specific requirements for these components. Also, different journals may accept images in various forms, while some are more restrictive (e.g., only electronic files accepted). Some journals may require figure captions to be in a certain font and size of type, and typed on a separate page. Again, the most important thing is to go to the journal's Web site and read its requirements carefully. If any material is reproduced from published material, be sure to obtain permission from the original publisher

> **Reality Check: Illustration Requirements**
>
> ### The Journal of Bone and Joint Surgery[3]
> - Limit of 10 images, must be in TIFF (tagged image file format) or EPS (encapsulated postscript file) format.
> - Images from a digital camera must have a minimum resolution of 300 ppi (pixels per inch); line-art drawings must have minimum resolution of 1200 ppi; size of 5 in. × 7 in. preferred.

Journal of Orthopaedic Trauma[2]

- TIFF, EPS, or PPT (Power Point) file. JPEG or GIFF files cannot be used.
- Resolution of at least 1200 dpi (dots per inch) for line art; at least 300 dpi for electronic photographs, radiographs, CT scans, and other scanned images.
- Fonts must be 8 point and sized consistently throughout artwork (recommended font: Helvetica).
- Figure legends should be less than 150 characters (or ca. 50 words).

Clinical Orthopaedics and Related Research[4]

- GIF and JPG format accepted, no greater than 144 dpi.
- Only black-and-white images, 4-color images, or a combination.
- Legends should be typed double-spaced on a separate page from text.

The Orthopedic Clinics of North America[5]

- TIF format, at least 3 in. × 5 in. size (preferably 5 in. × 7 in.).
- Halftone images must have resolution of at least 300 dpi; line art must be at least 1200 dpi; combination art must be at least 600 dpi.
- Hardcopy of each file must be included.

References

References should be placed at the end of the manuscript in the proper format. Authors are responsible for the accuracy of the references. Different journals may have different requirements for references, so be sure to familiarize yourself with them. Some style considerations commonly seen include: proper style for type of resource, listing of references in the order in which they appear in text or alphabetically, and use of abbreviations for journal titles. Most journals use the *American Medical Association Manual of Style* (AMA) for referencing style. There is reference managing software that could simplify your task, such as Reference Manager, EndNote and ProCite (see also Chapter 15).

> **Reality Check: Reference Managing Software**
> - Reference Manager: http://www.refman.com/
> - EndNote: http://www.endnote.com/
> - ProCite: http://www.procite.com/

Copyright Transfer and Author Agreement

A copyright transfer and author agreement allocates the copyright to the material that will appear in the journal. The journal should have some variation of copyright transfer and author agreement form that needs to be signed by all authors upon submission of the manuscript.

Financial Disclosure and Potential Conflict of Interest Statement

Authors will be required to disclose their financial support for their research and any potential conflict of interest. This can appear in the acknowledgment section at the end of the article before the references when published. The statement should have no bearing on whether your article is published, and is mainly to inform the readers.

> **Key Concepts: Following Instructions for Authors**
> The most important message to take away from this chapter is that it is absolutely pivotal that authors do their research on the manuscript requirements for any journal in which they wish their paper to be published. Instructions for authors are available at the Web sites of each journal, and the responsibility is on the author to comply with all set guidelines. Failure to follow the instructions can result in the return of your manuscript without review until it is in the correct format.

After Acceptance

After your manuscript has been formally accepted, some journals will send the corresponding author electronic page proofs—typeset material (usually as a PDF file) that looks just like the final journal pages and can be checked and corrected electronically or printed out and corrected manually if you are required to return hard copy of the proofs. The authors are responsible for ensuring that the proofs are accurate and error-free. The allowable changes are mainly typographical, and only the most critical changes to the accuracy of the content will be made. Also, the publisher has the right to refuse any changes that do not affect the accuracy of the content.

Conclusion

While the quality of your study is the most important thing, following the appropriate procedures is essential in getting it published. The Instructions for Authors are absolutely critical and must be followed for successful acceptance of your manuscript. The guidelines are available at the journal's Web site and you are responsible for ensuring that all aspects are complete. If the instructions are not followed, your manuscript will be returned to you without review until it is in the correct format. Thus, be sure to familiarize yourself with the various different guidelines set by different journals.

References

1. Aries Systems Corporation. Online Manuscript Submission and Peer Review. Available at: http://www.editorialmanager.com/homepage/home.htm. Accessed: December 16, 2009

2. Journal of Orthopaedic Trauma. Online Submission and Review System. Available at: http://edmgr.ovid.com/jot/accounts/ifauth.htm. Accessed: December 16, 2009

3. The Journal of Bone and Joint Surgery. Instructions to Authors. Available at: http://www2.ejbjs.org/misc/instrux.dtl. Accessed: December 16, 2009

4. Clinical Orthopaedics and Related Research. Author Resources. Available at: http://edmgr.ovid.com/corr/accounts/ifauth.htm Accessed: December 16, 2009

5. Orthopedic Clinics of North America. Guidelines for Manuscript Text Available at: http://www.orthopedic.theclinics.com/authorinfo. Accessed: December 16, 2009.

17

Formatting Your Paper: Title Page and More

Scott Wingerter

Summary

Other chapters have explained the process involved in the organization of your paper and include explanations of the issues necessary for the proper writing of a scientific manuscript. The purpose of this chapter is to describe how to correctly format a manuscript that is being submitted to a peer-reviewed journal. Here we briefly discuss the common sections and the general format of a research paper, focusing on the formatting rules and the specifics of the title page and cover letter that accompany your final submission.

Background Information

In the beginning stages of manuscript preparation, it is best to keep your original manuscript format simple and to not worry about specific requirements. There are common sections discussed later in this chapter that apply to most journals and will provide you with a general framework to use for any scientific manuscript. With today's simple-to-use word processing software, formatting changes can easily be made to a completed manuscript to make it comply with a journal's requirements.

Once you have chosen a journal to submit to, obtain the Instructions for Authors from that specific journal (see Chapter 16). The instructions are typically available on the journal's Web site and are also often included within the printed issues of the journal. The simplest approach to finding instructions online is to run an internet search for "Instructions for Authors" along with the name of the journal of interest. Large publishing groups provide complete lists of all of their journals with links to the corresponding Instructions for Authors.

> **Reality Check: Instructions for Authors**
> Groups such as Taylor & Francis (http://www.tandf.co.uk/journals/ifa.asp) and Elsevier (http://www.elsevier.com/wps/find /authorshome.authors) provide complete lists of all of their journals with links to the corresponding Instructions for Authors.

The important point to remember is to follow all instructions carefully, because some journals are looking for reasons not to publish your manuscript. Failure to follow simple formatting and submission instructions just gives them an easy reason to throw your paper out so as not to waste the reviewers' time. Always be sure to read these instructions several times and revisit them thoroughly prior to the final submission of the manuscript. You will be surprised at the number of items that are easily overlooked during the first reading. You may even want to ask a colleague to double-check that you have interpreted and followed the instructions accurately.

> **Key Concepts: Journal Guidelines**
> Follow all instructions set out by journals carefully and review the guidelines several times before the final submission of the manuscript so that your work is not rejected on the basis of lack of adherence to formatting guidelines.

General Format

Once you have selected the journal to which you are going to submit your paper, there are two issues to consider regarding the format of your finalized research paper:
1. The format of the manuscript itself.
2. The format of separate documents required for final submission.

First, we will discuss the format for the actual body of the paper. The format of a manuscript will vary depending on the type of research or paper being submitted. The most common types of published papers are original research and review articles. The format for a review article will depend on the topic, but its organization is typically based on different aspects of the area of research and the paper is not divided into specific sections with stipulated headings. A meta-analysis is a specific type of review article that includes quantitative analysis and will, therefore, require a more detailed description of the methods involved than a systematic review[1]. Another type of commonly published research is a surgical technique paper. An article on a new surgical technique is intended to teach the reader how to perform the procedure as well as to provide evidence for its efficacy. Accordingly, the format for a technique paper will typically include step-by-step directions for the procedure as well as a discussion of the technique's advantages and clinical results.

Jargon Simplified: Systematic Review and Meta-Analysis
Systematic review—"A critical assessment and evaluation of research (not simply a summary) that attempts to address a focused clinical question using methods designed to reduce the likelihood of bias."[2]
Meta-analysis—"An overview that incorporates a quantitative strategy for combining the results of several studies into a single pooled or summary estimate."[2]

For original research projects, whether basic science or clinical, a general format includes the following four major sections: Introduction, Materials and Methods (or possibly just Methods), Results, and Discussion. The Introduction provides background information about what is already known involving the subject and should include a succinct statement regarding the purpose of the present study (see Chapter 10). The Materials and Methods section is simply a description of the experimental design and should include a description of the statistical analysis used in the study (Chapter 11). The Results section provides nothing more than a summary of the experimental results (Chapter 12 and Chapter 13). You should not include any *interpretation* of the results within this section. The Discussion section provides the opportunity to interpret the results as well as identify the strengths and limitations of the study (Chapter 14).[3] A separate Conclusion(s) section with a concise summary of the results and implications can be included and may be required by some journals. More specific practical details regarding each of the commonly used sections have been discussed in the chapters indicated.

Other sections that will need to be considered for any paper format are an abstract (Chapter 9) and acknowledgments (Chapter 15). The abstract is discussed in more detail later in this chapter as well as in Chapter 9. The Acknowledgments section is not always required, but it provides you with the opportunity to recognize funding sources as well as colleagues who contributed to the research but did not meet the requirements for authorship. Some journals will have specific requirements regarding the disclosure of funding, but this section will typically be at the discretion of the author.

Finally, all papers will end with a References section (Chapter 15) that includes all of the literature cited within the manuscript; this section may also be labeled Literature Cited. Apart from the major division of referencing styles into the name–date or numbered systems, the precise formatting of references will vary greatly from journal to journal, so the proper style must be identified and correctly implemented. Software programs such as EndNote (Thomson, Stamford, CT) include an extensive list of commonly used citation styles and will format the references within your paper automatically. The most common format uses numbers (superscript or in brackets) at the end of the sentence related to the source of information. These numbers can be sequential within the paper and identified in the references in the order in which each source appeared in the

text. Alternatively, the list of references can be alphabetized and the corresponding number for each source in the alphabetized list is then used within the text.

Key Concepts: Sections to Be Included in Papers and in Submissions

Sections Included in Most Papers	Sections Included in Most Submissions
Title/Cover page	Cover letter
Abstract	Abstract
Keywords	Manuscript
Introduction	Figures
Materials and methods	Electronic version
Results	Financial disclosure
Discussion	Conflicts of interest statement
Conclusion	Transfer of copyright agreement
References	

The format of the separate documents required for final submission will vary between journals and between individual documents. Some of the commonly required sections or separate documents that you will need to consider are: title/cover page, abstract, possibly a mini-abstract, keywords, manuscript, key points, figures, and cover letter. Additional documents that must be completed and signed prior to publication are a transfer of copyright agreement and a financial disclosure or conflicts of interest statement. Each of these documents will have different requirements and formats, so specific information on what each includes is discussed below. The most important thing always to remember is to include all required sections in the exact format and in the order requested by the particular journal's instructions for authors.

Key Concepts: Required Documents
Whatever the individual journal's requirements are, it is essential to include **all** the necessary documents in the exact **format** and **order** stipulated.

Many journals now use online submissions that identify a list of all documents that are required for upload. Two of the common online submission systems are Editorial Manager and Rapid Review. Within the field of orthopaedic surgery, the *Journal of Bone and Joint Surgery* (*JBJS*), *Clinical Orthopaedics and Related Research* (*CORR*), the *Journal of Orthopaedic Trauma* (*JOT*), and *Spine* use Editorial Manager. A list of journals published by Lippincott Williams & Wilkins that use Editorial Manager can be found at http://www.lwwonline.com/pt/re/lwwonline/journalsEM.htm. The *Journal of the American Academy of Orthopaedic Surgeons* (*JAAOS*) uses Rapid Review.

If you are submitting your manuscript by mail, the same documents needed for online submission are typically requested. One major aspect that will be identified in the instructions for authors is the number of printed copies that you are required to submit. This number will vary between journals according to the number of reviewers that your paper will be sent to. In addition to the previously discussed sections, the journal will also often require you to include an electronic version of the paper and supporting documents on CD-ROM. The electronic versions can typically be saved as Word documents in a variety of file formats from other word-processing and text-handling programs. Consult the journal's Web site to determine which file formats are acceptable to that particular journal for text and also for images.

> **Key Concepts: Submitting Manuscripts by Mail**
> Submitting manuscript by mail will typically require the same documents needed for online submissions, except perhaps for the additional need for multiple printed copies depending on the number of reviewers that your paper will be sent to, and documents on a CD-ROM.

Abstract

Specific aspects of writing the abstract have been discussed in detail in Chapter 9, but some key points of formatting deserve mention here. The abstract is typically requested as a document separate from the manuscript. The requirements will vary greatly between journals, but the two most common requirements that you must identify and adhere to are the total number of words allowed and any requirements regarding subheadings/structure of the abstract. Some journals (e.g., *Spine*) may also require a mini-abstract that will be included in the journal's table of contents. The mini-abstract provides the reader with a very brief summary of your work (no more than 50 words). Finally, some journals, including *JBJS* and *CORR*, now require the identification of a level-of-evidence rating for your research within the abstract. The journal's instructions will provide you with a classification scheme to help you determine the level of your primary research question.

> **Jargon Simplified: Abstract, Structured Abstract, and Level of Evidence**
> **Abstract**—A summary of the entire manuscript provided at the beginning of the paper.
> **Structured abstract**—An abstract that is subdivided into prespecified sections.
> **Level of evidence**—A rating system for classifying the quality of a study.[4]

> **Key Concepts: Abstract Requirements**
> The two most common stipulations for abstracts are the total number of words allowed and the subheadings or structure of the abstract.

Keywords

The keywords are terms that you choose as representative of the main topics discussed in your paper. These words are used by many search engines to identify your work as a paper of interest for someone searching in this field. The title of your paper will often include some of the specific terms that will help other researchers find your article, but keywords give you the opportunity to categorize your work and include some more general terms as well. For example, in a research study involving patients undergoing total knee arthroplasty you might want to include keywords such as "osteoarthritis," "clinical trial," and "surgery," to help identify the patient base and general aspects of the research and treatment involved. In this case, the general term "total joint replacement" could be included instead of "total knee arthroplasty." You do not want your keywords to simply repeat the words of the title; you want to add to the spectrum of terms that will allow searchers to identify your article. Many journals will limit the number of words or terms you are allowed to provide, but regardless of the number, remember to choose them wisely.

When you are finalizing your paper, the keywords are sometimes included in the same file as the abstract, but some journals require the submission of a separate file. As with every other aspect of submission, be sure to read the instructions carefully and place the keywords in the appropriate location.

> **Key Concepts: Keywords**
> Keywords are used by others in the field to identify your research paper as an item of interest. Your keywords should not simply repeat the words of the title; they should include a range of terms that will help searchers to identify your article. Different journals will have different limitations on the number of keywords you can provide and where they are located: be sure these guidelines are followed.

> **Reality Check: Example Keywords**
> • **Title:** Randomized controlled trial of pain relief following total knee arthroplasty

- **Good keywords:** osteoarthritis, total joint replacement, knee replacement, clinical trial, surgery, analgesics
- **Bad keywords:** randomized controlled trial, pain relief, total knee arthroplasty

Manuscript

The manuscript refers to the primary text or body of the article. When submitting, the manuscript file may or may not include the figures depending on the chosen journal. If the journal requests the figures as separate files, you can include a note within the text indicating where you would prefer the figures to appear, but the final placement will be at the discretion of the editors. In addition to identifying the preferred location of the figures, many journals will request the inclusion of figure legends either within the text or at the end of the manuscript document. The final formatting of the section headings, such as Introduction or Discussion, will also typically be handled by the journal editors. However, familiarity with the journal will allow you to present your paper in a format that is consistent with the intentions of the final publication.

Complying with the journal's style requirements is important for all sections, but many of the requirements are most relevant to the manuscript portion of the paper. Some key factors that must be considered are line spacing, page numbering, font selection, and margins. The most common line spacing is double because the increased space between lines allows for easier reading and editing by the reviewers. The *New England Journal of Medicine* even requests triple spacing to further aid their reviewers. If spacing is not mentioned specifically in the instructions, consider double-spacing at least the manuscript portion of your paper for these reasons. Another requirement that improves the overall review process is the inclusion of page and line numbers. Numbering the lines and pages allows the reviewers to make comments specific to individual lines of text. A final requirement related directly to the review process is blinding of the paper. This means that you do not include author names or institutions anywhere in the manuscript file, in an attempt to reduce possible bias in the review process. If a blinded manuscript is not required, you should consider including some identifying information within the header. Some journals will have specific requirements, including the first author's last name and/or a short running title.

> **Jargon Simplified: Blinded Manuscript (Blinded Review)**
> Authors' names and affiliations are not included on the manuscripts so the reviewers are "blind" to the people or locations associated with the submission.

> **Key Concept: Manuscript Format**
> Things to consider when submitting your manuscript include the placement of figures and legends, line spacing, page numbers, font selection, and margins.

Key Points

A separate Key Points section is a specific requirement of *Spine* and may be found in other journals. Key points are three to five short statements that summarize what the authors believe to be most important about the paper and the research findings. These points are included in a box in bulleted format at the end of the article. The specific formatting involved with the final appearance of the key points is handled by the journal editors, but submitting a document with the statements in the format found in the final publication (e.g., in a bulleted list for *Spine*) will help your submission appear as though it belongs in the journal.

Figures

For most submissions, you will be required to submit your figures as separate files. These need to be of high-quality images with the highest possible resolution. You will also usually be given specific requirements for acceptable file types (e.g., ppt or tiff). If acceptable, a Microsoft PowerPoint file with each figure on a separate slide is often the easiest method for editing and organizing your images and text, especially if you are including multiple images within one figure. As mentioned previously, the figure legends will typically be covered in the manuscript portion of your submission. However, you can also include the legends in your figure files if you can maintain high resolution. When you are mailing a submission in, you may be required to submit high-quality glossy images instead of, or in addition to, high-quality image files on a CD-ROM.

Financial Disclosure / Conflicts of Interest Statement

You will always be required to identify in some manner sources of financial support of the research and any possible conflicts of interest related to the study. The journal will either provide you with a form to complete or require financial disclosure on the title page or within the cover letter. Bias related to conflicts of interest is currently a major focus of concern within the scientific community and the general population, so you will be required to make any relevant relationships known. The formatting of this information is extremely varied between journals as the information itself is more important than its format.

Jargon Simplified: Conflict of Interest
Any outside affiliation or activity, often financial, that may limit a researcher's ability to impartially evaluate his or her results poses a conflict of interest.

Transfer of Copyright Agreement

Another form that will be required prior to final publication is a Transfer of Copyright Agreement. Some journals will request this signature form with the initial submission, while others will allow you to wait until after your paper has been accepted. This form does not require any sort of formatting and is nothing more than an additional requirement of manuscript submission that must be remembered. The key point to identify regarding this agreement is whether or not the journal you are submitting to requires it with your initial submission; *JBJS*, *JOT*, and *Spine* all require it at initial submission, while *CORR* only requires it prior to publication.

Reality Check: Requirements for Major Orthopaedic Surgery Journals

Journal of Bone and Joint Surgery (*JBJS*)

Required:	Optional:
Title page	Cover letter
Blinded manuscript	Acknowledgment
IRB approval	Figures and/or tables
Copyright transfer and author agreement	
Potential conflict of interest statement	

Journal of the American Academy of Orthopaedic Surgeons (*JAAOS*)

Pre-submission requirements:	Full submission:
Authors' names and affiliations	Title page
Abstract	Abstract
Detailed outline	Body of the text, including bibliography, summary, references, figure legends, tables

Clinical Orthopaedics and Related Research (*CORR*)

Cover letter (template provided)
Title page
Abstract
Text (with separate pages for Introduction, Materials and Methods, Results, and Discussion and the first author's name, and with page number in the upper right corner of each page)
Acknowledgments
References
Tables
Legends

Journal of Orthopaedic Trauma (*JOT*)

Required:	Optional:
Unblinded title page	Cover letter
Blinded manuscript (with structured abstract)	Acknowledgment
Copyright transfer	Figures and/or tables

Spine

Title page
Structured abstract, key words, and key points
Mini-abstract/précis
Text (with running head)
References
Tables and figures
Copyright transfer form

Title Page

This page can be referred to as either the cover page or the title page. The term title page more accurately represents its purpose, while the term cover page has been accepted as it is commonly the first page of the manuscript. Considering that most submissions will also include a cover letter, we will use the term title page to help differentiate the two more clearly.

The title page format is straightforward and fairly consistent, but requirements do vary. The only item that will be mandatory on all title pages is the full manuscript title. Almost all title pages will also be required to include all authors' names and affiliations. Some journals, including *JAAOS*, include the title page when your paper is sent for blinded review, so only the title of the manuscript is to be included. In addition to authors' names and affiliations, an unblinded title page will need to include identification of a corresponding author along with this author's mailing address, telephone number, fax number, and e-mail address. The corresponding author will typically be the first author or the senior author, but the person selected should be one who can be contacted easily and consistently so that vital information regarding your submission is not missed.

Jargon Simplified: Corresponding Author
One selected author who will receive additional information and questions following submission and/or publication.

Inclusion of the manuscript title and authors' information will satisfy the requirements for the title page of most journals. Some other specific considerations for certain journals are a short running title and financial disclosure information. A running title is a shortened version of your title that will be included in the header region of the final publication. If a journal requests a running title, there will be a limit on the number of words or total characters allowed. For example, *CORR* sets a limit of 80 spaces (letters and blanks) for your full title and 40 spaces for your running title. As discussed previously, all journals will require financial disclosure within your submission, but some journals will also specifically require that this disclosure be part of the title page.

The most important formatting issue to remember for your title page is spelling. You are fully responsible for the accuracy of the spelling of each author's name and affiliation information. Furthermore, you must verify prior to submission that you have included all authors' names in the desired order.

> **Key Concepts: Title Page Checklist**
> - Full title
> - Short title (if requested)
> - Authors' names and highest degrees
> - Authors' affiliations
> - Corresponding author contact information
> - Financial disclosure (if requested)

Cover Letter

A cover letter is exactly what it sounds like—a letter that acts as the cover sheet for your manuscript submission. While not all journals require a cover letter, it is highly recommended for many reasons. The letter is typically addressed to the editor of the journal and provides an opportunity to make a good first impression of professionalism. This letter also allows you to provide more direct contact information and clearly identify that all requirements regarding submission have been met. Some journals will have specific requirements regarding the content of your cover letter. *CORR*, for example, has detailed requirements for a cover letter and provides a manuscript template available online. The journal's instructions specifically state that "manuscripts will not be published and may be returned without review unless this cover letter is included."[5]

Two of the most important considerations of your cover letter are whom to address and your own contact information. You must do everything you can to find a specific person to address your cover letter to and identify them specifically in the salutation of the letter. Your letter must then also include contact information for the journal to contact you with further questions.

After a specific contact has been identified and your information is included, the rest of the cover letter may vary and will remain fairly simple. The body of your letter will typically include the title of your paper, the name of the journal being submitted to, and identification of what is enclosed (as requested in the guidelines of the Instructions to Authors). You may consider using formatting such as

bold text for your manuscript title to help clarify the specifics of your work. Do not, however, use text formatting excessively in the letter. Underlining and italics should be avoided. The purpose is to identify a key point and not overwhelm the reader. A final element of the body of your letter should be a statement thanking the journal editors for consideration of your paper.

There are also some general format and appearance issues to consider. A proper letter format should include the date of the letter and a contact address at the top of the letter. The body of the letter should be written in a block paragraph format (i.e., no first-line indents) with an extra line space between paragraphs, and you should always double-check your spelling and grammar. If submitting by mail, always print your letter on department letterhead and high-quality paper. Finally, a good cover letter for your initial submission should not exceed one page. The purpose of the letter is to introduce your work and the letter should be kept concise.

> **Key Concepts: Cover Letter Checklist**
> - Letterhead/high-quality paper
> - Addressed to a specific person
> - Correct spelling and proper grammar
> - Block paragraph format
> - Double spacing between paragraphs
> - Corresponding author contact information
> - Thank the editors for their consideration.

Reality Check: How, and How Not, to Write a Cover Letter

Example of a Good Cover Letter
Your letterhead
Date
Contact name
Contact address
Dear _(Contact name)_:
We would like to submit the attached original scientific research entitled "**(title)**" for review for publication in a future issue of (journal name) . This manuscript is not under review elsewhere, and all authors have reviewed and approved the submitted version.
Following the guidelines of the Instructions to Authors for (journal name) , an original manuscript, [include here a list of all other required enclosures, such as title page, extra copies of the manuscript, an electronic version, glossy figures, etc.] are enclosed. If you need any additional copies or have any questions, please contact me at (email address/phone number) .
Thank you for your time and consideration of our manuscript for publication. We look forward to hearing from you soon.
Sincerely,
Your name
Your title

Example of a Bad Cover Letter

Date

Journal name

Contact address

To Whom It May Concern:

We would like to submit the attached research for publication in a future issue of your journal. We feel that it is high-quality work and deserves inclusion in your journal.

We have included one copy of the text for your review. If you have any questions, please contact me.

Please let us know when our paper will be published.

Sincerely,

Your name

Conclusion

The most important points to remember regarding the format of your manuscript submission are to obtain the instructions from your targeted journal and to follow all of those instructions carefully. It is critical to submit your manuscript with well-organized supporting documents and to not undervalue the importance of spelling and grammar within these forms and letters. Your cover letter and title page will be among the initial items seen by a journal's reviewers, so be sure to make a strong first impression.

Suggested Reading

AMA Manual of Style. A Guide for Authors and Editors. 10th ed. New York: Oxford University Press; 2007

Brand RA. Writing for Clinical Orthopaedics and Related Research. Clin Orthop Relat Res 2003; (413):1–7

Elsevier's Guide to Publication. Available at: http://www.elsevier.com/wps/find/authorsreview.authors/howtosubmitpaper. Accessed April 24, 2009

Perneger TV, Hudelson PM. Writing a research article: advice to beginners. Int J Qual Health Care 2004;16(3):191–192

Wright TM, Buckwalter JA, Hayes WC. Writing for the Journal of Orthopaedic Research. J Orthop Res 1999;17(4):459–466

References

1. Bhandari M, Devereaux PJ, Montori V, Cinà C, Tandan V, Guyatt GH; Evidence-Based Surgery Working Group. Users' guide to the surgical literature: how to use a systematic literature review and meta-analysis. Can J Surg 2004; 47(1): 60–67

2. Guyatt GH, Rennie D, eds. User's Guides to the Medical Literature: A Manual for Evidence-based Clinical Practice. Chicago, IL: AMA Press; 2001

3. Zeiger M. Essentials of Writing Biomedical Research Papers. New York: McGraw-Hill; 1991

4. Wright JG, Swiontkowski MF, Heckman JD. Introducing levels of evidence to the journal. J Bone Joint Surg Am 2003;85-A(1): 1–3

5. Clinical Orthopaedics and Related Research. Author Resources. Available at: http://edmgr.ovid.com/corr/accounts/ifauth.htm. Accessed December 30, 2009

18

Grammar Police: The *Dos* and *Don't*s of Writing

Eric Morrison

Summary

While study quality and results are important in research, the proper communication of the information is of equal significance. Proper grammar and writing conventions are essential in academic writing to effectively communicate study findings to the scientific community. The purpose of this chapter is to provide a review of the main elements of grammar and writing conventions, including punctuation, diction and spelling, and writing strong sentences and paragraphs.

Introduction

We have all likely learned the material at one point in our lives, but over time we may forget the rules of proper writing. While these rules change very little over time, everyday casual usage of language through speech changes rapidly and varies across different geographical regions and cultures. The information in this chapter (based on US usage) has been collected from different sources that are very thorough on the subject matter. We hope you will be able to use this chapter as a condensed reference for writing your research paper.

Punctuation Details

Periods (.)

Periods are the most common form of punctuation at the end of sentences. Use a period to end sentences that are statements or neutral commands.

Periods are also used for abbreviations. Sometimes conventions vary between different styles or countries (e.g., PhD and MD could be written as Ph.D. and M.D.) Apply the following general rules when including abbreviations:

1. Do not use abbreviations in the written text too generously. You do not want your writing to come across as lazy, although it is acceptable to use abbreviations to be concise. Make sure that you write out the words completely, followed by the abbreviation in parentheses, the first time you mention it. You cannot assume that all of your readers know what the abbreviation stands for. You may need to use abbreviations more often in tables or figures where space is restricted.
2. Abbreviations ending in lowercase are generally followed by periods (**Table 18.1**).

> **Key Concepts: When using "e.g." and "i.e."**
> * The abbreviation "e.g." stands for the Latin term *exempli gratia*, which means "for example."
> * The abbreviation "i.e." stands for the Latin term *id est*, which means "that is."
> Use "e.g." to give an *example*:
> People who suffer from osteoporosis must ensure that they consume foods rich in calcium (e.g., milk).
> Use "i.e." to *specify and explain*:
> This operation may result in unfortunate outcomes (i.e., death).

3. Abbreviations in all capital letters, such as acronyms for studies and organizations, do not have periods (**Table 18.2**).
4. Do not add an additional period when an abbreviation with a period ends a sentence.

> **EXAMPLE** The surgery took place at 10:00 a.m.

5. Periods are generally used for place name abbreviations except for mailing codes (**Table 18.3**).[1]
6. Do not use periods with units in the metric system and other scientific symbols (**Table 18.4**).

Table 18.1 Common abbreviations ending in lower case

Mr.	Mrs.	Dr.	Sept.	etc.
p.m. / a.m.	cf.	et al.	i.e.	e.g.

The use of periods with simple abbreviations [truncations] ending in lower case is universal; in British-based usage, periods are not used with *contractions*—short forms in which the final letter of the full word is the final letter of the abbreviated form (e.g., Dr).

Table 18.2 Examples of common abbreviations that are in all capital letters

NCAA	NATO*	FBI	USA	UN
IHFRC	TV	MLA	CBC	RCMP

* When an abbreviation formed form initial letters makes a pronounceable word it is termed an acronym and with use often comes to be written as a normal word (Nato, laser, radar).

Table 18.3 Period use in name abbreviations (top line) and mailing codes (bottom line)

B.C.	P.E.I.	Nfld.	N.Y.	Mass.
BC	PE	NF	NY	MA

Table 18.4 Common metric system units and other scientific symbols

km	cm	kg	ml	kJ	C	Hz	Au	Zr

Periods are never used as part of the abbreviations of SI units, though they commonly are with "customary" units (in., lb., etc.).

Question Marks (?)

Use a question mark to end sentences that are direct questions.

INCORRECT	CORRECT
Does the patient have an inter-trochanteric hip fracture.	Does the patient have an inter-trochanteric hip fracture?

You can also place a question mark at the end of a statement to turn it into a question. Phrasing a question in this format usually signals doubt.

STATEMENT	QUESTION
The patient has an inter-trochanteric hip fracture.	The patient has an inter-trochanteric hip fracture?

Note that you can also include question marks in the middle of sentences, though not typically in formal writing unless they are found within a quotation in the middle of a sentence.

EXAMPLE	Question 3 on the patient follow-up interview form stated, "How would you rate your pain on a scale from 1 to 10?"; we have now deleted this question.

Do not use a question mark for indirect or reported questions. Instead, use a period.

INCORRECT	CORRECT
The patient wondered how he would feel after surgery?	The patient wondered how he would feel after surgery.
The physician asked how the patient fractured her hip?	The physician asked how the patient fractured her hip.

Exclamation Points (!)

Use exclamation points at the end of strong commands and emphatic statements. However, you should use them sparingly in formal writing.

EXAMPLE	Sample size matters!

Commas (,)

1. Use commas to punctuate a series of three or more items.

EXAMPLE	This study included sites from North America, South America, Europe, Asia, Africa, and Australia.

> **Key Concepts:**
> Note that a comma is included before the coordinating conjunction (i.e., "and") in this example.

2. Use a comma to set off introductory elements.

EXAMPLE	Although the center screened 100 patients with hip fractures, only 40 of them were eligible for the study.

> **Jargon Simplified: Clauses**
> **Clause**—An expression including a subject and predicate, but not necessarily constituting a complete sentence.
> **Independent clause**—A clause that can stand by itself as a sentence.
> **Dependent clause**—A clause that cannot stand by itself as a sentence.

3. Use commas to set off nonessential modifiers (supplementary information added in a sentence that is not essential to the basic meaning of the sentence).

EXAMPLE	Dr. Schmidt, the Principal Investigator, enrolled five patients in the study.

4. Use commas when introducing a quotation.

EXAMPLE	Prof. Ballintyn wrote, "Caring about the patient significantly contributes toward the care of the patient."

5. Use commas with titles and degrees.

EXAMPLE	Dr. D. Leanage, MD Martin Luther King, Jr.

6. Use commas when writing dates.

EXAMPLE	The patient sustained his injury on February 12, 2007.

Do not use commas if the date is inverted (12 February 2007) or only the month and year are written (February 2007).

7. Use commas in addresses.

EXAMPLE	293 Wellington Street North, Hamilton, ON.

Apostrophes (')

Apostrophes can take the place of absent letters in contractions. However, contractions should be used sparingly in academic writing, if used at all.

EXAMPLE	can't (cannot) isn't (is not) it's (it is)

Use apostrophes to signal possession for nouns.

EXAMPLE	The patient's leg is broken.

Key Concepts: Correct Use of the Apostrophe
- For nouns that do not already end in an *s*, add *'s* at the end of the word. (e.g., Dr. Smith's patient)
- For nouns that do end in an *s*, simply add an apostrophe after the *s*. (e.g., Dr. Williams' patient)
- Be careful when spelling these homonyms (words that sound the same, but have different meanings):

It's = It is	Its = a possessive pronoun
You're = You are	Your = a possessive pronoun

Semicolons (;)

The semicolon is uncommonly used, often because its purpose is poorly understood. As a general rule, semicolons should have complete sentences on both sides. You can use semicolons to join two complete sentences that are closely related.

EXAMPLE	Patients receiving treatment A were pleased with the results of their procedures; patients receiving treatment B often required revision surgeries.

Note that using a comma instead of a semicolon in this case would result in a *comma splice*. You must either use a semicolon or place a period and start a new sentence.

Jargon Simplified: Comma Splice
Incorrectly linking two complete sentences together by using a comma.

You can also use a semicolon between items in a series if one or more items contain internal punctuation. The results section of a research study is a good place to use semicolons.

EXAMPLE	The risk ratios for secondary outcome measures were: implant failure, 0.30 (95% CI, 0.16 to 0.58; $P < 0.001$); malunion, 1.06 (95% CI, 0.32 to 3.57); pulmonary embolus, 1.10 (95% CI, 0.26 to 4.76); compartment syndrome, 0.45 (95% CI, 0.13 to 1.56); and infection, 0.98 (95% CI, 0.21 to 4.76).[2]

Colons (:)

A colon must have a complete sentence in front of it, but both sentences and nonsentences may follow it. Only if a complete sentence follows a colon should you capitalize the first letter after the colon.

Use a colon to introduce a list.

EXAMPLE	Three main variables were important in assessing quality of life for patients in the study: pain level, mobility, and ability to perform daily activities.

You can also use a colon to introduce further elaboration or explanation.

EXAMPLE	Dr. Smith is the most experienced orthopaedic surgeon in the study: He has performed over two thousand procedures of this type.

You may use a colon to introduce a quotation.

EXAMPLE	Dr. Johnson described his experience working as a physician in developing countries: "In all the locations where I have worked, the clinics are fully staffed by competent medical professionals. However, these facilities are in great need of supplies and medications."

Dashes (—)

Dashes can be used to set off modifiers, parenthetical material, or to indicate changes in thoughts and feelings. In general, dashes create an informal tone and should not occur frequently in academic writing. Instead of using dashes, simply use commas, colons, or parentheses.

Parentheses ( )

Use parentheses around supplementary or explanatory information.

EXAMPLE	Over 200 experienced orthopaedic surgeons took part in the study (each surgeon had completed more than 50 Gamma nail procedures in his/her career).

Key Concepts: Rule for Using Parentheses
A complete sentence in parentheses within another sentence does not begin with a capital letter or end with a period

Parentheses are often used in the Results section of scientific articles.

EXAMPLE	Of 204 included articles, the mean number of citations per year was 2.04 (95% confidence interval 1.6 to 2.4; range 0–20.9).[3]

You can also use parentheses to clearly mark items in a series.

EXAMPLE	Five patient interview forms were included in the packet: (1) patient follow-up week one, (2) patient follow-up week two, (3) patient follow-up one month, (4) patient follow up three months, and (5) patient follow-up six months.

Key Concepts
Avoid unnecessary parentheses to prevent your sentences from becoming overly complicated and difficult to interpret. Furthermore, some readers tend to skim over comments in parentheses.

Brackets [ ]

Use brackets inside quotations to include additional material that is necessary for the reader to understand the quotation.

EXAMPLE	"We estimate that this number [of hip fractures] will increase to more than 300,000 this year."

Writing Strong Sentences

Critical Components of Sentences

A sentence basically consists of two parts: the subject and the predicate. The subject of the sentence is what acts or is described. The predicate tells something about the subject.

Sentences can be classified into two categories: *major sentences* and *minor sentences*. Major sentences must at least contain a subject and a verb. Minor sentences are usually exclamations, short questions of one or two words, or common idiomatic expressions that are not typically suitable for academic writing.

EXAMPLE	*The patient* <u>broke her femur.</u>
	Subject + <u>predicate</u>

Problems with Sentences

Subject–Verb Agreement

Subjects and their corresponding verbs must agree both in number and in person. Usually this skill comes naturally to most writers. However, be careful when words intervene between the subject and verb.

INCORRECT	CORRECT
Each of the patients have a fractured tibia.	Each of the patients has a fractured tibia.

Note: The subject is *each*, and it corresponds with the verb *has*.

Irregular Verb Conjugations

Irregular verbs pose difficulties in any language, and English is no exception. Misuse of the tenses of irregular verbs gives the impression of illiteracy and some care needs to be devoted to getting them right.

Table 18.5 lists some common irregular verbs and the forms of their various tenses. Although many of these examples may seem straightforward, poor speech habits can sometimes obscure the difference between slang and formal English.

Double Negatives

In some languages, such as Spanish and French, it is appropriate to use double negatives; the English language does not use double negatives. For example, the Spanish phrase, "No hice nada" directly translates to "I didn't do nothing." French would also use a double negative in this case: "Je n'ai fait rien." However, the intended meaning is "I did

Table 18.5 Common irregular verbs

Present tense	Past tense	Past participle	Present tense	Past tense	Past participle
Awake	awoke, awakened	awakened	lose	lost	lost
Be	was, were	been	pay	paid	paid
Beat	beat	beaten	ride	rode	ridden
Begin	began	begun	ring	rang	rung
Bend	bent	bent	rise	rose	risen
Bite	bit	bitten, bit	run	ran	run
Blow	blew	blown	say	said	said
Break	broke	broken	see	saw	seen
Bring	brought	brought	set (to place)	set	set
Build	built	built	shake	shook	shaken
Burst	burst	burst	shrink	shrank	shrunk
Buy	bought	bought	sing	sang	sung
Catch	caught	caught	sink	sank	sunk
Choose	chose	chosen	sit (to be seated)	sat	sat
Come	came	come	slide	slid	slid
Cost	cost	cost	speak	spoke	spoken
Do	did	done	know	knew	known
Draw	drew	drawn	lay (to place something)	laid	laid
Drink	drank	drunk	lead	led	led
Drive	drove	driven	leave	left	left
Eat	ate	eaten	lend	lent	lent
Fall	fell	fallen	lend	lent	lent
Find	found	found	lie (to recline, to rest on a surface)	lay	lain
Flee	fled	fled	spend	spent	spent
Fly	flew	flown	spring	sprang	sprung
Forget	forgot	forgotten	stand	stood	stood
Freeze	froze	frozen	steal	stole	stolen
Get	got	gotten	strike	struck	struck
Give	gave	given	swim	swam	swum
Go	went	gone	take	took	taken
Grow	grew	grown	teach	taught	taught
Hang (to suspend)	hung	hung	tear	tore	torn
Hang (to execute)	hanged	hanged	tell	told	told
Hear	heard	heard	throw	threw	thrown
Hide	hid	hidden	wear	wore	worn
Hold	held	held	weave	wove	woven
Keep	kept	kept	write	wrote	written

nothing" or "I didn't do anything." When writing in English, make sure that you only include one form of negation in each sentence. Including more than one form of negation confuses the reader about whether your intended meaning is positive or negative.

INCORRECT	CORRECT
The patient cannot hardly wait to start exercising again.	The patient can hardly wait to start exercising again. **or** The patient cannot wait to start exercising again.
This was something that none of these surgeons had never seen before.	This was something that none of these surgeons had ever seen before.

Comma Splice

A comma splice occurs when two separate independent clauses are mistakenly joined together with a comma.

EXAMPLE (incorrect)	Hip fractures have an associated mortality rate of 30%, they have devastating consequences for patients and their families.

To fix this sentence, do one of the following:
1. Replace the comma with a colon or semicolon.

EXAMPLE	Hip fractures have an associated mortality rate of 30%; they have devastating consequences for patients and their families.

2. Replace the comma with a period and start a new sentence.

EXAMPLE	Hip fractures have an associated mortality rate of 30%. They have devastating consequences for patients and their families.

3. Add an appropriate coordinating conjunction (i.e., "and") to remedy the comma splice.

EXAMPLE	Hip fractures have an associated mortality rate of 30%, and they have devastating consequences for patients and their families.

Sentence Fragment

Most simply stated, a sentence fragment is an incomplete sentence. Although it may begin with a capital letter and end with a period, it lacks a critical component. The most common sentence fragments lack a verb. Often sentence fragments can be corrected by joining two clauses together.

INCORRECT	CORRECT
Each year, almost 300,000 North Americans suffer hip fractures. A very serious medical condition.	Each year, almost 300,000 North Americans suffer hip fractures, which are treated as very serious medical conditions.

Run-On Sentence

A run-on sentence exists when two independent clauses are joined together without appropriate punctuation. It is also appropriately referred to as a "fused sentence," because the independent clauses are fused together instead of having a conjunction to link them together. You can fix a run-on sentence by separating the sentence into two sentences or by adding a conjunction with appropriate punctuation.

INCORRECT	CORRECT
Randomized trials of alternative forms of internal fixation for managing patients with femoral neck fractures also remain inconclusive, although a previous meta-analysis comparing various internal fixation methods in hip fractures reported "nonsignificant" differences in alternative approaches, our meta-analysis suggests that a single large compression screw and sideplate performed 5-fold better in reducing revision rates when compared with the current standard of multiple cannulated screws.	Randomized trials of alternative forms of internal fixation for managing patients with femoral neck fractures also remain inconclusive. Although a previous meta-analysis comparing various internal fixation methods in hip fractures reported "nonsignificant" differences in alternative approaches, our meta-analysis suggests that a single large compression screw and sideplate performed 5-fold better in reducing revision rates when compared with the current standard of multiple cannulated screws.[4]

INCORRECT	CORRECT
Dr. Mahoney explained to the patient that a hip fracture is a serious medical emergency on Monday.	On Monday, Dr. Mahoney explained to the patient that a hip fracture is a serious medical emergency.

In the incorrect example it appears that hip fractures are particularly serious on Mondays!

Vague Reference

Avoid phrasing sentences in a vague manner, as the reader could interpret your message differently than you had intended.

EXAMPLE	The doctor took the patient and his things into the operating room.

You must be able to answer this question easily: Whose things? The doctor's things or the patient's things?

graphs do not stand out to the reader as much as those at the beginning and the end.

- Mention important points in shorter sentences. The message can be lost among a great deal of information in a long sentence.

Appropriate Sentence Length

Sentences typically range between 15 and 25 words in length. It is perfectly acceptable to include sentences shorter than or longer than this amount, as it adds variety to the text. However, consistently writing sentences that are too short or too long can be detrimental to creating a piece of good writing. Generally, shorter sentences can be found in more informal writing (e-mails, popular writing, narratives, etc.), while longer sentences tend to be found in formal and specialized writing (e.g., research papers). However, writers of research papers sometimes cram more points into a sentence than they should, destroying the unity of the sentence in the process.

Key Concepts: Appropriate Sentence Length
- If a sentence is too long, the main ideas may not stand out from all the supporting details. Try to break long sentences down into multiple smaller sentences, or edit the sentence to make it more concise.
- If sentences are consistently too short, then the links between your main ideas may not be clear. Try combining a group of consistently short sentences with coordinating conjunctions, and build up your sentences using appropriate elaboration.
- Try varying sentence length and structure to eliminate monotonous writing.

Keep in mind that the end of the sentence is the most emphatic position because it leaves the reader with your most important point. Another way of rephrasing that last sentence would be: Leave your reader with your most important point by remembering that the most emphatic position is the end of the sentence. It just depends on what you wish to emphasize most: in this case either "leaves the reader with your most important point" or "the most emphatic position is the end of the sentence." There is no right or wrong version, but it is best to write the sentence in a way that prepares the reader for the subsequent sentence. The second most emphatic position in a sentence is the beginning position. The middle of the sentence is the least emphatic position. Keep in mind that this principle applies to the layout of paragraphs as well.

Key Concepts
- The end of the sentence is the most emphatic position. The beginning of the sentence is the next most emphatic position.
- Place an important sentence at the end or the beginning of a paragraph. Sentences in the middle of para-

Underlining and Italics

Italics may be occasionally used to emphasize important components of text. Authors should be careful not to overuse italics in their writing.

EXAMPLE	In several countries, the title of *professor* is commonly preferred instead of the title of *doctor* by physicians who have both MD and PhD degrees.

You can also emphasize certain sentences or particular parts of a sentence through repetition and punctuation.

Pronouns

Pronouns are generic terms that can substitute for a noun. **Table 18.6** gives common types of pronouns and provides examples

When referring to organizations, do not use plural pronouns.

INCORRECT	CORRECT
The hospital takes good care of their patients.	The hospital takes good care of its patients.

Use the relative pronouns *who* and *whom* to refer to people. Use the relative pronoun *that* to refer to other things.

The pronoun "their" should not be used in cases where the singular can be used (e.g., he/she or his/her). However, it is occasionally used in "gender neutral" statements and to keep writing concise. EXAMPLE: An orthopaedic surgeon who uses their training to teach others is always welcome at our hospital.

Table 18.6 Common types and examples of pronouns

Personal pronouns	I, you, he, she, it, we, they
Possessive pronouns	my, your, her, his, its, our, their
Objective pronouns	me, you, him, her, it, us, them, whom
Indefinite pronouns	everybody, some, one, several, each
Relative pronouns	who, whoever, which, that
Interrogative pronouns—introduce questions	who, which, what
Demonstrative pronouns	this, that, such
Intensive pronouns	a personal pronoun plus -*self* or -*selves* (himself, ourselves): He himself asked that question

INCORRECT	CORRECT
Did patient fracture *their* leg?	Did the patient fracture *his* or *her* leg?

Do not use the word *myself* unless you have already used the word *I* earlier in the sentence.

Sometimes people mistakenly use *I* instead of using *me*, because they had always been taught to do so. Use *I* for the subject of the sentence. Use *me* for the object of the sentence.

INCORRECT	CORRECT
The assistant handed surgical tools to Dr. McDermott and I.	The assistant handed surgical tools to Dr. McDermott and me.

> **Key Concepts: Using *me* or *I***
> Try removing other names from the sentence to see whether what you have written is correct. If you were to write "The assistant handed surgical tools to Dr. McDermott and I," change it and see if it makes sense: "The assistant handed surgical tools to I." Obviously, this doesn't sound correct, and *me* is the correct word to use.

Subordinating Conjunctions

Subordinating conjunctions link subordinate (dependent) clauses to the main independent clause when a coordinating conjunction is not needed. For instance, you would not write the following sentence: Even though the parents were illiterate, but their children may read well. This sentence does not require the coordinating conjunction *but* because it already has the subordinating conjunction *even though*.

EXAMPLES	Subordinating conjunctions: after, although, as, as if, as long as, as though, because, before, even if, even though, if, if only, in order that, now that, once, provided

Coordinating Conjunctions

Coordinating conjunctions can be used to join words or phrases.

EXAMPLES	Coordinating conjunctions: and, but, for, nor, or, so, yet

Parallelism

Similarity or parallelism in grammatical structure must exist for two or more words, phrases, or clauses linked together.

NONPARALLEL	PARALLEL
Of all endurance sports, the patient prefers <u>to run</u> and <u>cycling</u> the most.	Of all endurance sports, the patient prefers <u>running</u> and <u>cycling</u> the most. *or* Of all endurance sports, the patient prefers <u>to run</u> and <u>to cycle</u> the most.

To run and cycling links a verb and a noun. This is referred to as **faulty parallelism**. To correct this problem, place linked words in the same grammatical form.

Limit Linking Verbs

Linking verbs join the subject of the sentence with the predicate, but they do not convey action. Linking verbs indicate states and provide additional information about the subject. The most commonly used linking verb is "to be" and all of its conjugated forms and tenses (i.e., *am, is, are, was, were,* etc.). Other examples of linking verbs include *become, remain, seem, prove, act, get, grow, feel, look, appear, taste, sound,* and *smell.* Overuse of linking verbs, especially forms of the verb "to be," weakens your writing. Instead of using linking verbs like "is," "are," and "were" try substituting more active verbs.

WEAK	STRONGER
Dr. Smith is a hip fracture specialist.	Dr. Smith specifically treats hip fractures.

In cases where removing forms of "to be" disrupts the meaning of your sentence, you do not need to make changes. The grammar police will not arrest you! However, limiting their use wherever possible helps to strengthen your writing.

Active versus Passive Voice

Whenever possible, you should write in the active voice instead of the passive voice. When using the active voice, the agent of the action is the subject of the sentence. The subject is underlined in the following examples.

PASSIVE	ACTIVE
Patients less than 18 years of age were excluded from the study [by us].	We excluded patients less than 18 years of age from the study.
Falling down the stairs was mentioned by the patient as one of her fears.	The patient mentioned falling down the stairs as one of her fears.

When the passive voice is used, the receiver of the action becomes the subject of the sentence. Generally the passive voice is less specific and less direct than the active voice and therefore its use results in wordiness and does not produce fully descriptive writing. However, when writing scientific research articles, you may sometimes need to write in the passive voice to avoid naming yourself or certain individuals.

Writing Strong Paragraphs

Unity

It is important to maintain unity within a paragraph and within the overall piece of writing. The best way to begin writing a paragraph is to write a topic sentence. The topic sentence is the first sentence in the paragraph. It should relate directly to the overall message of your piece of writing. Likewise, the rest of the paragraph should correspond directly with the topic sentence of the paragraph. All the subsequent points, examples, and further explanations should not deviate from the theme of the topic sentence.

Transitional Terms

Transitional terms are useful to direct the reader smoothly through the text. Use the transitional terms listed in **Table 18.7** to help guide your reader easily through your writing .[1]

Quotations and Paraphrasing

Quotations are an exact copy from another source. Paraphrasing involves taking content from another source, but transforming it into new words. You must reference both properly to give credit to the original author. Introduce quotations by using commas or colons.

Table 18.7 Examples of transitional terms

Terms showing addition of one point to another	and, also, another, in addition, further, besides, moreover
Terms showing similarity between ideas	again, equally, in other words, in the same way, likewise, similarly
Terms showing difference between ideas	but, although, conversely, despite, even though, however, yet, though, in contrast, whereas, nevertheless, in spite of, still, otherwise, on the contrary, on the other hand
Terms showing cause and effect or other logical relations	as a result, because, consequently, for, hence, of course, since, then, therefore, thus
Terms introducing examples or details	for example, in particular, namely, specifically, for instance, to illustrate, that is
Terms expressing emphasis	chiefly, especially, more important, indeed, mainly, primarily
Terms showing relations in time and space	after, afterward, at the same time, before, earlier, in the meantime, later, meanwhile, simultaneously, then, while, subsequently, behind, beyond, farther away, here, nearby, in the distance, next, there, to the left

Diction and Spelling

Spelling Errors

Despite the efforts that have gone into creating word-processing programs with built-in spell-check functions, spelling mistakes still sometimes occur. *Always* proofread your writing, and also try to get someone else to proofread for errors.

Furthermore, be aware of some words that are commonly confused because they sound similar. These words are referred to as *homophones* or *homonyms* (**Table 18.8**).

Key Concepts: Common Issues with Spell-Checking Your Work

Sometimes you know the material so well that your mind automatically corrects the mistake while you are reading, which can cause you to miss some spelling mistakes.

Sometimes you might misspell your intended word as another correct word, for example, if you mean to write et al but instead write *at al*. Because *at* is an actual word, the spell-check will not highlight this error.

Sometimes the spell-check will actually change your misspelled word to the word that it assumes you are attempting to spell. Often it replaces the mistake with the correct word, but sometimes it does not.

Table 18.8 Common homonyms/homophones

accept (to receive)	affect (to influence)	all ready (prepared)
except (other than)	effect (result in)	already (by this time)
ascent	aisle	led
(a movement up)	isle	lead
assent (agreement)		
it's	bear	manner
its	bare	manor
birth	board	boarder
berth	bored	border
borne	break	by
born	brake	buy
		bye
capital	complement	council
capitol	compliment	counsel
course	desert [verb]	die
coarse	dessert	dye
discreet	forth	hear
discrete	fourth	here
heard	hole	past
herd	whole	passed
patience	piece	plain
patients	peace	plane
pore	pray	presence
pour	prey	presents
principle	rain	right
principal	rein	rite
	reign	write
road	sight	stationary
rode	site	stationery
rowed	cite	
their	to	whose
they're	too	who's
there	two	

Capitalization

Words belonging to the following categories should begin with a capital letter:

1. Specific persons and things.
2. Specific places and geographical regions.
3. Days of the week, months, holidays.
4. Historical events, documents, periods, movements.
5. Government offices or departments and institutions.
6. Political, social, athletic, and other organizations and associations and their members races, nationalities, and their languages.
7. Religions, their followers, and terms for the sacred.

Wordiness

It is crucial to write your research in a concise manner. Sometimes your writing may be restricted to a certain amount of space, so you must present your ideas as clearly and concisely as possible. Even when space is not an issue, wordiness obscures the message you are attempting to convey through your writing.

The following are some common wordy phrases that you can often omit or make more concise:
The reason why ...
has/are/is made ...
The occurrence of ...

It is frequently possible to reduce such wordy phrases to a single word.[5]

WORDY	CONCISE
at all times	always
at the present time	now, yet
because of the fact that	because
due to the fact that	because
for the purpose of	for
in order to	to
in the event that	if
in the final analysis	finally

Redundancy

Avoid common expressions that are redundant.

circle around	consensus of opinion
continue on	cooperate together
final completion	frank and honest exchange
the future to come	important essentials
puzzling in nature	repeat again
return again	revert back
square/round in shape	surrounding circumstances

Avoiding Gender Bias

Do not unnecessarily refer to gender or favor one gender over another.[5]

INCORRECT	CORRECT
male nurse	nurse
female orthopaedic surgeon	orthopaedic surgeon
businessman	businessperson
chairman	chair, chairperson
manpower	personnel, human resources
craftsman	craftsperson, artesian
layman	layperson
mankind	humankind, humanity, human beings, humans

Choosing Politically Correct Terminology

Avoid using *labels* for people.

INCORRECT	CORRECT
The cancer patient	The patient with cancer, the patient who has cancer
The autistic child	The child with autism, the child who has autism
Wheelchair bound, confined to a wheelchair	Uses a wheelchair

Use proper terminology to specify racial and ethnic identities.

> **Key Concepts: Racial and Ethnic Groups**
> • Grouping several distinct cultures as "Asian" or "Hispanic" could be interpreted offensively if you are making generalizations across a group of distinct cultures that only share similar physical appearances or languages.
> • Preferences for politically correct terms change over time.

Another important example illustrating the change of acceptable language is the terminology used for people with developmental disabilities. The following sequence illustrates the evolution of several terms that people have used over time:

The term idiot (previously used as a scientific term for a person with an IQ < 20) → slow → mentally retarded → mentally handicapped → mentally challenged → *having a developmental disability (current preferred politically correct term).*

> **Key Concepts: Be Politically Correct**
> According to current language preferences, people are said to *have a developmental disability* (note that in common everyday language some people consider labeling individuals as *developmentally disabled* offensive terminology). The term *mental retardation* is now used almost exclusively in scientific context.

Avoiding Jargon and Clichés

Clichés are overused, ready-made phrases. They contribute very little to the sentence and only add wordiness. Below are a few examples of some commonly used clichés that you should avoid using in formal writing.

EXAMPLES	It goes without saying • it stands to reason • last but not least • needless to say • by leaps and bounds • as a matter of fact • as a last resort • all things being equal • in the long run • slowly but surely.

International Spelling Variations

Several differences in spelling exist among English-speaking countries. Note that Canadian spelling shares similar characteristics with American spelling (*-ize* as opposed to the commonly British *–ise*) and with British spelling (*-our* and *-re* as opposed to the American *–or* and *–er*) (see **Table 18.9**). Authors should be aware of these variations and prepare their manuscripts according to the variant of English in which the journal publishes.

Table 18.9 International spelling variation

American	Canadian	British*
Analyze	analyze	analyse
Behavior	behaviour	behaviour
Caliber	calibre	calibre
Canceled, cancelled	cancelled	cancelled
Center	centre	centre
Check (for payment)	cheque	cheque
Color	colour	colour
Criticize	criticize	criticise
Favor	favour	favour
Hemorrhage	haemorrhage	haemorrhage
Kilometer	kilometre	kilometre
Liter	litre	litre
Organize	organize	organise
Paralyze	paralyze	paralyse
practice (verb)	practice	practise
Realize	realize	realise
Tire (for wheel)	tire	tyre
Traveling	travelling	travelling
Vapor	vapour	vapour

* Both -ise and -ize forms are in use in British English and both equally correct if used consistently. The -yze/-yse distinction between American and British usage is absolute.

References

1. Messenger WE, de Bruyn J, Brown J, Montagnes R. The Canadian Writer's Handbook. 4th ed. Toronto: Oxford University Press; 2005
2. Bhandari M, Guyatt GH, Tong D, Adili A, Shaughnessy SG. Reamed versus nonreamed intramedullary nailing of lower extremity long bone fractures: a systematic overview and meta-analysis. J Orthop Trauma 2000;14(1):2–9
3. Bhandari M, Busse J, Devereaux PJ, et al. Factors associated with citation rates in the orthopedic literature. Can J Surg 2007;50(2):119–123
4. International Hip Fracture Research Collaborative. Surgical Management of Hip Fractures—Options and Evidence. Available at http://www.ihfrc.ca/main.php?page=overview&intro=y. Accessed: September 2007
5. Aaron JE, McArther M. The Little, Brown Compact Handbook. First Canadian edition. Don Mills, ON: Addison Wesley Longman; 1997

19

How to Address Reviewer's Comments: *Dos* and *Don'ts*

Rad Zdero, Emil H. Schemitsch

Summary

When your manuscript has been submitted for possible publication to an academic journal, it is an asset to be familiar with the ways in which such journals function during the review process. This chapter provides an outline of the journal "system," with details about the various individuals who compose the organizational system typical of any academic journal. We also discuss tips that should be considered by authors when composing a response letter to reviewers with examples of wrong and right responses. After reading this chapter, the reader will hopefully understand that there is an artistic and creative aspect in knowing how to respond effectively to reviewers so that a research paper has the best chance of actually getting published.

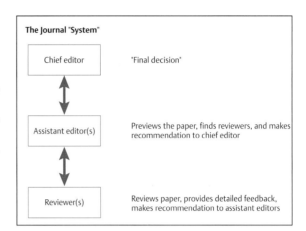

Fig. 19.1 A simplified organizational chart for a typical academic journal, regardless of discipline.

Introduction

One of the most exciting events in research happens when that e-mail or letter arrives from the editor's desk informing you that your manuscript has been accepted for publication in a scientific journal. In that moment, you realize that all your effort has not been in vain. Your scientific and technical discoveries will no longer remain a well-kept secret shared by you and your coauthors alone. Your journal article will soon be helping and influencing fellow surgeons, researchers, and engineers in their own endeavors to enhance surgical techniques, improve orthopaedic devices, and make a deposit at the scientific community's worldwide "bank of knowledge." But, before that happens, there is just one little obstacle to overcome—a band of folks known as "reviewers," who have the power to permit or prevent your article's publication. The aim of this chapter is to give you some practical tools for dealing deftly with reviewer's comments so that you can get that worthwhile article published.

Knowing the Journal "System"

It is always helpful to know a little about the way academic journals function, so that you can better deal with both the practical and emotional aspects of seeing your article—your "baby"—prodded and poked by a faceless "system"

called "the journal." **Figure 19.1** illustrates a simplified organizational chart for a typical academic journal, regardless of discipline.

Chief Editor

At the top is the big boss and the keeper of the gate. This person is more formally known by a variety of titles, such as chief editor, editor-in-chief, or editor, depending on the journal's preference. This individual is usually an internationally recognized expert in the field with an MD or PhD (or academic equivalent) who has years of experience, many academic publications to their name, and familiarity with all the cutting-edge developments in the discipline. The chief editor is not simply an administrative person who happens to have been hired to be the journal's editor. From a scientific standpoint, then, he or she is your peer. This is the main person responsible for finally deciding whether or not your article is fit for publication in the journal.

Assistant Editor(s)

At the chief editor's side there will usually be a small team of assistant or deputy editors to help manage the many hundreds or thousands of article submissions received each year from researchers hoping to see their papers published. They, too, are acknowledged experts in the field with excellent academic credentials and are involved in ongoing research. Because a journal might publish content on several subspecialties in the field (e.g., an orthopaedic journal might publish, say, in the areas of arthroplasty biomechanics, surgical techniques, and biomaterials), it is not uncommon for each of the assistant editors to be exclusively responsible for all articles related to their particular subspecialty. Their main job is often to provide a cursory preliminary reading of your submitted article to make sure there are no major mistakes in formatting (e.g., missing information, wrong bibliographical referencing style) or major problems with content (e.g., the information in your study falls outside the usual scope of the journal) that would make a full review of your article a waste of everyone's time and energy. In such situations, the assistant editor will usually communicate with you within a few days of your original submission, informing you of any major issues that need to be sorted out before they will go ahead and start the review process. If everything is okay, then the next step will be for the assistant editor to find usually two to four reviewers willing to take on your paper.

Reviewer(s)

Eventually, your article will find its way to a group of several reviewers who will give your paper detailed consideration and who will provide specific written feedback to the assistant editor by a certain deadline (usually 2–6 months after initial submission). But who really are these dreaded "reviewers" who strike fear into the hearts of humble researchers everywhere, whose great hope is simply to see their paper published in a reputable journal? And what do they actually do when they "review" your paper?

Reviewers, in reality, are also your peers. They themselves are clinicians, academics, and/or engineers. They manage clinics, teach at universities, and/or direct research groups. They have MDs and PhDs or the equivalent. They have previously submitted (and often published) several papers in the same journal to which you are submitting your article and, therefore, have gained a certain amount of academic credibility. And that is why they have become trusted, voluntary, recruits for that journal. Truth be told, it is often the case that authors submitting an article to a journal have much more experience and expertise in the field than the reviewer assessing their work. But just as often, it is the other way around. Moreover, the researcher should be aware that while some journals hide the names of the authors from the reviewer (i.e., blind review), others do allow the reviewer knowledge about the authors' identities. However, the names of the reviewers are never revealed to authors. That is just part of the process of allowing your work to be evaluated by a group of your scientific peers, whether more or less experienced than yourself. Also, reviewers are virtually never paid for reviewing articles, but do this on a strictly voluntary basis as a way of further contributing to the scientific quest. So, there is no need to be intimidated by reviewers. Just remember: they are you!

Reviewers can be compared with the liver of the journal "system": they filter out all the low-quality research work and make sure the journal rejects it, while allowing the quality research to remain. First, reviewers are usually conscientious. They will read your paper carefully, sometimes several times to make sure they fully understand what your research project is all about, often making notes along the way. Second, reviewers assess articles related to their own subspecialty. They are simply one of several people looking at your article from a variety of angles to give it the broadest assessment possible. They will not necessarily be experts on every aspect of your paper. For example, a paper on the biomechanical stability of a new fracture fixation device for orthopaedic trauma may be evaluated by one or two surgeons looking at its clinical viability and one or two engineers looking at its mechanical and material feasibility. Third, reviewers look for strengths and flaws in your paper, both in format and content. They might ask themselves such questions as: "Is the paper clear, concise, and comprehensive?" "Does it conform to the journal's basic formatting requirements?" "Are the methods and materials used appropriately in addressing the clinical or engineering problem at hand?" "Are the results being interpreted properly and presented clearly?" "Does the study contribute something new to the field?"

Finally, the reviewer is working under a deadline. Reviewers are often given several months to do an initial review on a paper, whereas a 4- to 6-week timeline is not unusual for a revised resubmission. Because of this time constraint, and with their own research, teaching, and/or clinical programs to attend to, sometimes reviewers cannot give your paper all the attention it might deserve. However, the chief editor and assistant editors are often quick to give future assignments to reviewers from their roster who consistently provide quality reviews and equally quick to drop reviewers who consistently do poor jobs.

Key Concepts: Reviewers
Reviewers are your peers!

Key Concepts: Improvement
There is always room for improving your article!

Tips for Responding to Reviewers

Once your article has been reviewed fully, the corresponding author will receive an e-mail or letter from the chief editor or assistant editor informing them of the journal's decision regarding the paper. Few papers are "accepted" outright without any changes required by the journal. If a paper is "rejected" altogether, the journal will often still be courteous and provide you with the reviewers' comments to help you improve the manuscript on your own and hopefully succeed in publishing it elsewhere. However, most papers that eventually get published by the journal are initially categorized as "accepted with revisions" or "reject and resubmit" and will require numerous improvements based on reviewers' comments. In these cases, the authors will be invited by a certain deadline to revise and resubmit their paper. This is to be accompanied by a detailed line-by-line response to the reviewers' comments, indicating exactly how the manuscript has, or has not, been changed. Your response letter to the reviewers will be read both by the assistant editor and also by the original reviewers, to ensure that all their original concerns have been addressed. The following tips should be considered "best practice" guidelines and not rigid rules in how to reply to reviewers.

Start Off Well

It is advisable to start your response letter on a positive note, showing your appreciation to the editors and reviewers for their time and energy spent on assessing your work and indicating any specific things about your response. For example, you may start off with something like, "The authors wish to thank the editor and reviewers for their time and effort in evaluating our manuscript for potential publication. We appreciate the chance to have submitted our work to you. We have attempted to address each of the concerns mentioned point-by-point below and hope that they are adequate in this regard. Please note that our responses below are given in bold text following each of the reviewers' initial comments."

Don't Take It Personally

Reviewers are just doing their job and, usually, have no particular agenda other than improving your manuscript. Their criticisms of your work should not be taken to mean that your efforts have been futile and that you have no future as a researcher. Rather, take their comments as a reminder that there is always room for improving your article. And remember that reviewers are human too. They can make mistakes in judgment, they can misunderstand certain aspects of your paper, they can have biases for and against certain research approaches and conclusions, they might not be able to do as thorough a job as possible of reviewing your paper because of other research obligations, and they have their own specialty which can cause them to have blind spots.

Read the Reviewer's Comments Carefully

Read the reviewer's comments several times. This will help to make sure you really understand the specific items they actually want you to address and it might help you identify the philosophical theme that may be present in most of their comments about your paper. It can even reveal the subspecialty of the reviewer. For example, surgeons will often focus on clinical relevance, while engineers will focus on the physics of the test set-up or surgical instrumentation.

Be Thorough

Some reviewers will write long paragraphs with a multitude of comments about your paper buried deep within. It can help to break down the reviewer's comments into specific subpoints. Respond to each subpoint individually, even going so far as to number your responses (e.g., "Firstly …," "Secondly …," "Thirdly …," etc), which will help you organize your thoughts and appear organized to the reviewer. Also, make sure to respond to every significant comment the reviewer makes, even when they are general or positive remarks that do not require changes to your manuscript (e.g., "We thank the reviewer for their accurate introductory summary of our research paper").

Be Concise

Do not use an elephant gun to kill a mouse. No one likes long-winded responses to rather straightforward remarks. Get to your point quickly. Avoid getting into long philosophical discussions about the meaning of your paper or in your attempts to justify certain aspects. Keep your responses simple and straightforward. Moreover, do not use excessively long quotations either from your own manuscript or from outside sources that you may be citing to support your point.

Be Honest

Honesty is the best policy. Do not invent information or data just to please the reviewer in the hope that you will get your paper published. If certain information that they request is now currently unavailable, then say so. This might include patient demographics that were never provided by a donor institution, experimental data that were never actually collected, or specimens that have been disposed of so that tests cannot be repeated.

Be Diplomatic

A kind word really does go a long way. Always be polite and courteous in all situations. Because reviewers are human and not always entirely objective, it is possible that a polite tone may bias the reviewer in your favor, especially on technical issues that they are undecided about. You may wish to use phrases like "Please consider instead ...," "We agree with the reviewer that ...," and "We thank the reviewers for their ...."

Choose Your Battles Wisely

In some cases, you may have a fundamental disagreement with the reviewer about the meaning of one of your results or the appropriateness of your experimental methodology. Before you respond, count the cost. Ask yourself "Is my pride getting in the way of improving the paper?" "Would making the change the reviewer suggests really alter the message of the paper?" "Is this a fundamental issue or not?"

Different Comments Deserve Different Responses

For simple formatting and wording issues, it is recommended that authors make all changes suggested by the reviewer, even if it seems to alter your communication "style." For technical issues, it is suggested that authors make any and all changes suggested, if possible, unless the required specimens, data, or patients are no longer available to permit this. For philosophical issues, it is recommended that authors make all changes requested by reviewers, that is, unless you have some sort of major disagreement with the reviewer. Then it is advisable to provide an alternative suggestion and write something like "If this is a major issue for the reviewer, we would defer to the editor on this matter."

Divide and Conquer

The corresponding or lead author should not feel pressured to make all the revisions on a paper all by herself or himself, especially if there is a substantial amount of work involved. Many hands make light work, as the saying goes. Include your coauthors in the process, so that everyone can gain some experience in responding to reviewers. It is best to divide the work on the basis of coauthors' specialties (e.g., clinician, statistician, engineer). Each coauthor will bring their expertise and, for certain matters, can answer the reviewer better than other coauthors.

Make It Easy for the Reviewer

The reviewers will be happy if you make the review process easy for them. Therefore, do not make the reviewer hunt around in the manuscript for the exact changes you made. Indicate exactly what changes you made and where the reviewer can find them in the new revised version. Always indicate the page, paragraph, and/or line number of your change, depending on the journal's requirements for response letters. Moreover, whenever possible, it is always better to include the actual quotation from your manuscript (if it is not too long) showing your change, rather than just saying "completed as requested."

Always Change Something

Show the reviewers you take them seriously, by making the changes requested, even small ones. Always assume the reviewer wants something changed in your manuscript, even if they do not say so explicitly. Therefore, whenever possible, always make some sort of change to the manuscript based on the reviewer's comments. This might need to be only minor style or wording changes, showing a formula explicitly, or adding a clarifying sentence.

Get Another Pair of Eyes

When in doubt about the content or the tone of one of your responses, have someone else check it out, particularly one of your coauthors who is familiar with the project. This may include situations when you are unsure of some of the technical issues you are responding to, when you are unsure of communication issues if English is not your first language, or when you are in disagreement with the reviewer about a major aspect of your paper.

Know the Right People

It's all about who you know. Sometimes, for example, journals will ask you to suggest potential reviewers of your paper either because their roster of volunteer reviewers is currently limited or because they trust your judgment as to who the experts are in your subspecialty that can do a good and fair job of reviewing your work. Sometimes, in addition, journals do not have a "blind review" policy, allowing the reviewer to know the names of the paper's authors. If you approach this correctly, both of these things can work in your favor. So, suggest to the assistant editor potential reviewers you know personally in your field, if not stipulated otherwise.

Know When to Switch Journals

Sometimes journals are not always totally clear about whether they want your paper to be revised and resubmitted or not. In such situations, you will need to know how to read between the lines. For example, the assistant editor will always tell you clearly if your paper has been "rejected" outright. It is best not even to contest the decision in this case, but rather move on to another journal. However, if the paper has not been totally "rejected," the assistant editor may hint or advise you whether it is worth your while to make revisions for a resubmission.

Be on Good Terms with the Chief and Assistant Editors

Put your best foot forward. Develop a good rapport with the editors of a journal, particularly one to which you often submit articles. This will give you increased personal credibility which, though not securing you an unfair advantage, can make the review process go more smoothly. For example, make sure to write a polite cover letter identifying them by name, e-mail them directly if you have any questions or concerns, accept the chance to act as a volunteer "reviewer" for the journal whenever possible, or make a point of introducing yourself personally at scientific conferences.

Don't Give Up

If at first you don't succeed, try again. Don't get discouraged if your paper is totally rejected. Everyone has a paper rejected at some time. Pick yourself up, make changes to your paper based on the reviewers' comments, and submit it to a different journal. Sometimes it might take submission to two or three different journals before a paper is finally accepted, especially if it is a truly novel work that may be hard for some reviewers to fully embrace.

Examples of Wrong and Right Responses

Below are three examples of typical reviewer remarks, which cover the main categories of comments often found in article reviews, namely, formatting/wording issues, technical issues, and philosophical issues. They are each followed by a sample of a wrong way and a right way for you to respond to the critique. Using the tips in the Response Letter Checklist (**Fig. 19.2**), can you identify how many of these tips were ignored (in the wrong responses) or heeded (in the right responses) to the following reviewer comments?

Response Letter Checklist

☐ Start off well
☐ Don't take it personally
☐ Read the reviewer's comments carefully
☐ Be thorough
☐ Be concise
☐ Be honest
☐ Be diplomatic
☐ Choose your battles wisely
☐ Different comments deserve different responses
☐ Divide and conquer
☐ Make it easy for the reviewer
☐ Always change something
☐ Get another pair of eyes
☐ Know the right people
☐ Know when to switch journals
☐ Be on good terms with the chief and assistant editors
☐ Don't give up

Fig. 19.2 Your response letter checklist.

Formatting or Wording Issues

The reviewer writes: "In the Conclusion, the statement on page 17, lines 2–3 can be improved by specifying that the reconstructed ligament had lower linear stiffness (not just saying there was a difference)." Your **wrong** response: "The authors do not feel that this suggestion by the reviewer is important at all and wonder why the comment was even made. So we have not made any changes." Your **right** response: "The authors have adjusted this remark to now read: 'Intact specimens, however, showed higher linear stiffness than reconstructed specimens, which suggests that the present reconstruction method may adversely affect wrist biomechanics during normal hand activities' (page 17, lines 4–6)."

Technical Issues

The reviewer writes: "While doing a post-hoc power analysis cannot be used as part of the design criterion, it would still be useful to present such an analysis to put the results into context. Simply saying that testing 12 pairs of specimens should be enough is not adequate." Your **wrong** response: "The new requested information is in the revised manuscript." Your **right** response: "The authors have now performed a post-hoc power analysis as suggested by the reviewer and now report it in this section: 'The post-hoc power analysis yielded a value of 0.88, indicating a high probability that all actual statistical differences were detected using 12 pairs of specimens, i.e., that type II error was avoided' (see page 15, lines 189–191)."

Philosophical Issues

The reviewer writes: "I have serious concerns about the experimental nature of the study. The authors have not clearly shown that their methodology is appropriate for the question being investigated. Please either provide precedent from the literature and/or justify the methodology in more detail." Your **wrong** response: "The authors believe that their methodology is correct and would suggest to the reviewer that performing a simple Medline search would reveal similar studies to ours." Your **right** response: "The authors appreciate the reviewer's remarks and have sought to show that our methodology is appropriate. Firstly, several prior studies that are similar to ours (refs #32–35) have now been cited in the Methods section (page 5, line 18). Secondly, we have now also added to the text the following paragraph about the mechanical principles of our experimental set-up: 'The physics of the methodology in question is based on …' (see page 5, lines 25–30)."

Conclusion

This chapter has endeavored to give you some background insight into how journals approach the article review process. Moreover, some practical tips have been offered for how to respond appropriately in writing to the improvements recommended and criticisms given by reviewers. The reader has hopefully understood that, beyond mere technical execution, there is an artistic and creative aspect in knowing how to respond effectively to reviewers so that a research paper has the best chance of actually getting published.

Suggested Reading

Day RA, Gastel B. How to Write and Publish a Scientific Paper. 6th ed. Santa Barbara, CA: Greenwood Press; 2006

Körner A. Guide to Publishing a Scientific Paper. New York, NY: Routledge; 2008

20

Getting Your Research Accepted at Scientific Meetings: Writing the Abstract

George Mathew, Sheila Sprague

Summary

Writing an abstract involves extracting information from your research paper and summarizing it in a brief and concise manner. An abstract is written either for submission to a conference or for a scientific article, and may or may not be structured depending on the requirements of the conference or publication. Generally, an abstract should be written after the entire manuscript is completed. The purpose of this chapter is to guide you in preparing an effective abstract for submission to specialty meetings.

Introduction

Reviewers' primary function is to decide whether your podium or poster presentation will be accepted. They often appraise your submission based solely on your title and abstract. Keep in mind that reviewers often have to rate more than 100 abstracts and that not all reviewers are fluent in English. Thus, they will appreciate a clear, simple, and straightforward structured abstract. This will strengthen the distinctiveness of your work in comparison with other studies.

> **Jargon Simplified: Poster Presentations versus Podium Presentations**
>
> **Poster versus podium presentation:** Orthopaedic meetings often have poster and podium presentations. In a poster presentation, the investigators prepare a poster summarizing their research methods and outcomes. The poster is displayed during the meeting. Investigators may be asked to give a brief oral summary of their study. They should also be available throughout the meeting to address any questions that the meeting attendees have about their research. In contrast, a podium presentation is a short oral presentation given by the investigator during a scientific session. The presentations are given in front of an audience using PowerPoint. Attendees may ask the investigator questions following their presentation.[1]

A compelling abstract contains the questions or purposes, the methods, results, and conclusions of the article. Thus, it is important to catch the reader's attention by making the title and abstract as concise, accurate, and readable as possible.

> **Key Concepts: The Importance of Abstracts**
>
> Titles and abstracts are used by reviewers in the peer-review process to determine the acceptance of research studies for presentation at national and international meetings.

Titles: Selecting a Title

The title is essential for bringing attention to an abstract, poster, or podium presentation. As the title may be the only factor that can captivate the reader's attention, it must be as accurate, informative, and complete as possible. The title is also strongly emphasized in meeting programs, and an effective title will draw a larger crowd to your podium or poster presentation.

> **Key Concepts: Tips for Writing Titles**
>
> - Be as descriptive as possible and use specific rather than general terms, for instance, gamma nail rather than intramedullary nail.
> - Use simple word order and common word combinations, for instance: "distal radial fracture" is more commonly used than the eponyms "Colle's" or "Barton's."
> - Avoid using abbreviations; they could have different meanings in different fields.
> - Avoid using acronyms and initialisms, for example: "Ca" for calcium could be mistaken for "CA," which means cancer.
> - Write taxonomic names in full, such as *Staphylococcus aureus* rather than *S. aureus.*
> - Refer to chemicals by their common or generic names instead of their formulas.
> - Avoid the use of Roman numerals in the title as they can be interpreted differently, for instance part III could be mistaken for factor III.

Abstracts: Selecting the Most Important Information

Authors need to critically assess their manuscripts and choose the most important aspects of their study that are appropriate for inclusion in the abstract.

Key Concepts: Pertinent Information

The purpose of the abstract is to give the maximum amount of pertinent information in the minimum amount of space.

Once the abstract is ready, it can be helpful to ask a colleague who is not involved in the research to assess it. This will ensure that the content is clear and understandable.

Key Concepts: Abstracts

The abstract must outline the most important aspects of the study while providing only a limited amount of detail on its background, methodology, and results.

Abstract Preparation: Structure

Abstracts that are being submitted to specialty meetings and journals should preferably have a structured format. Structured abstracts have several advantages: they help authors summarize the different aspects of their work, they make the abstract clearer, and make it easier for peer reviewers and readers to assess the contents of the manuscript or presentations. A structured abstract[2,3] should include an Introduction (or Background and Purpose), Methods, Results, and Conclusions. This closely follows the IMRaD (Introduction, Methods, Results and Discussion) format that was introduced in the early 20th century[3] and is currently used in about two-thirds of structured abstracts published in major medical journals.[4,5] This format is recommended for original papers,[6,7] where the "D" represents discussion instead of conclusions in your abstract. Even if structured abstracts may tend to be longer, they are considered more informative and clearer by their readers if they implement this format.[8] Before you begin preparing for your abstract, remember to check the requirements on abstract structure.

It is interesting to note that a structured abstract is not a requirement at many meetings such as EFORT (European Federation of National Associations of Orthopaedics and Traumatology) and COA (Canadian Orthopaedic Association). Additionally some journals, such as the *Journal of Bone and Joint Surgery*, British Volume, do not require a structured abstract.

Key Concepts: Abstract Structure

The abstract structure varies between meetings, journals, and articles. Authors should ensure that the abstract in their manuscript is consistent with the requirements of the meeting or journal of choice.

The abstracts that are submitted to meetings and journals are typically structured as follows:
- **Introduction/background:** This section should place the study into the context of the current knowledge of its field and list the purpose of the article; in other words, the authors should summarize why they performed their research.
- **Methods:** This part should summarize how the study was performed and mention the different techniques employed. It should also include details of any statistical tests employed.
- **Results:** This section should describe the main findings of the study.
- **Conclusions:** A brief summary of the content of the abstract and the potential implications of its results.

For further details on the requirements of any meeting, you should check the relevant "Instructions for Abstract Submissions."

Reality Check: Submission Instructions for Authors.

The following is an example of instructions for authors from the Orthopaedic Research Society.[9]
1. SUBMISSION DEADLINE: The deadline for electronic submission of abstracts is Wednesday, September 5, 2007 at 5:00 PM Central Time.
2. ABSTRACT LIMIT: There are no restrictions on the number of abstracts you may submit or present.
3. CHARACTER LIMIT: There is a limit of 7,500 characters for the text of your abstract submission. This includes title, abstract body, authors, institutions, tables, images and all spaces.
4. SPECIAL CHARACTERS and FORMATTING: If you copy and paste the title and/or body from your word processor, special characters or formatting will not transfer. You will have to replace special characters and/or insert formatting tags using the character palette. To access the palette, click on the "Special Characters" button located on the Title/Body page.
5. TABLES: Tables may be used, however graphic support is unavailable. For each row in the table, 50 characters will be deducted from the total character count. Tables can be edited or deleted at any time before the submission deadline.
6. TITLE: The title should be entered in "Mixed Case" (not UPPERCASE) letters. Do not use quotes or formatting tags in the title.
7. ABSTRACT BODY: Nonproprietary (generic) names should be given the first time a drug is mentioned in the body of the abstract and should be written in lowercase letters, e.g., acetaminophen. The first letter of a proprietary name is always capitalized, e.g., Tylenol. Do not mention support of work by a research grant.

8. AUTHORS: Please enter all authors in the order they should appear in the heading of the abstract. You should ensure that the name of the presenting author appears in the first author position. Other than name and e-mail address, you do not have to provide comprehensive contact information on co-authors but you may do so if you like. If you (the Contact Author) are not the Presenter of an abstract, you will need to provide comprehensive contact information on the Presenter.

9. INSTITUTIONS: Enter all department and institutional affiliations. Department is an optional field. Only three (3) institutional affiliations will be allowed per author. You do not need to enter institutions in a particular order to be able to designate author affiliations.

10. KEYWORDS FOR CD-ROM: Up to five (5) keywords should be selected. You are required to select at least two (2) keywords.

11. ABSTRACT PROOF: Carefully check the proof of your abstract. Make sure all special characters and formatting are displaying properly in your proof. If you find errors, return to the appropriate page by clicking on the page name in the sidebar menu, and make your corrections.

12. SUBMITTING YOUR ABSTRACT: If you have not completed all required sections/items you will not be able to submit your abstract. In the case of missing items, you will be prompted to enter the missing information. When all required information is entered and saved, go to the "Proof & Submit" page to submit your abstract.

13. TECHNICAL SUPPORT: If you have any difficulty with the submission process that you cannot resolve yourself, please call or e-mail Scholar One Technical support. The e-mail address and phone number are available from anywhere on the site by clicking on the "Technical Support" link located in the upper right-hand corner of each page.

Key Concepts: Characteristics of an Abstract

1. Around 250 words (variable, depending on journal/meeting).
2. Begins with one or two sentences of Introduction or Background, usually specific information.
3. The bulk of the abstract is the data. This can be a combination of the Methods and Results. The summation of the data is given along with the technique used to obtain the data. Specific details about procedure and results are omitted unless they are especially relevant.
4. At the end are one or two sentences of Discussion or Conclusions, explaining what the data means and summarizing the work.
5. The abstract (either at the very beginning or the very end) usually contains a phrase/sentence talking about the importance of the work being done, or how it affects the world or science.

Reality Check: An Example of a Submitted Abstract
Example of an abstract submitted to Australian Orthopaedic Association Scientific Meeting, Melbourne, 2002.[10]

Effect of Surgical Approach on Fracture Healing: Comparison of Minimal Invasive Approach (MIS) to Conventional Open Reduction And Internal Fixation Technique (ORIF) in a Sheep Tibial Shaft Fracture
M. Schüetz, A. Schmeling, K. Ito and N. Haas. Charité - Campus Virchow, Humboldt University, Berlin, Germany.michael.schuetz@charite.de

Introduction: The goal of this study was to examine the effect of a minimal invasive approach (MIS) in comparison to that with conventional open reduction internal fixation (ORIF) with regard to fracture healing.

Method: Twelve sheep were bilaterally operated on the hind limbs as a paired comparison in randomized order. To every sheep leg a high speed reproducible closed soft tissue injury was induced on the lateral tibial compartment. Then a simple transverse shaft fracture was created with a specially designed 4pt bending impact device. In both approaches, an internal fixator was used for stabilization. For the MIS technique, the fracture device and the internal fixator were applied on the periosteum through two 2 cm medial longitudinal skin incisions. For the ORIF technique a 20 cm medial longitudinal skin incision was made and the fracture was reduced with a bone clamp prior to stabilization. Fracture healing was monitored with radiographs every two weeks, and weight bearing on each leg was measured weekly. Six sheep were killed at six weeks and another six at 12 weeks. After hardware removal, the tibiae were biomechanically tested for stiffness (torsion and 4pt bending) and strength (4pt bending) and then prepared for histological analysis. Statistics were calculated using a paired t-test with a significance level of $p < 0.05$.

Results: No statistically significant difference was found between MIS and ORIF groups in regard to the biomechanical properties of the sheep tibiae at six or 12 weeks. All tibiae of the six week group and all except one tibia of the 12 week group failed through the original fracture site (one exception failed through a screw hole). There was no significant difference in weight bearing between the MIS and ORIF treated legs. This sheep received an operation due to screw pull-out and loss of reduction at two weeks. Hence, weight bearing of the opposite leg was preferred, but the mechanical properties of both tibiae at 12 weeks were similar to the other sheep.

Conclusions: The biomechanical and histological data did not show a statistically significant increase in fracture healing. One reason for this may be that our model is not sensitive enough to show these differences (too low soft tissue injury or fracture severity, inappropriate anatomy or fast fracture healing in sheep). On the other hand these results may reflect an overestimation of MIS benefits, since it is a more technically demanding procedure than that with ORIF.

In relation to the conduct of this study, one or more of the authors is in receipt of a research grant from a non-commercial source.

Let us "debrief" the sample abstract in the above example.

1. **Length**: This abstract is 466 words long. This is longer than the 350-word limit for most meetings, but is within the acceptable limit of 7500 characters (example: the *Orthopaedic Research Society* annual meeting criteria). Remember to keep the word count for your abstract within the specific meeting/manuscript criteria.
2. **Introduction**: The abstract begins with an introduction (background) that is one sentence long. Note that the information is specific and relates to the research topic.
3. **Methods/Results**: "Twelve sheep were bilaterally operated on the hind limbs as a paired comparison in randomized order." "Fracture healing was monitored with radiographs every two weeks, and weight bearing on each leg was measured weekly."
   - Note that individual pieces of data are given usually in one sentence.
   - The end result of the experiment is stated without providing a *P*-value.
     "No statistically significant difference was found between MIS and ORIF groups in regards to the biomechanical properties of the sheep tibiae at six or 12 weeks."
   - Also note that the technique used is mentioned but not described in detail.
     "For the ORIF technique a 20 cm medial longitudinal skin incision was made and the fracture was reduced with a bone clamp prior to stabilization."
4. **Discussion**: The discussion is the interpretation of the results in relation to the hypothesis/topic provided.
   "The biomechanical and histological data did not show a statistically significant increased in fracture healing."
   - The authors have then speculated on the reasons for the above conclusion.
5. **Importance**: Note that the importance of the study has not been specifically mentioned.

Key Concepts: Tips on Writing Abstracts
- Check the length of the abstract: Abstracts should not exceed the required word limit. Abstracts that are too long lose their function as summaries of the full article, and excess words may be omitted by some indexing services.
- Include synonyms for words and concepts that are in the title: for instance, if referring to "juxta-articular" in the title mention "periarticular" in the abstract (if appropriate).
- As in the title, use simple word order and common word combinations.
- Make sure the salient points of the manuscript are included, but be consistent; the abstract should only reflect those points covered in the manuscript.
- Minimize the use of abbreviations.
- Do not cite references.

Writing an Abstract for a Work-In-Progress

It is recommended that an abstract be written after the entire manuscript is completed.[11] This is because the process of writing will often change one's thoughts regarding the paper. Thus, you will be saving time if you write your abstract based solely on the final version of your manuscript. Only after careful consideration of the data and a synthesis with the literature can an author (or authors) truly write an effective abstract. However, you may occasionally be required to write an abstract for an ongoing research study.

Key Concepts: Presenting Preliminary Data
First, report the set of data that you have. The more actual data you provide the better the abstract will be.

When writing about ongoing research, remember to mention how the study will actually be done and what importance it has. Perhaps briefly mention the technique involved, but do not elaborate on it too much. An abstract is never a place to discuss technique in depth. If you do, people can tell that it has not been done.

Spend more time on background, and more time on importance. State clearly what experiments will be performed and how as if they have been done, but never write results and/or discussion for work that has not been done as this is unethical. In other words, you can say that X was analyzed by Y method even if the work has not yet been done, but you cannot say X was analyzed to give you Z.

Be conservative in your estimates regarding how much work will be done. Never overstate your case.

Reality Check: SPRINT[12]

Study to Prospectively Evaluate Reamed Intramedullary Nails in Tibial Fractures (S.P.R.I.N.T.)
Introduction: While surgeons agree that intramedullary nails are the treatment of choice, the use of reamed versus non-reamed intramedullary nails in decreasing rates of re-operation remains controversial. Controversy is most intense for a sub-group of patients, those with open fractures. No large randomized trials have definitively addressed the optimal nailing technique for patients with tibial fractures.

Primary Objective: To evaluate the impact of reamed and non-reamed intramedullary nailing on rates of re-operation in 900 patients with closed and open tibial shaft fractures. Secondary outcomes include return to work, functional status and health-related quality of life. **Overview of Important Methodological Issues in the Trial**: We are conducting the largest, multi-center, randomized clinical trial of reamed versus non-reamed intramedullary nails in the management of patients with tibial shaft fractures. Currently 105 surgeons are randomizing patients from 24 centers throughout North America and the Netherlands. Special features of this study design include 1) a proscription to re-operation before 6 months, 2) central randomization and thus ensured concealed allocation, 3) adequate sample size to limit Type II error rate, 4) comprehensive collection of data, and 5) central adjudication for all primary outcome events reported by participating centers. We describe our challenges with patient enrollment, limiting crossovers, and study event adjudication.

The purpose of this abstract is to present the methodology of the SPRINT trial. The authors provide a brief description of the rationale for the trial ("No large randomized trials have definitively addressed the optimal nailing technique for patients with tibial fractures."). The authors clearly state the primary objective and secondary objectives of the study. In addition, the authors provide an overview of the important methodological considerations for the trial and provide discussion on several of the challenges they are currently facing.

Even though the trial was underway, the authors did not present the preliminary data. The authors presented the definitive results of the SPRINT trial upon the trials completion at the Orthopaedic Trauma Association's annual meeting in October 2007.[13,14]

Although there is no specific mention regarding the importance of the study, the significance of the methodological issues in the trial is mentioned and these are listed ("special features of this study design include …").

Submission of Abstracts to Scientific Meetings

Key Concepts: Abstract Submission
1. Remember to adhere to the submission deadline.
2. Decide on the format: podium or poster.
3. Check whether the study has been approved by the Institutional Review Board (IRB) or ethics committee.
4. Check FDA approval when using devices/implants.
5. Prepare a summary sentence describing the abstract.
6. Decide who will be the presenting author.
7. Check that all coauthors have reviewed the abstract.

In the following are two practical examples of abstract guidelines, one from the Japanese Pediatric Orthopaedic Association (JPOA) and the other from the American Association of Orthopaedic Surgeons (AAOS).

Reality Check: Japanese Pediatric Orthopaedic Association Guidelines[15]
Important Dates
Deadline for Abstract Submission: Monday July 16, 2007
Notification of acceptance: By the middle of August, 2007
Guidelines for Abstract Submission
1. All submissions must be made on line using the UMIN Registration System. Submissions made via email or fax will not be accepted.
2. Select "Oral Presentation" or "Poster" for your preferred presentation type. Please note that the final decision regarding presentation type will be made at the discretion of the Organizing Committee.
3. All correspondence from the Registration Secretariat, including confirmation of abstract registration and notification of selection, will be sent via email.
4. First author must be a presenting author.
5. A maximum of 10 author names, including presenting author, may be listed on each paper.
6. You may enter up to 5 affiliations for the presenting author and coauthors. Make sure to select the correct affiliation number when entering the names of presenting author and coauthors.
7. The number of words in the abstract title must be 30 or less. If the title is 31 words or more you cannot submit your abstract.
8. If you want to include symbols (i.e., +, −, &, Greek letters (e.g., μ), superscripts (i.e., Na^+), subscripts (i.e., H_2O), italics, bold, or underline in your abstract, please follow the instructions and use codes provided when you enter the abstract data.
9. The number of words in the abstract body must be 240 or less. You will not be able to submit your abstract if the abstract body is 241 words or more in length.
10. The total number of words including abstract body, abstract title, and the names and affiliations of authors, must not exceed 320 words. You will not be able to submit your abstract if the total number of words is 321 words or more in length.
11. You cannot include figures or diagrams in your abstract.
12. Please make a note of your password and registration number. You will need your password and registration number to edit or delete your submission.
Please ensure that you read through and understand the above guidelines for abstract submission before submitting your abstract.
Privacy Policy: Information collected will not be given to or shared with any third party agencies, organizations or institutions. This information will be used for program contact purposes only.

Abstract Submission
Deadline: Monday July 16, 2007

Inquiries
Please contact the 18th meeting of the Japanese Pediatric Orthopaedic Association Registration Secretariat: email jpoa2007@jtbcom.co.jp. Fax: +81-6-6456-4105.

Reality Check: American Association of Orthopaedic Surgeons Guidelines[16]

Step 1: Type, Title, and Classification

You must first decide whether you have a preference for your presentation format—podium or poster. The AAOS Program Committee will take your preference into account, however, they cannot guarantee that your preference will be accommodated.[16] Next, you must answer a series of questions about your abstract, including whether your research subjects are living humans or animals. If the answer is "yes," you must indicate whether an IRB or ethics committee has approved your study. If you practice outside of the United States, where IRB or ethics committee approval is not required, indicate that the study was "Not approved, or not submitted" and explain the reasons why in the space provided.

If you practice in the United States, you must also indicate whether the US Food and Drug Administration (FDA) has approved all the devices and pharmaceuticals for the use described in your study or why your study does not describe the use of devices or pharmaceuticals. Finally, you must submit a summary sentence describing your abstract and select the category that best describes the content of your research. The summary sentence will be used in the Annual Meeting Final Program, if your abstract is accepted. The 12 categories of research include the following: adult reconstruction—hip; adult reconstruction—knee; sports medicine/arthroscopy; hand/wrist; foot/ankle; shoulder/elbow; rehabilitation medicine; trauma; spine; practice management/nonclinical; pediatrics; and tumors/metabolic bone disease. You may also elect to choose a second and third category that describes your abstract.

Step 2: Presenter and Coauthors

This step requires you to enter the last and first names of the presenter as well as the authors and co-authors of the abstract. Once you do this, the AAOS will search its database for the city and state of the people whose names you have entered, so that you can confirm that the database has identified the correct people. If the database contains more than one person with the same name, you will need to select the correct entry on the basis of the city and state. You may enter the names of people who are not already in the system by adding them to the database.

Step 3: Review and Submit Abstract

Finally, you must enter your abstract, which can be a maximum of 250 words long. Each abstract has four parts, or fields. The Introduction should clearly state the problem and the purpose of the study. The Methods section should describe what was actually done. The Results should summarize the findings of the study. The Discussion/Conclusion should be based on the findings and relate to the stated purpose of the study (within the context of current scientific knowledge in the field). Do not list any authors' names, their institutions of origin, or the names of companies or products involved in the study. If you do, your abstract will be disqualified. Do not include any photographic material, radiographs, charts, graphs, or tables.

Jargon Simplified: Institutional Review Board (IRB)

A specially constituted review body established or designated by an entity to protect the welfare of human subjects recruited to participate in biomedical or behavioral research.

Evaluation of Submitted Abstracts

Generally a subcommittee evaluates submitted abstracts. The principles of evaluation apply to the majority of meetings. For example, at the AAOS, each abstract is reviewed by a subcommittee of four to nine orthopaedic surgeons practicing in the respective category (pediatrics, hand/wrist, etc.). A 10-point scale is used, ranging from superior to poor.

Key Concepts: Evaluation of Submitted Abstracts

Reviewers look for specific features, and grading is influenced by the following factors:
- Significance of the study
- Content and clarity of the abstract
- Specific number of cases or specimen studies
- Presence of clinical or research data to support the study's conclusions
- Minimum follow-up of 2 years per patient for results describing reconstructive procedures
- Description of new or modified techniques related to diagnosis, surgery, complications, or other phases of orthopaedic surgical problems

After the subcommittees have graded their assigned abstracts, the results are sent to the AAOS Program Committee. Each member of the committee is assigned up to three abstract categories. Committee members review the highest-rated abstract submissions and designate them as either paper or podium presentations based on the subject matter and your initial presentation preference. The abstract submission and acceptance process is competitive. It is important to frame the question in a manner that is relevant to the current practice of orthopaedics. The abstract should be written clearly and the standard scientific outline should be followed if you are to have the best chance of being accepted. Planning ahead is critical to meet the respective deadlines.

> **Key Concepts: Common Errors**
> * Missing the submission deadline
> * Failing to read the instructions for authors for the specific meeting/journal
> * Overlooking spelling and grammar errors—it is recommended that you ask a colleague who is experienced to read your abstract
> * Submitting an abstract before the study is completed with the data analyzed
> * Submitted abstracts with errors in the data analysis
> * Forgetting to mention coauthor

> **Reality Check: Orthopaedic Associations**
> 1. Annual American Academy of Orthopaedic Surgeons.
> 2. Annual Canadian Orthopaedic Association.
> 3. Annual British Orthopaedic Association.
> 4. Annual Australian Orthopaedic Association.
> 5. EFFORT—European Federation of National Associations of Orthopaedics and Traumatology.
> 6. SICOT—International Society of Orthopaedic Surgery and Traumatology.

Conclusion

Make sure your abstract is clear and concise and adheres to all guidelines provided by the meeting sponsor. Show your draft to colleagues for appraisal, and if you are not fluent in written English, allow others to edit your work.

Suggested Reading

Alexandrov AV. How to write a research paper. Cerebrovasc Dis 2004;18(2):135–138

Alexandrov AV, Hennerici MG. Writing good abstracts. Cerebrovasc Dis 2007;23(4):256–259

Taylor RB. The Clinician's Guide to Medical Writing. New York: Springer; 2005

References

1. Wittich WA, Schuller CF. Instructional Technology: Its Nature and Use. 4th ed. New York: Harper and Row; 1973
2. Taddio A, Pain T, Fassos FF, Boon H, Ilersich AL, Einarson TR. Quality of nonstructured and structured abstracts of original research articles in the British Medical Journal, the Canadian Medical Association Journal and the Journal of the American Medical Association. CMAJ 1994;150(10):1611–1615
3. Wong HL, Truong D, Mahamed A, Davidian C, Rana Z, Einarson TR. Quality of structured abstracts of original research articles in the British Medical Journal, the Canadian Medical Association Journal and the Journal of the American Medical Association: a 10-year follow-up study. Curr Med Res Opin 2005;21(4):467–473
4. Sollaci LB, Pereira MG. The introduction, methods, results, and discussion (IMRAD) structure: a fifty-year survey. J Med Libr Assoc 2004;92(3):364–367
5. Nakayama T, Hirai N, Yamazaki S, Naito M. Adoption of structured abstracts by general medical journals and format for a structured abstract. J Med Libr Assoc 2005;93(2):237–242
6. Pakes GE. Writing manuscripts describing clinical trials: a guide for pharmacotherapeutic researchers. Ann Pharmacother 2001;35(6):770–779
7. Pamir MN. How to write an experimental research paper. Acta Neurochir Suppl (Wien) 2002;83:109–113
8. Hartley J. Applying ergonomics to *Applied Ergonomics*: using structured abstracts. Appl Ergon 1999;30(6):535–541
9. Submission Instructions for Authors. Orthopaedic Research Society. Available at: http://ors2008.abstractcentral.com/abstract. Accessed on July 30, 2007
10. Example of an abstract submitted to Australian Orthopaedic Association Scientific Meeting, Melbourne, 2002. Available at: http://www.aoa.org.au/scical2002mlb.asp. Accessed on July 30, 2007
11. Brand RA. Writing for Clinical Orthopaedics and Related Research. Clin Orthop Relat Res 2003;413(413):1–7
12. Bhandari M, Sprague S, Swointkowski M, Tornetta P, Schemitsch EH, Guyatt GH on behalf of the S.P.R.I.N.T. Investigators. Study to prospective evaluate reamed intramedullary nails in tibial shaft fractures (S.P.R.I.N.T.) Control Clin Trials 2003;24(3):126S–127S
13. S.P.R.I.N.T. Investigators. (Bhandari M). A Randomized Trial of Reamed versus Non-Reamed Intramedullary Nail Insertion on Rates of Re-operation in Patients with Fractures of the Tibia. Orthopaedic Trauma Association (OTA) 23rd Annual Meeting, Boston, MA, October 2007
14. S.P.R.I.N.T. Investigators. (Tornetta P). A Randomized Trial of Reamed versus Non-Reamed Intramedullary Nail Insertion on Functional Outcome in Patients with Fractures of the Tibia. Orthopaedic Trauma Association (OTA) 23rd Annual Meeting, Boston, MA, October 2007
15. Japanese Pediatric Orthopaedic Association Guidelines for authors. Available at: http://jpoa2007.jtbcom.co.jp/en/gaiyou.html. Accessed on July 30, 2007
16. Jennie McKee. Sharpen your abstract for 2008 Annual Meeting. American Association of Orthopaedic Surgeons: Available at: www.aaos.org/news/bulletin/may07/clinical2.asp. Accessed on December 21, 2009

21

PowerPoint Presentations: Tips for Presenting Your Work

Tara M. Mastracci

Summary

This chapter provides a walkthrough on creating an effective PowerPoint presentation for your research project, with tips on presenting your work and what to include in your PowerPoint slides. By following the suggested guidelines you should be able to maximize your chances of giving a top-notch presentation.

> **Key Concepts: Keys to a Successful Presentation**
> - In-depth knowledge of the subject area
> - A structured approach to the presentation
> - Well-designed, concise, and simple slides
> - Practice, practice, practice!

Introduction

Scientific presentations have become an integral aspect of surgical training and a common obligation of academic surgical practice. Residents and fellows are routinely asked to present their research at rounds, didactic lectures, or scientific conferences. Whether it is scientific, clinical, or methodological research, the ability to organize, create, and deliver a scientific presentation is a valuable skill, but one that is frequently not taught in a systematic way.

Before the Presentation

Without question, the most important aspect of any presentation is your own in-depth understanding of the subject area. It will be expected that if you have conducted research in the area, you are likely to have a good understanding of the topic. However, before any presentation, a review of the current literature is recommended to determine whether any new publications may be relevant to your topic area. In addition, when you are presenting at a session with a moderator, he or she is likely to be knowledgeable in your subject area and it is advisable to review the literature that the moderator has published on the topic. Whether or not this review of the literature is included in the talk you are presenting, it is nonetheless one way of preparing for questions that might arise.

In addition to your being very well versed in the subject area, a successful presentation involves well-structured content, concise and simple slides, and plenty of practice.

The objective of this chapter is to explore these three points, and to provide some direction for the first-time presenter.

Structured Approach to the Presentation

Scientific presentations often have very strict time limits such that the presenter may have to explain the rationale, methods, and results of complex research within 10 minutes. Distilling months or years of research into a brief presentation requires a rigorous prioritization of the key points of the subject. Using the scientific method as headings in the talk is a traditional and well-accepted organizational method. Ultimately, the aim of the presentation should be to 'tell a story' that begins by grounding the listener in the cogent issues of the subject area and then proceeds systematically to reveal the methods used, results discovered, and lastly, the final conclusions made.

The Presentation

Introduction/Background

The introduction slides should be brief and succinct.[1,2] Novice presenters commonly attempt to include minutiae in the introductory portion of their presentation, creating a section that overwhelms and overshadows the research presented. The introduction should be geared toward the audience to whom it will be presented. If you are presenting to experts in the field, a very limited review is needed, while a more general audience that might not be conversant with the topic area would require a recapitulation of some of the "principles" that otherwise might be considered assumed knowledge. Introductory slides should be appropriately referenced, so that the interested listener can take note of where a more in depth review of the points can be found.

Research Question

Every research project ultimately stems from a research question, which helps to direct the research itself and set the expectations for the results that may be revealed. The research question is central to the project, and therefore should be included in the presentation. It is common for research questions in clinical research to be organized using the PICO format: population, intervention, comparator, and outcome.[3] For bench research, the PICO format can be adapted to include the same themes. In the presentation of either research question, it helps to outline the aims or objectives of the project, which can be included on a separate slide.

Methods

An explanation of the methods employed in the research should be provided. This would include any assumptions that may have been made prior to conducting the research, as well as a brief outline of the process used to achieve the results. All software and equipment should be listed. In addition, any standardized or prevalidated scoring systems, scales, or processes used that are not of your own design should be listed. Any unique elements to the design of your project should be included if they contribute to the outcome.

Results

The results section should be the most descriptive segment of your presentation. It is in these slides that the most pertinent results can be highlighted. Often researchers will include a descriptive element, where the characteristics of patients or study materials are described, and then proceed to the major findings of the research. The displayed results should be distilled in such a way that the findings are apparent. Liberal use of descriptive diagrams and simple tables is encouraged.

Summary

The summary slides may include a discussion of the findings, specifically highlighting their place in the context of the literature (i.e., compared with other previously published work). The implications of the research should also be included. Many researchers find that the summary is where future research directions can be discussed, which includes presenting any hypotheses that may lead to future research initiatives. Conclusions, if included, should not be overstated and should be supported by the results of the research.

Acknowledgments and Disclosure

Most researchers are now being asked by conference organizing committees to disclose any conflicts of interest at the beginning of their talk. This should include any industrial or other relationships that might be seen to influence your views on the topic. Disclosure should also include the funding source used for your research. Final acknowledgment slides can be included to give credit to mentors or students who contributed to the research.

Well-Designed, Concise, and Simple Slides

Ninety-five percent of electronic presentations are now given using Microsoft Office PowerPoint, so taking time to understand basic functions and explore the applications of this software is a valuable investment in your research career.[4] Among the many helpful tools embedded in the PowerPoint software is the presentation template tool, which can assist in creating a presentation as it provides a helpful guide to creating slides that are simple and well organized. Furthermore, many users' guides have been published that will aid in navigating presentation software, and a list of some of the more common references is provided at the end of the chapter.

In general, the goal of each slide should be to make your point with the fewest number of words possible[2] so as to maximize the "information density" on each slide. This means that lengthy descriptions that are filled with long sentences should be replaced with point-form summaries. Your message can be elaborated upon in the oral component of your presentation, if necessary. Also, adding diagrams and figures for illustrations throughout the PowerPoint presentation will allow you to present your research more effectively. In general, these slides are for highlighting the major points of your presentation, and they should be consistent with your verbal presentation. This means that the points on your slides should be read word-for-word to help the audience connect with your speech, but remember also to elaborate on the points in a natural speaking manner. When designing your slides, keep in mind that the audience will be simultaneously reading your presentation and listening to your explanation. Thus, it is crucial to simplify your message as much as possible.

> **Key Concepts: Presentation Tips**
> • Keep slides simple and concise
> • Use point form, avoid long sentences and paragraphs
> • Use diagrams and figures
> • Elaborate verbally on the points written on your slides

Punctuation and Grammar

Generally, it is accepted that periods are not required to complete points listed on slides. Other forms of punctuation may be used, sparingly, if they add to the information. Titles should have each main word with an initial capital letter, as well as the first word of every point; otherwise all points should be written in lower case lettering. The *AMA Manual of Style*[5] can be consulted for the current accepted abbreviations for units of measurement, etc. Abbreviations that are not widely used should be included only if they are preceded by their full form in the first instance (i.e., 'abdominal aortic aneurysm [AAA]'). Most importantly, all presentation software includes a spell-check tool, which should always be used to ensure the spelling and grammar are correct on your slides.

Labels and Figure Descriptions

Figures are very useful in scientific presentations because they can relay a great deal of information on a single slide. However, the audience will have only a limited amount of time to decipher the figure on an electronic presentation slide. Thus, verbal explanations should highlight the key components of the figures. Any legends or labels should be legible by the audience. If used sparingly, colored text can be used to highlight important words.

"Orphan Words" and Other Indiscretions

Slides for scientific presentations should be well organized and the contents should be expressed as simply as possible. Most presenters find that organizing thoughts in point form is useful, and PowerPoint is designed to maximize

this approach. Of course, oversimplification of complex concepts is an inherent risk of this format. Therefore, care should be taken to ensure that the oral presentation provides adequate detail for the outline that appears on screen. Allowing single words or word fragments ("orphan words") to continue onto the following line can expand the amount of space necessary for a thought, and lead to a more disorganized-looking slide. **Figure 21.1** shows common choices that can be made to maximize the communicativeness and presentability of a given slide. Use of the 'custom animation' tool should be minimized in scientific presentations as it detracts from the credibility of the presentation. Moreover, care should be taken to ensure that all lettering is in a uniform font.

Practice, Practice, Practice

Rehearsing your presentation prior to the day of delivering it is always a good idea.[1,2] It is often best to review the presentation with someone who is knowledgeable about the subject, such as a supervisor. This colleague would be best able to provide feedback about clarity and ensure that no major points are missed. On the other hand, rehearsing in front of nonexperts will provide information about style and comprehensibility. A general rule of thumb is to prepare one slide per minute of presentation. However, it is best to plan to speak more slowly for audiences that are not as familiar with the topic, which means allowing more time for the description of each slide. In general, reading from prewritten cards should be avoided; the best presentations are those in which eye contact can be made with the audience.

There are helpful cues that will assist an inexperienced speaker in a smooth presentation. The addition of an outline or key points from your talk onto each slide will orient both you and the audience, thus making the talk flow most efficiently. Providing a handout of your slides will again

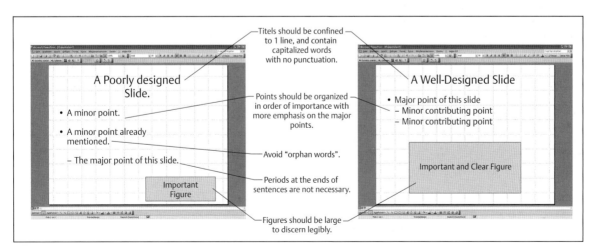

Fig. 21.1 Comparison of a well-designed and a poorly designed PowerPoint slide.

give the audience a guide to your talk and also remove visual gaze from you. Finally, physically standing where both you and the slides can be seen will allow for optimal understanding of your presentation by the audience.

Audiovisual materials can also provide unanticipated hurdles in a scientific presentation.[6] It is best to have more than one copy of the presentation available, in case of unexpected technical difficulties. As well, you should try to arrive early for your presentation to ensure that all figures and slides project well. This will also allow you to make any last-minute changes needed for your presentation.

> **Key Concepts: Presentation Tips**
> - Figures need verbal explanation accompanying them and legends should be legible by the audience.
> - Design your slide well to maximize effectiveness.
> - Practice prior to your presentation by delivering it to an expert and to a nonexpert.
> - Stand where the audience can see you and the slide at the same time.
> - Prepare extra copies of your presentation in case of unexpected technical difficulties and arrive early for your presentation so that you can test the equipment.

Conclusion

Making a scientific presentation is an essential skill for any clinician scientist. Following the simple guidelines provided in this chapter and using common sense will allow you to maximize your chances of giving a successful presentation.

Suggested Reading

Atkinson C. Beyond Bullet Points: Using Microsoft Office PowerPoint 2007 to Create Presentations That Inform, Motivate and Inspire. Richmond, WA: Microsoft Press; 2007

Finkelstein E. How to Do Everything with Microsoft Office PowerPoint 2003. Emeryville, CA: McGraw-Hill Osborne Media; 2003

Kosslyn SM. Clear and to the Point: 8 Psychological Principles for Compelling PowerPoint Presentations. New York: Oxford University Press; 2007

Lowe D. PowerPoint 2003 for Dummies. Hoboken: Wiley; 2003

Reynolds G. Presentation Zen: Simple Ideas on Presentation Design and Delivery. Berkeley, CA: New Riders Press; 2007

References

1. Collins J. Education techniques for lifelong learning: giving a PowerPoint presentation: the art of communicating effectively. Radiographics 2004;24(4):1185–1192
2. Broderick LS. Optimizing electronic presentations. Acad Radiol 2003;10(9):1045–1051
3. Haynes B, Sackett DL, Guyatt G, Tugwell P. Clinical Epidemiology: How to do Clinical Practice Research. New York: Lippincott Williams & Wilkins; 2006
4. Scarsbrook AF, Graham RN, Perriss RW. Expanding the use of Microsoft PowerPoint. An overview for radiologists. Clin Radiol 2006;61(2):113–123
5. American Medical Association. AMA Manual of Style. A Guide for Authors and Editors. 10th ed. New York: Oxford University Press; 2007
6. Kaplan NM. Suggestions for improving the effectiveness of oral presentations. J Investig Med 2002;50(6):419–420

22

Poster Presentations: Preparing an Effective Research Poster

Chad Coles

Summary

Poster presentations are becoming more and more popular in the scientific community. It is therefore important to have the knowledge and skills to prepare an effective poster. This chapter provides a comprehensive, yet practical list of suggestions to aid you in the poster-creating process, from choosing the appropriate background color to setting up your poster on the day of your presentation.

Introduction

The poster presentation is a very important medium for the dissemination of orthopaedic research knowledge. With increasing emphasis on well-conducted clinical trials and quality biomechanical and basic science research, growing numbers of abstracts are submitted each year to our national and international orthopaedic meetings. There are significant time constraints at these busy meetings and, even with the use of concurrent sessions, there is a limited amount of podium presentation time. The only remaining alternative is the increasingly utilized poster session, whereby hundreds or thousands of submissions can be viewed and discussed. Acceptance of your work for poster presentation should not be viewed as a "rejection" or sign that your project is not "worthy" of the podium, but should be embraced as an opportunity to convey the importance of your findings in this very different, and often more challenging format.

While entire volumes have been dedicated to this topic alone, this chapter will highlight key elements to be considered in the creation of an effective poster presentation. The "Suggested Reading" section of this chapter gives details of books that contain additional information and form the foundation for what is now common knowledge. The second text, in particular, contains excellent recommendations for the creation of figures and tables.

Why Are Posters Unique?

Unlike a completed manuscript, or even a podium presentation, a good poster is a highly condensed version of your project, conveying only the key details and the most important information to the viewer. It is not simply your carefully crafted abstract (see Chapter 20) printed on colored poster board; rather, the poster must be cleverly constructed to be truly effective in delivering your message. A poster is a visual tool and, as such, must be easily seen and interpreted by the passer-by. Colorful graphics and concise tables and figures assist in delivering your information. The poster must deliver your message for you, even in your absence. The average viewer, wandering by with beverage in hand, spends only a few seconds in front of each poster, *unless* something unique or of particular interest catches his or her eye: herein lies your challenge!

Preparation

Start early! Completing your research project was the easy part. Preparation of a good poster, particularly for the novice, requires significant thought, creativity, and patience. Several drafts and revisions of your layout may be required before the desired result is achieved. Revisiting the project after a few days or weeks may allow you to look at your poster with fresh eyes, and with new ideas for improving your presentation. You will want to seek the input of any coauthors, and you may choose to have other colleagues offer independent critique of your work prior to final printing. Depending on your familiarity with the software program selected (discussed later), a significant portion of your time may be expended in learning how to manipulate text and graphics for the desired visual effect. All of this can take a surprising amount of time until you have gained experience.

Instructions to Authors

Now that your work has been accepted for poster presentation, you must first read and adhere to the poster instructions particular to each meeting. These are typically included with your acceptance notification, and are also often available online. While you might think that these would be uniformly consistent, there are significant variations in poster size and content requirements for each organization, and these may vary from year to year as the meeting venue changes. For example, the 2010 American Academy of Orthopaedic Surgeons Annual Meeting[1] allows for a poster size of 4 feet × 8 feet, whereas other meetings, such as the 2010 Canadian Orthopaedic Association Annual Meeting[2] allowed a poster size of 4 feet × 4 feet, and the 2009 Orthopaedic Trauma Association Annual Meeting[3] allowed even smaller poster sizes of only 45 inches × 45 inches. The size restrictions will significantly impact on the content and layout of your poster. An oversized poster that overhangs the display space or infringes on neighboring posters looks just as amateurish as too small a poster that is dwarfed by the available space and adjacent displays.

> **Key Concepts: Follow Specific Poster Guidelines**
> Each organization may have different size and content requirements for posters, which may change from year to year or be specific to particular venues. A poster that is too large may infringe on neighboring posters, while a poster that is too small may look out of place in a larger area.

Many meetings now require a Food and Drug Administration (FDA) Approval Notice of any device or pharmaceutical described, as well as a disclaimer of any "off-label" use described. A financial support disclosure of project funding may also be required. While individual and institutional support is accepted by most organizations, others may forbid commercial funding.

> **Reality Check: Complying with Specific Instructions**
> Pay particular attention to poster display set-up and dismantling times. Failure to have an accepted poster displayed during the scheduled meeting times may result in the author(s) being banned from abstract submission in future years. There may also be a designated time for poster presentation during which your attendance at the poster is expected.

Color Scheme

While color selection is, in part, a personal choice, and may allow your poster to stand out in a "sea" of other posters, some general recommendations still stand. Color contrast between the background and text is critical for ease of viewing. Some presenters prefer the more traditional, white background with black lettering (**Fig. 22.1**).

While this provides excellent contrast for text and colored figures, the combination may lack the personality and visual impact you seek. Your poster may also fail to "stand out" on the typically white display boards. Another suggested combination is a dark background (royal blue, navy blue, teal green, forest green, or purple) with light text (white, yellow, golden yellow, ivory, light blue, or cyan)[1] (**Fig. 22.2**).

Brighter colors such as red and orange, while good for emphasis, do not make good background colors. Fluorescent colors are best avoided altogether. Avoid complicated, patterned backgrounds, though a subtle watermark is acceptable. A third color option is to use a colored background with white text boxes to highlight dark text (**Fig. 22.3**).

Colors add tremendously to your figures and graphics by enhancing visual appeal as well as lending clarity to charts and graphs. At most, two or three basic colors should be used on one poster, and there should be a consistent theme in all graphics. Obviously not all color combinations work well together, and some experimentation (and discretion) will be required.

> **Key Concepts: Recommendations for Color Selection**
> • Ensure color contrast between the background and text.
> • Bright colors such as red and orange are not preferable background colors.
> • Avoid fluorescent colors and patterned backgrounds.
> • Select two or at most three basic colors as a consistent theme.

Font Selection and Size

There are two main categories of fonts: serif and sans-serif. Serifs are the decorative lines added to the basic strokes of a letter (**Fig. 22.4**). Sans-serif fonts, such as Arial and Helvetica, are suitable for larger fonts or shorter lines of text such as titles and graph labels. Serif fonts, such as Times, are easier for the reader to follow along longer lines of smaller text, as the serifs guide the eye along a straight line.[4] An option for additional emphasis is to use a sans-serif font for the title and headings, and a serif font for text. Alternatively, a sans-serif font can be used throughout the poster for consistency, as a large enough font size will be used for the text to negate the benefit of serifs.

Font size should be large enough to allow easy reading from a distance. The title should be legible from 6 to 8 feet away, which correlates to 80- to 96-point font size. Text should be easily readable from a distance of 4 feet, requiring a minimum of 24-point font size. This includes text in figures and graphs. If there is not enough space to include what you have written, the solution is always to use fewer words, never smaller font size.

> **Key Concepts: Be Sure to Choose an Appropriate Font Size**
> • Ensure that font size is large enough to be read from a distance:
>   – The title should be legible from 6 to 8 feet away.
>   – Text should be legible from a distance of 4 feet.
> • If you have problems with space, use fewer words, *not* smaller font size.

Text should be single-spaced to facilitate reading and avoid waste of valuable space. Avoid long blocks of text in favor of multiple, shorter paragraphs, each focusing on a separate, important concept or detail. The start of a new paragraph is best signaled by a preceding empty line of text, rather than

"Alcohol use increases fracture risk in rats."

John A. Smith,[1] Susan B. Jones,[2] Michael C. Macdonald[3]

[1]University of Pointless Research, [2]Hospital for Sick Rodents, [3]Beer Brewers of Canada

Introduction

Much research has been conducted on the drinking habits of rats. [1]In particular, young, male rats have been identified as being at particular risk for excessive consumption. This same demographic has the highest incidence of trauma for the species (Figure 1).[2]

Many who care for these troubled rodents have suspected, for years, that alcohol consumption contributes to the incidence of disabling fractures in this population. This double-blinded, randomized controlled study was conducted to answer the following question: "Does alcohol use increase fracture risks in young, male rats?"

Methods

Institutional Review Board approval was obtained for this study. One hundred young, male, Wistar rats were randomized to one of two equally sized groups. Randomization was conducted by a blinded researcher (SBJ) drawing sealed, opaque envelopes containing either the letter "A" or "B". These formed the study groups (Figure 2).

Group A was permitted unrestricted access to beer (a fermented mixture of water, malted barley, and hops) with a 5 percent alcohol content[3]. Group B was permitted unrestricted access to a non-alcoholic beer (a non-fermented mixture of water, malted barley, and hops) with the same ratio of ingredients, nutritional and carbohydrate concentration, and flavour. Beverages were provided in identical, unlabeled bottles to prevent bias.

Prior to randomization, rats had been provided equal time for practice and training on a previously designed and validated, standardized obstacle course (Figure 3).

A sufficient time, equal for both groups, was permitted for consumption of the liquid refreshment. Rats were then videotaped and timed while negotiating the standardized obstacle course.

Length of time to complete the course, number of falls during course navigation, and other behaviors were carefully documented. Rats were then examined and x-rayed to document any fractures.

Results

Rats in Group A (beer) consumed significantly higher volumes than rats in Group B. While rats in Group B were able to successfully complete the maze, 17 rats in Group A failed to complete the course, or could not be bothered. Those rats in Group A who completed the maze required significantly more time than their sober counterparts. There were significantly more falls observed in Group A (243 falls, or 2.43 falls per rat) compared with only 17 falls in Group B (Figure 4).

There were 6 fractures observed in Group A. Four rats sustained femur fractures as a result of falls.
Two other rats sustained fifth metacarpal fractures after fighting with other rats. There were no fractures observed in Group B, which was statistically significant.

Conclusions

Alcohol consumption in rats was associated with the following findings:

- **Alcohol impaired performance times and task completion in rats**

- **Alcohol consumption was associated with a significant increase in the rate of falls**

- **Fracture risk was significantly increased in intoxicated rats**

While falls were directly responsible for the majority of fractures observed, other high-risk behavior was also observed to be linked to fracture risk. Further studies are planned to assess how long-term condition in the intoxicated state may improve performance and minimize injury risk. Several of the rats in Group A have already volunteered ...

Acknowledgements

We would like to thank the audiovisual department for their hours of work in video capture and editing, and custodial services for repeatedly cleaning up after the rats in Group A.

Disclaimer

While several of the rats in Group A sustained injuries while intoxicated, none of them seemed to mind. There were no fatalities.

References

1. Smith, JA, Johnson RP, Smart M, et al. Alcohol consumption patterns in rats. J Rat Sci. 1999;69:257-83.

2. National Institute for Rat Safety. 2006 Injury and Age Demographics. http://NIRS/2006_Statistics.html. Accessed September 1, 2007.

3. Mackenzie R and Mackenzie D, eds. Beer: The Art and Craft of Creation and Consumption. 3rd ed. Toronto, Canada. Smith & Maclaughlin; 2004.

Fig. 22.1 A poster with traditional dark lettering on a white background.

indenting the first line of the new paragraph. This maintains valuable clear space on your poster and helps keeps readers from losing their place in an endless block of text. Text can either be aligned only to the left margin, leaving an uneven edge along the right side of the paragraph, or more frequently justified, which maintains a cleaner, crisper appearance. Caution should be exercised when using justified text in narrow columns as excessive interword spaces can appear unsightly.

Organization and Layout

Your poster should follow a clear and logical order for the reader. This is typically from top to bottom and from left to right. Information should be organized into columns for ease of reading, both to avoid readers getting lost along a long line of text and also to facilitate their viewing of the poster in a crowd, moving along logically from one column to the next rather than struggling to see past adjacent viewers (**Fig. 22.5a,b**).

> **Key Concepts: Properly Organize Your Poster for Ease of Reading**
> • Make sure your poster has a clear and logical structure.
> • Present information from top to bottom and from left to right.
> • Use columns to organize your information.

Charts and figures should be used to replace and supplement text wherever possible. These should be interposed within the text as referenced to avoid the need to "skip around" the poster. Every effort should be made to maintain a smooth, logical flow. If possible, symmetric place-

"Alcohol use increases fracture risk in rats."

John A. Smith,[1] Susan B. Jones,[2] Michael C. Macdonald[3]

[1]University of Pointless Research, [2]Hospital for Sick Rodents, [3]Beer Brewers of Canada

Introduction

Much research has been conducted on the drinking habits of rats. [1]In particular, young, male rats have been identified as being at particular risk for excessive consumption. This same demographic has the highest incidence of trauma for the species (Figure 1).[2]

Many who care for these troubled rodents have suspected, for years, that alcohol consumption contributes to the incidence of disabling fractures in this population. This double-blinded, randomized controlled study was conducted to answer the following question: "Does alcohol use increase fracture risks in young, male rats?"

Methods

Institutional Review Board approval was obtained for this study. One hundred young, male, Wistar rats were randomized to one of two equally sized groups. Randomization was conducted by a blinded researcher (SBJ) drawing sealed, opaque envelopes containing either the letter "A" or "B". These formed the study groups (Figure 2).

Group A was permitted unrestricted access to beer (a fermented mixture of water, malted barley, and hops) with a 5 percent alcohol content[3]. Group B was permitted unrestricted access to a non-alcoholic beer (a non-fermented mixture of water, malted barley, and hops) with the same ratio of ingredients, nutritional and carbohydrate concentration, and flavour. Beverages were provided in identical, unlabeled bottles to prevent bias.

Prior to randomization, rats had been provided equal time for practice and training on a previously designed and validated, standardized obstacle course (Figure 3).

A sufficient time, equal for both groups, was permitted for consumption of the liquid refreshment. Rats were then videotaped and timed while negotiating the standardized obstacle course.

Length of time to complete the course, number of falls during course navigation, and other behaviors were carefully documented. Rats were then examined and x-rayed to document any fractures.

Results

Rats in Group A (beer) consumed significantly higher volumes than rats in Group B. While rats in Group B were able to successfully complete the maze, 17 rats in Group A failed to complete the course, or could not be bothered. Those rats in Group A who completed the maze required significantly more time than their sober counterparts. There were significantly more falls observed in Group A (243 falls, or 2.43 falls per rat) compared with only 17 falls in Group B (Figure 4).

There were 6 fractures observed in Group A. Four rats sustained femur fractures as a result of falls.
Two other rats sustained fifth metacarpal fractures after fighting with other rats.
There were no fractures observed in Group B, which was statistically significant.

Conclusions

Alcohol consumption in rats was associated with the following findings:

■ **Alcohol impaired performance times and task completion in rats**

■ **Alcohol consumption was associated with a significant increase in the rate of falls**

■ **Fracture risk was significantly increased in intoxicated rats**

While falls were directly responsible for the majority of fractures observed, other high-risk behavior was also observed to be linked to fracture risk. Further studies are planned to assess how long-term condition in the intoxicated state may improve performance and minimize injury risk. Several of the rats in Group A have already volunteered ...

Acknowledgements

We would like to thank the audiovisual department for their hours of work in video capture and editing, and custodial services for repeatedly cleaning up after the rats in Group A.

Disclaimer

While several of the rats in Group A sustained injuries while intoxicated, none of them seemed to mind. There were no fatalities.

References

1. Smith, JA, Johnson RP, Smart M, et al. Alcohol consumption patterns in rats. J Rat Sci. 1999;69:257-83.

2. National Institute for Rat Safety. 2006 Injury and Age Demographics. http://NIRS/2006_Statistics.html. Accessed September 1, 2007.

3. Mackenzie R and Mackenzie D, eds. Beer: The Art and Craft of Creation and Consumption. 3rd ed. Toronto, Canada. Smith & Maclaughlin; 2004.

Fig. 22.2 A poster with the same content and layout as in **Fig. 22.1** but with a more interesting dark-colored background with light lettering.

"Alcohol use increases fracture risk in rats."

John A. Smith,[1] Susan B. Jones,[2] Michael C. Macdonald[3]

[1]University of Pointless Research, [2]Hospital for Sick Rodents, [3]Beer Brewers of Canada

Introduction

Much research has been conducted on the drinking habits of rats. [1]In particular, young, male rats have been identified as being at particular risk for excessive consumption. This same demographic has the highest incidence of trauma for the species (Figure 1).[2]

Many who care for these troubled rodents have suspected, for years, that alcohol consumption contributes to the incidence of disabling fractures in this population. This double-blinded, randomized controlled study was conducted to answer the following question: "Does alcohol use increase fracture risks in young, male rats?"

Methods

Institutional Review Board approval was obtained for this study. One hundred young, male, Wistar rats were randomized to one of two equally sized groups. Randomization was conducted by a blinded researcher (SBJ) drawing sealed, opaque envelopes containing either the letter "A" or "B". These formed the study groups (Figure 2).

Group A was permitted unrestricted access to beer (a fermented mixture of water, malted barley, and hops) with a 5 percent alcohol content[3]. Group B was permitted unrestricted access to a non-alcoholic beer (a non-fermented mixture of water, malted barley, and hops) with the same ratio of ingredients, nutritional and carbohydrate concentration, and flavour. Beverages were provided in identical, unlabeled bottles to prevent bias.

Prior to randomization, rats had been provided equal time for practice and training on a previously designed and validated, standardized obstacle course (Figure 3).

A sufficient time, equal for both groups, was permitted for consumption of the liquid refreshment. Rats were then videotaped and timed while negotiating the standardized obstacle course.

Length of time to complete the course, number of falls during course navigation, and other behaviors were carefully documented. Rats were then examined and x-rayed to document any fractures.

Results

Rats in Group A (beer) consumed significantly higher volumes than rats in Group B. While rats in Group B were able to successfully complete the maze, 17 rats in Group A failed to complete the course, or could not be bothered. Those rats in Group A who completed the maze required significantly more time than their sober counterparts. There were significantly more falls observed in Group A (243 falls, or 2.43 falls per rat) compared with only 17 falls in Group B (Figure 4).

There were 6 fractures observed in Group A. Four rats sustained femur fractures as a result of falls.
Two other rats sustained fifth metacarpal fractures after fighting with other rats.
There were no fractures observed in Group B, which was statistically significant.

Conclusions

Alcohol consumption in rats was associated with the following findings:

■ **Alcohol impaired performance times and task completion in rats**

■ **Alcohol consumption was associated with a significant increase in the rate of falls**

■ **Fracture risk was significantly increased in intoxicated rats**

While falls were directly responsible for the majority of fractures observed, other high-risk behavior was also observed to be linked to fracture risk. Further studies are planned to assess how long-term condition in the intoxicated state may improve performance and minimize injury risk. Several of the rats in Group A have already volunteered ...

Acknowledgements

We would like to thank the audiovisual department for their hours of work in video capture and editing, and custodial services for repeatedly cleaning up after the rats in Group A.

Disclaimer

While several of the rats in Group A sustained injuries while intoxicated, none of them seemed to mind. There were no fatalities.

References

1. Smith, JA, Johnson RP, Smart M, et al. Alcohol consumption patterns in rats. J Rat Sci. 1999:69:257-83.

2. National Institute for Rat Safety. 2006 Injury and Age Demographics. http://NIRS/2006_Statistics.html. Accessed September 1, 2007.

3. Mackenzie R and Mackenzie D, eds. Beer: The Art and Craft of Creation and Consumption. 3rd ed. Toronto, Canada. Smith & Maclaughlin; 2004.

Fig. 22.3 Illustrating the use of a colored background with white text boxes for clarity.

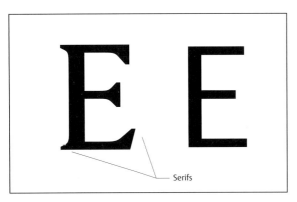

Fig. 22.4 Serif and sans-serif fonts.

ment of graphics will create a pleasing visual effect and add balance to your poster.

Graphics

Graphics should be briefly referred to in the text (i.e., "Figure 1" or "Table 1") and be placed so as not to interrupt the flow of ideas. Visual aids are intended to replace long blocks of text, and must be self-explanatory. Each figure or table legend should provide sufficient descriptive information to stand alone, without requiring the viewer to read the body of the text to understand the significance. Many viewers may choose to look only at your graphics, and not to read the text.

Any photographs should be of good quality and high resolution to avoid loss of detail with enlargement to poster

---

a

"Alcohol use increases fracture risk in rats."

John A. Smith,[1] Susan B. Jones,[2] Michael C. Macdonald[3]

[1]University of Pointless Research, [2]Hospital for Sick Rodents, [3]Beer Brewers of Canada

Introduction

Much research has been conducted on the drinking habits of rats. [1]In particular, young, male rats have been identified as being at particular risk for excessive consumption. This same demographic has the highest incidence of trauma for the species (Figure 1).[2] Many who care for these troubled rodents have suspected, for years, that alcohol consumption contributes to the incidence of disabling fractures in this population. This double-blinded, randomized controlled study was conducted to answer the following question: "Does alcohol use increase fracture risks in young, male rats?"

Methods

Institutional Review Board approval was obtained for this study. One hundred young, male, Wistar rats were randomized to one of two equally sized groups. Randomization was conducted by a blinded researcher (SBJ) drawing sealed, opaque envelopes containing either the letter "A" or "B". These formed the study groups (Figure 2). Group A was permitted unrestricted access to beer (a fermented mixture of water, malted barley, and hops) with a 5 percent alcohol content[3]. Group B was permitted unrestricted access to a non-alcoholic beer (a non-fermented mixture of water, malted barley, and hops) with the same ratio of ingredients, nutritional and carbohydrate concentration, and flavour. Beverages were provided in identical, unlabeled bottles to prevent bias.

Prior to randomization, rats had been provided equal time for practice and training on a previously designed and validated, standardized obstacle course (Figure 3).A sufficient time, equal for both groups, was permitted for consumption of the liquid refreshment. Rats were then videotaped and timed while negotiating the standardized obstacle course.

Length of time to complete the course, number of falls during course navigation, and other behaviors were carefully documented. Rats were then examined and x-rayed to document any fractures.

Results

Rats in Group A (beer) consumed significantly higher volumes than rats in Group B. While rats in Group B were able to successfully complete the maze, 17 rats in Group A failed to complete the course, or could not be bothered. Those rats in Group A who completed the maze required significantly more

---

b

"Alcohol use increases fracture risk in rats."

John A. Smith,[1] Susan B. Jones,[2] Michael C. Macdonald[3]

[1]University of Pointless Research, [2]Hospital for Sick Rodents, [3]Beer Brewers of Canada

Introduction

Much research has been conducted on the drinking habits of rats. [1]In particular, young, male rats have been identified as being at particular risk for excessive consumption. This same demographic has the highest incidence of trauma for the species (Figure 1).[2] Many who care for these troubled rodents have suspected, for years, that alcohol consumption contributes to the incidence of disabling fractures in this population. This double-blinded, randomized controlled study was conducted to answer the following question: "Does alcohol use increase fracture risks in young, male rats?"

Methods

Institutional Review Board approval was obtained for this study. One hundred young, male, Wistar rats were randomized to one of two equally sized groups. Randomization was conducted by a blinded researcher (SBJ) drawing sealed, opaque

Results

Rats in Group A (beer) consumed significantly higher volumes than rats in Group B. While rats in Group B were able to successfully complete the maze, 17 rats in Group A failed to complete the course, or could not be bothered. Those rats in Group A who completed the maze required significantly more time than their sober counterparts. There were significantly more falls observed in Group A (243 falls, or 2.43 falls per rat) compared with only 17 falls in Group B (Figure 4).

There were 6 fractures observed in Group A. Four rats sustained femur fractures as a result of falls.
Two other rats sustained fifth metacarpal fractures after fighting with other rats. There were no fractures observed in Group B, which was statistically significant.

Conclusions

Alcohol consumption in rats was associated with the following findings:

■ **Alcohol impaired performance times and task completion in rats**

■ **Alcohol consumption was associated with a significant increase in the rate of falls**

■ **Fracture risk was significantly increased in intoxicated rats**

While falls were directly responsible for the majority of fractures observed, other high-risk behavior was also observed to be linked to fracture risk. Further studies are planned to assess how long-term condition in the intoxicated state may improve performance and minimize injury risk. Several of the rats in Group A have already volunteered …

Fig. 22.5a, b
a A single-column layout is difficult to follow.
b A multiple-column layout improves ease of reading.

size. Images aligned with your columns of text give a smooth, professional appearance. Consider adding a narrow border to your photos to give a crisp edge, and provide contrast from backgrounds of similar color or brightness. Be very wary of images from the Internet, which are typically of lower resolution to allow high download speeds. These low-quality images will look fine on your poster proof, but do not enlarge well on a full-size poster and will appear very pixelated. Font size for figure labels should remain sufficiently large to be read at a comfortable distance, typically 20 to 24 point.

Tables can be an effective way to display your data, but must not be overly crowded or complicated. Do not attempt to display all of your data: select the key elements you feel are important to let readers understand the message of your poster. Again, keep a similar-sized font for table legends and values.

> **Key Concepts: Use Clear and Concise Tables**
> • Avoid crowded or complicated tables.
> • Include only key elements from your data.

Colorful graphs and figures are an excellent way to visually present your results. Choose a few contrasting colors, and be consistent throughout your poster. Keep figures simple and free of clutter. Direct labeling of your graph is more effective than using complicated legends and symbols. Keep axis labels short, and avoid vertical text for ease of reading (**Fig. 22.6a,b**).

Poster Title

The title is the most important determinant of whether the remaining information on your poster is read. As such, it deserves the largest font size on the poster (80 to 96 point), and should be easily legible from a distance of 6 to 8 feet. The title must attract ("You need to read this") as well as inform the reader ("This is what this poster is about").[5] Ideally, the title should not exceed one line for ease of reading. The title can either describe the research question posed ("Does alcohol use increase fracture risk in rats?") or can equally well deliver the answer to the question ("Alcohol use increases fracture risk in rats"). Avoid the use of more complex titles and the use of the colon, which adds length to the title but little added value[4]: "Alcohol use increases fracture risk: an in vivo study using rats." Use "Sentence case" instead of "Title Case" or "ALL CAPITALS" for ease of reading.

Put careful thought into your title selection to attract, and maintain your desired audience. "Catchy" is acceptable, but do not get too "cute"; you want your research

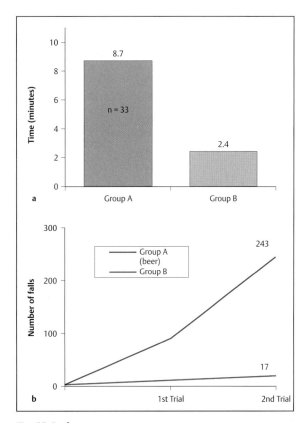

Fig. 22.6a, b
a An example of a simple, clearly labeled figure presented as a bar graph.
b An example of a simple, clearly labeled figure presented as a line graph.

and results to be taken seriously (with the exception of "examples" used throughout this chapter!).

> **Key Concepts: Importance of the Title**
> The title may be the only part of your poster that many viewers will read, so make it count!

Authors and Affiliations

The list of authors is typically included below the title. The font size should be smaller than that of the title, typically 60-point font, as the purpose of the poster is not self-promotion. Inclusion of the authors' first names may facilitate conversation and discussion during the poster session. Hospital or academic affiliations should also be included. If there are multiple affiliations, then superscript numbers should be used after the author's name, with the affiliations following on a separate line in 40-point font (**Fig. 22.7**).

John A. Smith,[1] Susan B. Jones,[2] Michael C. Macdonald[3]

[1]University of Pointless Research, [2]Hospital for Sick Rodents, [3]Beer Brewers of Canada

Fig. 22.7 Example of how to display authors' names and their affiliations.

Institutional logos can also be placed adjacent to the title, while taking care not to overpower the poster with excessive size. Again, be wary of the quality of logos available online. A photographed or scanned version will preserve image quality far better on enlargement.

Disclosure

Depending on the meeting and location, an FDA Approval Notice of any device or pharmaceutical described in the poster, as well as a disclaimer of any "off-label" use must be included. Particularly if "off-label" use is described, this disclaimer ought to precede the remaining poster information. Otherwise, the notice can follow at the end of the poster, in less-valuable space.

Introduction

The Introduction should briefly outline the background information on the subject of interest, including the importance of your project. The purpose of the study should be clearly stated and be easily identified. Consider the use of **bold type** to highlight the research question for the viewer. Aside from the title, the Introduction and Conclusions sections may be the only other sections read, and should therefore contain the most important information you want to convey.

> **Key Concepts: Importance of the Introduction**
> It is critical that both the Introduction and Conclusions sections contain the most important information from your study.

Methods

The Methods section should be concise. This should contain only the details that are critical to understanding the design of the study and to allowing that the validity of the results can be confirmed. Since a poster is a visual tool, any information that can be conveyed in a photograph (such as any testing apparatus or device studied) or in a schematic or diagram (to outline key steps in your study) should be presented in that form. Any opportunity to replace text with an appropriate visual aid should be exploited.

Results

The Results section is an important component of your poster, and should include the pertinent and important results of your study. Visual aids such as tables and figures are excellent ways to portray your results, as some viewers will not read the actual text.

Conclusions

If viewers are interested in your title, they will at least read your conclusions. The Conclusions section should be supported by your data. There is no space for lengthy discussion, and this is not the place for speculation. Clearly present the most important conclusions of your research that are supported by your data. A few, key points are best. These can be further highlighted with bullets, bold font, or text boxes.

> **Key Concepts: Include a Short and Concise Conclusion**
> • Avoid lengthy discussion and speculation.
> • Present the most important conclusions.
> • Consider using bullets, bold font, or text boxes.

Acknowledgments

Remember to acknowledge those who have contributed to the multiple stages of your work. This is an appropriate place to describe sources of funding.

References

Any sources cited in your poster should be appropriately referenced according to the American Medical Association format.[6] Font size for this section can be considerably smaller, especially if multiple sources are cited, as the truly curious can take a step or two forward if they must.

The Completed Poster

These are the traditional components of a scientific poster that viewers are expecting to see. Slight variations may be required, depending on the material you are presenting. A sample of a completed poster layout is shown (**Fig. 22.8**).

Software

There are many excellent graphics packages available for a very professional poster presentation. Probably the most familiar platform for many is Microsoft PowerPoint, which can produce quite reasonable posters, and was used for the examples shown throughout this chapter. The maximum width of a poster in PowerPoint is 56 inches, which would obviously not be a suitable choice if a larger poster size is required. Other software packages such as Adobe Illustrator, CorelDRAW, and Photoshop (to name but a few) are much more powerful publishing tools but, for that reason, a novice will require a considerably longer time to master them. Your final poster will typically need to be converted to Portable Document Format (PDF) for printing. Check

"Alcohol use increases fracture risk in rats."

John A. Smith,[1] Susan B. Jones,[2] Michael C. Macdonald[3]

[1]University of Pointless Research, [2]Hospital for Sick Rodents, [3]Beer Brewers of Canada

Introduction

Much research has been conducted on the drinking habits of rats.[1] In particular, young, male rats have been identified as being at particular risk for excessive consumption. This same demographic has the highest incidence of trauma for the species (Figure 1).[2]

Many who care for these troubled rodents have suspected, for years, that alcohol consumption contributes to the incidence of disabling fractures in this population. This double-blinded, randomized controlled study was conducted to answer the following question: "Does alcohol use increase fracture risks in young, male rats?"

Methods

Institutional Review Board approval was obtained for this study. One hundred young, male, Wistar rats were randomized to one of two equally sized groups. Randomization was conducted by a blinded researcher (SBJ) drawing sealed, opaque envelopes containing either the letter "A" or "B". These formed the study groups (Figure 1).

Figure 1. Study design showing equal randomization to Group A and Group B.

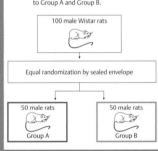

Group A was permitted unrestricted access to beer (a *fermented* mixture of water, malted barley, and hops) with a 5 percent alcohol content[3]. **Group B** was permitted unrestricted access to a non-alcoholic beer (a *non-fermented* mixture of water, malted barley, and hops) with the same ratio of ingredients, nutritional and carbohydrate concentration, and flavour. Beverages were provided in identical, unlabeled bottles to prevent bias.

Prior to randomization, rats had been provided equal time for practice and training on a previously designed and validated, standardized obstacle course (Figure 2).

Figure 2. Rat Obstacle Course

A sufficient time, equal for both groups, was permitted for consumption of the liquid refreshment. Rats were then videotaped and timed while negotiating the standardized obstacle course.

Length of time to complete the course, number of falls during course navigation, and other behaviors were carefully documented. Rats were then examined and x-rayed to document any fractures.

Results

Rats in Group A (beer) consumed significantly higher volumes than rats in Group B. While rats in Group B were able to successfully complete the maze, 17 rats in Group A failed to complete the maze, or could not be bothered. Those rats in Group A who completed the maze required significantly more time than their sober counterparts. (Figure 3).

Figure 3. Increased time required to for Group A to complete maze

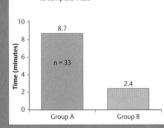

There were significantly more falls observed in Group A (243 falls, or 2.43 falls per rat) compared with only 17 falls in Group B (Figure 4).

Figure 4. Significantly more falls observed in Group A (beer)

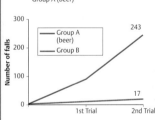

There were 6 fractures observed in Group A. Four rats sustained femur fractures as a result of falls. Two other rats sustained fifth metacarpal fractures after fighting with other rats. There were no fractures observed in Group B, which was statistically significant. (Figure 5).

Figure 5. Statistically significantly increased risk of fractures in Group A (beer)

	Femur Fractures	5th Metacarpal Fractures
Group A	4	2
Group B	0*	0*

* < 0.000001

Conclusions

Alcohol consumption in rats was associated with the following findings:

- **Alcohol impaired performance times and task completion in rats**
- **Alcohol consumption was associated with a significant increase in the rate of falls**
- **Fracture risk was significantly increased in intoxicated rats**

While falls were directly responsible for the majority of fractures observed, other high-risk behavior was also observed to be linked to fracture risk. Further studies are planned to assess how long-term condition in the intoxicated state may improve performance and minimize injury risk. Several of the rats in Group A have already volunteered ...

Acknowledgements

We would like to thank the audiovisual department for their hours of work in video capture and editing, and custodial services for repeatedly cleaning up after the rats in Group A.

Disclaimer

While several of the rats in Group A sustained injuries while intoxicated, none of them seemed to mind. There were no fatalities.

References

1. Smith, JA, Johnson RP, Smart M, et al. Alcohol consumption patterns in rats. J Rat Sci. 1999;69:257-83.

2. National Institute for Rat Safety. 2006 Injury and Age Demographics. http://NIRS/2006_Statistics.html. Accessed September 1, 2007.

3. Mackenzie R and Mackenzie D, eds. Beer: The Art and Craft of Creation and Consumption. 3rd ed. Toronto, Canada. Smith & Maclaughlin; 2004.

Fig. 22.8 Example of completed poster layout.

with your printing company, in advance, to confirm compatibility with your software selection.

Printing of the Poster

Most major copying and printing companies can produce a quality poster with reasonable advance notice, typically 24 hours. Your institution may also have a printing department familiar with scientific poster printing, and with reasonable pricing. Plan ahead to avoid last-minute panic! Ensure the company you choose supports the software package you have selected, and confirm in advance the length of time needed to print your poster. Some print shops may have technical limits, with a maximum printing width of 36 inches, which is important to know in advance. A matte finish will avoid glare when viewing your poster from an angle. Lamination adds durability and wrinkle and stain resistance to your poster, but also cost and the likelihood of glare. Newer materials, such as vinyl, may be a good compromise between matte finish and durability. Budget for approximately $10 per square foot (plus tax!) and add an additional 30% for lamination. Costs can quickly add up to hundreds of dollars, which is one disadvantage of poster presentations.

> **Key Concepts: Plan Ahead**
> Plan ahead to avoid last-minute panic! Ensure the company you choose supports the software package you have selected, and confirm in advance the length of time needed to print your poster.

Transportation of the Poster to the Meeting

Most printed posters can be carefully rolled and stored in a cardboard poster tube. More durable, plastic carriers are available at most art supply stores. As many meeting destinations require air travel, you may wish to confirm with your air carrier about size restrictions for carry-on baggage. You may also wish to consider a domestic or international courier service as a means of getting the poster to the meeting quickly and safely. It is wise to carry a backup of your final poster PDF file in a safe location, in the event of loss of the printed poster. Most larger copying and printing stores can reprint your poster at your destination, but for a price.

> **Key Concepts: Have a Back-up Plan**
> If you baggage check your poster during air travel, you may never see it again! Have a backup copy on disk, stored in a separate location.

Setting Up the Poster

Respect the designated setting-up and dismantling times for poster displays. Your poster will be assigned a number and corresponding display board location. This is not up for negotiation or trade, in an attempt to gain a better vantage point, or to be next to your colleague. Mount your poster within your designated space using Velcro, or tacks. Bring your own supply, as these will typically not be provided on site. Mount your poster sufficiently high to be visible, with the key area of the poster at eye level for comfortable viewing. Do not forget to reclaim your poster after the meeting is complete. If you must leave the meeting early, prior to completion of the poster display times, designate a colleague or coauthor (or two!) to collect your poster at the appropriate time. Do not take your poster down prematurely.

Presentation

Not all meetings will have a designated poster presentation time, but if they do then your presence is expected. This is your opportunity to showcase your work. Your dress and demeanor should be appropriate. Chewing gum and coffee should be avoided. You may choose to present your poster in a one- or two-minute presentation, or simply stand off to the side, and engage viewers after they have had an opportunity to digest some of the information contained in your poster. Make use of your figures and tables when discussing results.

> **Reality Check: Keep Business Cards on Hand**
> This is an excellent opportunity to discuss your work with others in your field of interest. These interactions may spark new ideas, and generate new contacts for future endeavors. Keep your business cards on hand for those you meet (and wish to make future contact with!).

Handouts

It is useful to have reprints of your research available for those who are truly interested. These can be copies of your manuscript, or alternatively a color reprint of your poster on letter-size paper, as long as the necessary font size does not become unreadable. These can be contained in a manila envelope securely suspended below your poster display. Alternatively, a PDF version of your poster can be posted online, with reference to the link on your poster or handout. Once again, it is helpful to have business cards on hand, as the poster session is a great way to make contacts.

Contact Information

Place your name and contact information on the back of your poster in case you forget to take down your poster at the end of the meeting (although most organizations will not return abandoned posters) or in the event of loss.

Conclusion

The aim of this chapter is to effectively prepare you for creating a poster presentation. By following the guidelines suggested in this chapter, you should be able to generate a poster that justifies all the hard work that you placed into your research endeavors.

Suggested Reading

Briscoe MH. Preparing Scientific Illustrations: A Guide to Better Posters, Presentations, and Publications. New York: Springer; 1996

Gosling PJ. Scientist's Guide to Poster Presentations. New York: Kluwer Academic; 1999

References

1. American Academy of Orthopaedic Surgeons 2010 Annual Meeting. Participants Instructions. Available at: http://www3.aaos.org/education/anmeet/accepted/Guidelines/Poster_Instructions.pdf. Accessed January 1, 2010
2. Canadian Orthopaedic Association 2010 Annual Meeting. Scientific Session Audiovisual Guidelines. Available at: http://www.coaannualmeeting.org/websites/coa2010/index.php?p=2. Accessed January 1, 2010.
3. Orthopaedic Trauma Association 2009 25th Annual Meeting. Participants Instructions. Instructions for Preparation of Poster Presentations. Available at: http://www.ota.org/meetings/09AM/poster%20instructions%20June%202009.pdf. Accessed January 1, 2010.
4. Briscoe MH. Preparing Scientific Illustrations: A Guide to Better Posters, Presentations, and Publications. New York: Springer; 1996
5. Lewison G, Hartley J. What is in a title? Numbers of words and the presence of colons. Scientometrics 2005;63(2):341–356
6. Iverson C, Christiansen S, Flanagin A, et al. American Medical Association Manual of Style: A Guide for Authors and Editors. 10th ed. New York: Oxford University Press; 2007

23

Be Consistent: Present and Publish the Same Results

Boris A. Zelle

Summary

In this chapter we discuss the role of meeting abstracts and the significance of subsequent full-text publication. Meeting abstracts are frequently referenced, but this is problematic when no follow-up journal papers are published or publication is inconsistent with what is presented at scientific meetings. Here we survey the current practice in research publication and its consistency with presented abstracts, examine the effects of poor follow-up publication (or lack thereof), and provide strategies to help improve consistency of full-text writing and abstracts for potential authors.

Introduction

Conference presentations are the major forum for dissemination of new research results. Abstracts presented at such meetings have an important impact on medical care. The quality of a publication depends on both the quality of the work and the reporting. A paper presented at a scientific meeting should accurately reflect the final results of the study. Meeting abstracts should provide sufficient information on the study's research question, study design, primary outcome measures, sample size, statistical analysis, results, measures of precision, and a conclusion.

Impact of Meeting Abstracts

Abstracts from scientific meetings can have a significant impact on clinical practice and ongoing research as they are frequently referenced in textbooks, at scientific meetings, at instructional course lectures, during rounds, and in expert committees. It has been suggested that as many as 53–63% of the chapters of major orthopaedic textbooks included results from abstracts presented at scientific meetings. Thus, it is evident that abstracts presented at scientific meetings are truly significant.[1] While awaiting peer-reviewed publication of the full-text paper, clinicians and researchers may rely on the contents of meeting abstracts to make judgments regarding their future research and/or patient care. In addition, meeting abstracts are commonly used sources for systematic literature reviews and meta-analyses. With improved indexing in standard databases and the use of Internet resources, meeting abstracts are widely available to investigators who are performing a meta-analysis. Given the recently increased interest among the medical community in evidence-based medicine, it can be assumed that the results of such systematic reviews will have a significant impact on clinicians' opinions and their treatment protocols. For these reasons, abstracts presented at scientific meetings should report on final study results and include the appropriate level of quality and accuracy. Moreover, abstracts should be consistent with any subsequent full-text publication.

> **Key Concepts: Availability of Meeting Abstracts**
> With improved indexing and Internet resources, meeting abstracts are widely available and have an important impact on education, patient care, and planning of research projects.

Although meeting abstracts are very meaningful to researchers and clinicians, it has been questioned whether abstracts from scientific meetings should be used to guide clinical practice. Recent publications have emphasized the lack of accurate reporting in meeting abstracts, the low rate of subsequent full-text publication following abstract presentation, and the great inconsistency between meeting abstracts and subsequent full-text publication. For these and other reasons, some peer-reviewed journals even prohibit referencing of abstracts in papers that they publish.[2]

From Abstract to Full-Text Publication

Podium presentations at scientific meetings provide an important forum for the dissemination of the most recent scientific advances. Subsequent publication of a full-text publication in a peer-reviewed journal should be the expected outcome of such presentations. Additionally, presenters should report on completed projects that have undergone critical data analysis and appropriate peer review.

Compared with podium presentations at scientific meetings, publication in peer-reviewed journals has several potential benefits. The investigator usually reaches a larger readership compared with a scientific meeting and the investigators are able to describe their research in more detail. Moreover, there is a lucrative incentive for authors to publish a full-text article because of the corresponding benefit of academic promotion.

However, a large number of studies presented at scientific meetings do not make the transition to a subsequent full-text publication. The publication rates of full-text articles after presentation of abstracts at international meetings have been reported to range from 11% to 78% (see Chapter 2).[3-12] This emphasizes that a significant number of papers presented at research meetings are of low scientific quality and will not pass the more challenging and rigorous peer-review process of medical journals. In addition, it can be assumed that a portion of the meeting abstracts will report preliminary data of ongoing studies and some of the authors involved will choose not to pursue the completion of the study. Moreover, some authors may not be willing to make the time commitment for completing a full-length manuscript because of their busy clinical practice responsibilities. The presentation of incomplete studies and the lack of subsequent full-text publication results in several problems. One problem is that investigators citing meeting abstracts are at risk of quoting studies that will never become full-text literature in a medical scientific journal; another is that researchers and clinicians who apply the results of meeting abstracts into research and clinical practice may rely on low-quality data or incomplete studies.

Why is Consistency between Meeting Abstract and Subsequent Full-Text Publication Important?

As discussed above, meeting abstracts have a great impact on education, research, and clinical practice. They represent an important source of information for clinicians and scientists by serving as data for systematic literature reviews. Over the last few years, technology has made meeting abstracts more widely available to researchers and scientists. With improved indexing of medical databases, even researchers who did not attend the scientific meeting can assess the meeting abstracts. Many researchers make their most recent abstracts from scientific meetings available either on their homepage or via typical Internet searches.

The increased availability of meeting abstracts requires the appropriate level of quality and accuracy for reporting purposes. Inconsistencies between meeting abstracts and subsequent full-text publications can easily be detected by other researchers. Discrepancies between meeting abstracts and subsequent full-text publication will jeopardize the credibility of the authors in question. In addition, unexplained discrepancies will confuse the reader as to whether the abstract or the full-text publication reflects the correct data. Finally, submission of a full-text manuscript to a scientific journal will not be well received by the reviewers and editors if the data are inconsistent with prior meeting abstracts.

Key Concepts: Consequences of Inconsistency
1. Authors who report inconsistent data will jeopardize their credibility.
2. Inconsistencies between meeting abstracts and subsequent full-text publications will confuse researchers who are reviewing the literature.
3. Presentation of confusing preliminary data will mislead other researchers.

Literature on Consistency of Reporting

Over the last few years, the accuracy of reporting study results has gained increased interest in the scientific community. Weintraub in 1987 evaluated the consistency between abstracts and the subsequent full-text publication in 33 randomly selected papers from the *Journal of Pediatric Surgery*.[13] Only 30% had the same title and authors as their abstract. In addition, 45% of the meeting abstracts had sample sizes that were inconsistent with their corresponding full-text papers. The change of sample size ranged from 75% fewer cases to 210% more patients. Finally, the conclusions were consistent in only 23 of 33 papers; data and conclusions in the full-text publication were commonly observed to be weaker than in the abstract.

In an observational study, in 2002 Bhandari et al. evaluated the full-text publication rate of abstracts presented at the 1996 Annual Meeting of the American Academy of Orthopaedic Surgeons, the factors predicting the ultimate publication as a full-text manuscript after presentation of the abstract, and the consistency between abstracts and subsequently published full-text manuscript.[1] The authors divided inconsistencies into *minor* (differences in study title, number of authors, presentation of all outcomes, authors' interpretation of their own data) and *major* inconsistencies (discrepancies in the study objective and/or hypothesis, study design, primary outcome measure, any secondary outcome measure, sample size, statistical analysis, study results, and measures of precision such as standard deviation and confidence interval). The investigators reported that 159 (34%) of the 465 abstracts were followed by publication of a full-text article. The mean time to publication was 17.6 ± 12 months. Abstracts that were followed by subsequent full-text publication had a significantly higher sample size, and were significantly more often of North American origin. Discrepancies between abstracts and subsequent full-text publication were common.

With regard to minor inconsistencies between the abstracts and the subsequent full-text publication, final conclusions were consistent with the abstract 96.2% of the time. The title of 43.4% of the abstracts differed from that of the final published study. Authorship changed 29.6% of the time, including the addition of authors (18.2%), the removal of authors (6.3%), or both (5.0%). With regard to major inconsistencies, there was a high level of consistency between the abstracts and the final publications with respect to the study objective (99.4%) and study design (98.7%). The primary outcome measure changed 13.2% of the time and the sample size changed in 18.2% of the studies. Interestingly, the sample size decreased from the abstract to the final publication 8.8% of the time; the magnitude of the decrease in sample size ranged from 1% to 73%; and most authors did not explain the decreased sample size. Also, 18.9% of the results in the presented abstracts were inconsistent with the subsequent full-text publications. The time between presentation of the abstract and publication of the paper was a statistically significant independent predictor of inconsistencies between the abstracts and subsequent full-text publications. An increase in the delay until publication significantly increased the likelihood of an inconsistency.

In a subsequent study in 2003, Sprague et al., from the same research group as Bhandari et al., investigated the reason why certain abstracts presented at the 1996 Annual Meeting of the American Academy of Orthopaedic Surgeons were never published.[14] In their survey, the investigators contacted the 306 authors of the presented abstracts that were not followed by a subsequent full-text publication; 199 (65%) of the contacted authors responded to the questionnaire. The main reasons why these studies were never published were recorded as follows: (1) lack of sufficient research time (46.5%); (2) the study was still in progress (31.0%); (3) the responsibility for writing the manuscript belonged to someone else (19.7%); (4) difficulties with coauthors (16.9%); (5) manuscript publication had low priority beside other responsibilities (12.7%). Another interesting finding concerned the problem of locating the final full-text manuscript because of inconsistencies between abstracts and full-text publication with regard to authorship and study title. Thus, 86.1% of the published titles in the full-text papers were inconsistent with the title of the meeting abstract, and the authorship changed in 59.7% of cases.

Another study investigated the consistency between poster abstracts and the actual poster presentation at the Annual Meeting of the American Academy of Orthopaedic Surgeons in 2004.[15] This investigation showed discrepancies between the poster abstracts and the subsequent poster presentation in 76% of the posters presented. The most common change included a change in authorship, which occurred in 49% of the posters presented. Other remarkable inconsistencies included a change of the poster title (34%), changes of the numerical values of the study results (30%), and change of the sample size (15%).[15]

In a study published in 2006, Preston et al. evaluated the consistency between papers presented at the Orthopaedic Trauma Association and their subsequent full-text publication.[16] The study hypothesis remained the same in 99.3% but only 56.3% of the published full-text publications had the same sample size as the presented abstract. Of the studies published, 18.2% reported a sample size smaller than stated in the previously presented abstract. The final con-

clusion of the study changed 6.6% of the time. Only 10% of the authors explained the discrepancy between the previously published abstract and the subsequent full-text publication.[16]

What Can We Learn from These Investigations?

It has been shown that discrepancies can frequently be found and that they may involve any section of the paper. In some cases, inconsistencies between the meeting abstracts and subsequent full-text publication may be unavoidable and are part of the submission and peer-review process. Thus, the title may be changed at the request of a peer-reviewer or the journal; the sample size may change as the result of a peer-reviewer's request to narrow the inclusion criteria; the conclusions may be re-phrased as the peer-reviewers may find that the conclusions do not accurately reflect the finding of the study. Unfortunately, in some cases, these changes do not result in any significant improvement of the quality of the manuscript, but rather the peer-reviewers' personal opinions on the study are incorporated. Since the review and publication process is often very long and ongoing, many investigators may legitimately choose to ease off any resistance to changes to expedite the publication process. In most cases, however, changes made during the review process certainly do improve the quality of the paper and should be incorporated into the full-text publication. Appropriate acknowledgment of these changes should be made to avoid confusion for the reader.

While a few minor discrepancies between meeting abstract and subsequent full-text publication appear unavoidable, data from the literature suggest that most discrepancies result from poor study planning and inappropriate timing of presentation. The following issues may influence the consistency between meeting abstract and subsequent full-text publication: (1) presentation of preliminary data in meeting abstracts; (2) confusion over authorship responsibilities; and (3) selective reporting.

Submission of Preliminary Data

Submission of preliminary data appears to be a major issue and is clearly misleading readers, abstract reviewers, and those attending meeting. Sprague et al. recorded that almost one-third of authors who presented meeting abstracts without follow-up of subsequent full-text publication reported that the study was still ongoing, even several years after the podium presentation.[14] It appears that at the time of the meeting authors are still in the process of data collection and continuation of patient enrollment. This is strongly supported by the significant discrepancies of sample sizes and the numerical changes of the study results reported by previous investigators.[1,13,15,16] Preston et al. showed that as many as 56.3% of the sample sizes presented in meeting abstracts were inconsistent with the full-text publication and only 10% of authors explained these inconsistencies.[16] Bhandari et al. identified a significant problem by comparing the sample sizes of abstracts with the sample sizes in full-text publication.[1] In some cases the investigators encounter all patients eligible for the study and report this number in the meeting abstracts. However, in the subsequent full-text publication, the investigators report the number of patients who were truly reevaluated at follow-up and tend to omit the number of patients lost to follow-up, giving the impression that the follow-up rate was 100%. This dubious reporting practice will certainly bias the study results, mislead the reader, and jeopardize the authors' reputation for honesty and integrity.

> **Key Concepts: When to Submit your Abstract**
> Submit your abstract for a podium presentation *after* completion of data collection and data analysis.

Confusion over Authorship

With regard to authorship, the data from the literature suggest that authorship and author responsibilities are not clearly defined by many research groups. Sprague et al. reported that almost 17% of authors of meeting abstracts that were not followed by a subsequent full-text publication reported difficulties with coauthors as the reason for publication failure, and almost 20% reported that the responsibility for the manuscript belonged to someone else.[14] The poor clarification of authorship is also reflected by the high inconsistency of attribution of authorship that has been reported by other investigators.[1,13,15,16] The contribution of authors has become a topic of renewed interest. Rennie et al. (2000) advocated explicit reporting of each author's contribution in an appendix to every full-text paper published in the *Journal of the American Medical Association* to limit problems that are typical of irresponsible authorship, such as honorary authorship, ghost authorship, or duplicate and redundant publication as described and discussed in Chapters 2 and 7.[17]

> **Key Concepts: Criteria for Authorship**
> The International Committee of Medical Journal Editors (ICMJE; found at http://www.icmje.org) has clearly defined the contribution that is required to be credited with authorship[18]:
> * Authorship credit should be based on (1) substantial contributions to conception and design, or acquisition of data, or analysis and interpretation of data; (2) drafting the article or revising it critically for important intellectual content; and (3) final approval of the version to be published. Authors should meet conditions 1, 2, and 3.

> * Acquisition of funding, collection of data, or general supervision of the research group, alone, does not justify authorship.
> * All persons designated as authors should qualify for authorship, and all those who qualify should be listed.
> * Each author should have participated sufficiently in the work to take public responsibility for appropriate portions of the content.

> **Key Concepts: Authorship**
> 1. Ensure that guidelines for authorship are clearly defined.
> 2. Avoid including ghost authors.
> 3. Avoid including honorary authors.
> 4. Changing authorship means changing data.

In reality, it appears that changes of authorship may be made according to which of the authors remain affiliated with the institution, according to which authors are actually attending the meeting, and apparently according to political issues. This, however, is inappropriate research practice and the senior authors need to be responsible and aware that it is not at their discretion to include or exclude coauthors as there are clear guidelines for authorships as defined by the ICMJE.

> **Reality Check: Problems with Authorship**
> The authors of an experimental study presented their results at a meeting; they received an award; and subsequently published their manuscript in a scientific medical journal. The authors' names have been encoded in capital letters for obvious reasons.
> * Abstract: A, B, C, D, E, F
> * Award: B, A, C, D, E, G, F
> * Manuscript: B, A, C, E, G, F
> Author A was the lead author in the abstract, but for the award paper and the full-text manuscript author B became lead author. Author D was mentioned in the abstract and the award paper, but was not credited authorship in the full-text manuscript. Author G was not mentioned in the abstract, but was credited authorship in the award paper and the full-text publication.

Selective Reporting

Selective reporting may lead to significant differences in the outcome. For example, comparison of two treatment regimens may not show any significant differences between two groups for the main outcome measure. Thus, authors may conclude that both treatment regimens are equally effective. However, the authors may include multiple secondary outcome measures in their investigation, some of which may show a significant difference between the two groups. If the authors re-define their main outcome measure, they may conclude that one treatment regimen is superior. In this situation, it must be realized that with an increased number of outcome measures, the likelihood of finding significance in any of the recorded outcome measures automatically increases. Thus, appropriate mathematical adjustments of the *P*-value are to be made when several outcome measures are recorded.

What Can We Do to Increase Consistency and Accuracy?

Investigators who are in the process of publishing their research must be aware of the importance of accurate reporting of their results. High-quality abstracts will be well appreciated by peers and will assist other researchers in obtaining the most valuable information. Since Internet resources and online databases are widely available, inconsistencies and inaccuracies are quickly recognized by peers. Significant discrepancies between abstract and subsequent full-text publication will jeopardize the reputation and integrity of the publishing authors. Authors, peer-reviewers, editors, and meeting committees should be aware of the importance of consistency and should carefully scrutinize papers during the publication process.

Authors presenting studies at scientific meetings should ensure that their abstract and presentation accurately reflect the final results of the study. Presentation of preliminary data should be avoided or at the very least clearly labeled as such. If meeting abstracts are followed by subsequent full-text publication, any discrepancies should be explained to the reader and the previous abstract must be cited appropriately. Educators and instructors teaching young investigators and students need to guide their trainees in the publication process and stress the importance of consistency. To improve the quality of their meeting abstracts, authors should include sufficient and accurate information on the study objective/hypothesis, study design, primary outcome measure, sample size, statistical analysis, results for primary outcome measure, measures of precision, and conclusions. Some authors may find it helpful to structure their abstracts systematically. It has been suggested that structured abstracts are better in quality, more informative, and easier to read.[19-23] Quality criteria for abstracts have been developed and include[24]:

- Years of study duration and length of follow-up.
- Results of the main outcome measures; avoid selective reporting.
- Quantification of results with numerators, denominators, odds ratios, and confidence intervals where appropriate.
- Absolute differences rather than relative differences.
- For randomized trials, analysis is identified as intent-to-treat or evaluable patient analysis.
- For surveys, response rate is provided.
- For multivariate analysis, factors controlled for in the model are briefly summarized.

- Conclusions are drawn only from data contained within the abstract.

Authors should check their abstract carefully prior to submission to ensure that it fulfills these quality criteria. Moreover, authors may consider writing their full-text manuscript and the meeting abstract at the same time so as to minimize inconsistency and inaccuracy.

> **Key Concepts: Prepare Your Abstracts and Manuscripts at the Same Time**
> If you write your abstract and the full-text manuscript at the same time, you can most likely avoid any inconsistencies.

Meetings committees also play an important role in optimizing the accuracy and consistency of reporting. Meetings committees have several options to improve the quality of reporting by requesting structured abstracts. In addition, meetings committees should allow authors a sufficient number of words for the abstract to ensure accurate reporting of study methodology and study results. Guidelines that request specific quality criteria as mentioned above would further improve the quality of reporting. These can be requested in a check list that the authors have to complete at the time of abstract submission. As well, the author guidelines should emphasize the necessity of study completion at the time of abstract submission. Abstracts that suggest preliminary data should be scrutinized carefully. Requesting a publication-ready manuscript that will be handed to the session moderator for all accepted papers will also enforce accurate and consistent reporting.

Lastly, editors of medical journals and their peer-reviewers play an important role in ensuring accurate and consistent reporting. Journal editors and peer-reviewers should scrutinize submitted manuscripts for consistency with previously published meeting abstracts and request explanations for any inconsistency. Requesting previously published abstracts may facilitate this process. The importance of accurate reporting should be a part of the author guidelines as well.

Conclusion

Of many factors that contribute to high-quality research, one is consistency between meeting abstracts and subsequent full-text publishing. Authors need to appreciate the significance of follow-up papers after abstracts have been presented, and be mindful of the effects on their credibility if there are discrepancies between their abstracts and full-text papers. There are many examples of poor reporting practices in the literature that remind us of the significance of consistency. There are also many important players in the publishing process that help ensure accuracy and consistency of reporting. Thus, it is up to you, the author, to learn from the works of others and ensure that appropriate reporting practices are observed.

Suggested Reading

Bhandari M, Devereaux PJ, Guyatt GH, et al. An observational study of orthopaedic abstracts and subsequent full-text publications. J Bone Joint Surg Am 2002;84-A(4):615–621

Scherer RW, Dickersin K, Langenberg P. Full publication of results initially presented in abstracts. A meta-analysis. JAMA 1994; 272(2):158–162

Sprague S, Bhandari M, Devereaux PJ, et al. Barriers to full-text publication following presentation of abstracts at annual orthopaedic meetings. J Bone Joint Surg Am 2003;85-A(1): 158–163

References

1. Bhandari M, Devereaux PJ, Guyatt GH, et al. An observational study of orthopaedic abstracts and subsequent full-text publications. J Bone Joint Surg Am 2002;84-A(4):615–621
2. Brand RA. Writing for Clinical Orthopaedics and Related Research. Clin Orthop Relat Res 2003; (413):1–7
3. Riordan FA. Do presenters to paediatric meetings get their work published? Arch Dis Child 2000;83(6):524–526
4. Daluiski A, Kuhns CA, Jackson KR, Lieberman JR. Publication rate of abstracts presented at the annual meeting of the Orthopaedic Research Society. J Orthop Res 1998; 16(6): 645–649
5. Gorman RL, Oderda GM. Publication of presented abstracts at annual scientific meetings: a measure of quality? Vet Hum Toxicol 1990;32(5):470–472
6. Nguyen V, Tornetta P III, Bkaric M; Orthopaedic Trauma Association. Publication rates for the scientific sessions of the OTA. J Orthop Trauma 1998;12(7):457–459, discussion 456
7. Byerly WG, Rheney CC, Connelly JF, Verzino KC. Publication rates of abstracts from two pharmacy meetings. Ann Pharmacother 2000;34(10):1123–1127
8. Scherer RW, Dickersin K, Langenberg P. Full publication of results initially presented in abstracts. A meta-analysis. JAMA 1994;272(2):158–162
9. Juzych MS, Shin DH, Coffey JB, Parrow KA, Tsai CS, Briggs KS. Pattern of publication of ophthalmic abstracts in peer-reviewed journals. Ophthalmology 1991;98(4):553–556
10. Wang JC, Yoo S, Delamarter RB. The publication rates of presentations at major Spine Specialty Society meetings (NASS, SRS, ISSLS). Spine 1999;24(5):425–427
11. Hamlet WP, Fletcher A, Meals RA. Publication patterns of papers presented at the Annual Meeting of The American Academy of Orthopaedic Surgeons. J Bone Joint Surg Am 1997;79(8):1138–1143
12. Jackson KR, Daluiski A, Kay RM. Publication of abstracts submitted to the annual meeting of the Pediatric Orthopaedic Society of North America. J Pediatr Orthop 2000;20(1):2–6
13. Weintraub WH. Are published manuscripts representative of the surgical meeting abstracts? An objective appraisal. J Pediatr Surg 1987;22(1):11–13
14. Sprague S, Bhandari M, Devereaux PJ, et al. Barriers to full-text publication following presentation of abstracts at annual orthopaedic meetings. J Bone Joint Surg Am 2003;85-A(1): 158–163
15. Zelle BA, Zlowodzki M, Bhandari M. Discrepancies between proceedings abstracts and posters at a scientific meeting. Clin Orthop Relat Res 2005; (435):245–249
16. Preston CF, Bhandari M, Fulkerson E, Ginat D, Egol KA, Koval KJ. The consistency between scientific papers presented at the Orthopaedic Trauma Association and their subsequent full-text publication. J Orthop Trauma 2006;20(2):129–133
17. Rennie D, Flanagin A, Yank V. The contributions of authors. JAMA 2000;284(1):89–91
18. International Committee of Medical Journal Editors. Uniform Requirements for Manuscripts Submitted to Biomedical Journals: Writing and Editing for Biomedical Publication. Available at http://www.icmje.org/. Accessed: December 15, 2009.
19. Ad Hoc Working Group for Critical Appraisal of the Medical Literature. A proposal for more informative abstracts of clinical articles. Ann Intern Med 1987;106(4):598–604
20. Dupuy A, Khosrotehrani K, Lebbé C, Rybojad M, Morel P. Quality of abstracts in 3 clinical dermatology journals. Arch Dermatol 2003;139(5):589–593
21. Froom P, Froom J. Deficiencies in structured medical abstracts. J Clin Epidemiol 1993;46(7):591–594
22. Narine L, Yee DS, Einarson TR, Ilersich AL. Quality of abstracts of original research articles in CMAJ in 1989. CMAJ 1991;144 (4):449–453
23. Taddio A, Pain T, Fassos FF, Boon H, Ilersich AL, Einarson TR. Quality of nonstructured and structured abstracts of original research articles in the British Medical Journal, the Canadian Medical Association Journal and the Journal of the American Medical Association. CMAJ 1994;150(10):1611–1615
24. Winker MA. The need for concrete improvement in abstract quality. [editorial] JAMA 1999;281(12):1129–1130

Glossary

A-priori hypothesis
A hypotheses developed and stated before data analysis.

Abstract
A summary of the entire paper, provided at the beginning of the paper.

Attrition bias
Bias resulting from the number and management of deviations from protocol and loss to follow up.[1]

Blinding
"The participant of interest is unaware of whether patients have been assigned to the experimental or control group. Patients, clinicians, those monitoring outcomes, judicial assessors of outcomes, data analysts, and those writing the paper can all be blinded or masked. To avoid confusion the term *masked* is preferred in studies in which vision loss of patients is an outcome of interest."[2]

Blinded manuscript (blinded review)
Author names and affiliations are not included on the manuscripts so the reviewers are "blind" to the people or institutions associated with the submission.

Case–control study
"A study designed to determine the association between an exposure and outcome in which patients are sampled by outcome (that is, some patients with the outcome of interest are selected and compared to a group of patients who have not had the outcome), and the investigator examines the proportion of patients with the exposure in the two groups."[2]

Case series
"A study reporting on a consecutive collection of patients treated in a similar manner, without a control group. For example, a surgeon might describe the characteristics of an outcome for 100 consecutive patients with cerebral ischemia who received a revascularization procedure."[2]

Clause
An expression including a subject and predicate but not necessarily constituting a complete sentence.

Cohort studies
"Prospective investigation of the factors that might cause a disorder in which a cohort of individuals who do not have evidence of an outcome of interest but who are exposed to the putative cause are compared with a concurrent cohort who are also free of the outcome but not exposed to the putative case. Both cohorts are then followed to compare the incidence of the outcome of interest."[2]

Comma splice
Incorrectly linking two complete sentences together by using a comma.

Composite end point
An end point that is comprised of two or more outcomes.

Concealment
"Randomization is concealed if the person who is making the decision about enrolling a patient is unaware of whether the next patient enrolled will be entered in the treatment or control group. If randomization was not concealed, patients with better prognoses may tend to be preferentially enrolled in the active treatment arm resulting in exaggeration of the apparent benefit of therapy (or even falsely concluding that treatment is efficacious)."[2]

Conflict of interest
Any outside affiliation or activity, often financial, that might limit a researcher's ability to impartially evaluate his or her results.

CONSORT
Consolidated Standards of Reporting Trials. This encompasses various initiatives developed by the CONSORT Group to alleviate problems arising from inadequate reporting of randomized controlled trials.[3]

Continuous variable
"A variable that can theoretically take any value and in practice can take a large number of values with small differences between them"[2]

Corresponding author
One selected author who will receive additional information and questions from the journal following submission.

Detection bias
"Biased assessment of outcome."[1]

Dichotomous variable
"A variable that can take one of two values, such as pregnant or not pregnant, dead or alive, having suffered a stroke or not having suffered a stroke."[2]

Double-blind
When two parties are blinded to the participants' group allocation (e.g., patients and outcome assessors, patients and investigators, and so on).

Fabrication
Occurs when investigators report false or made-up results.[4]

Falsification
A type of fabrication that includes manipulating research materials to obtain specific results, or altering or excluding data in the report such that the results are not accurately represented.[4]

Ghost authorship
A ghost author is someone who has made significant contributions to the research and who meets the criteria for authorship, but who is not listed as an author.[5]

Honorary authorship
[Also known as guest or gift authorship] An honorary author is someone who is named as an author despite failing to meet the criteria for authorship.[5]

IMRaD format
A structured format for articles—Introduction, Methods, Results, and Discussion.

Incidence rate
"Number of new cases of disease occurring during a specified period of time; expressed as a percentage of the number of people at risk."[2]

Independent clause
A clause that can stand by itself as a sentence.

Institutional Review Board (IRB)
An IRB is a specially constituted review body established or designated by an entity to protect the welfare of human subjects recruited to participate in biomedical or behavioral research.

Intention-to-treat principle
"Analyzing patient outcomes based on which group into which they were randomized regardless of whether they actually received the planned intervention. This analysis preserves the power of randomization, thus maintaining that important unknown factors that influence outcome are likely equally distributed in each comparison group."[2]

Levels of evidence
A rating system for classifying the quality of a study.[6]

Levels of evidence for therapeutic studies:

Level I
- High-quality randomized controlled trial with statically significant difference or no statically significant but narrow confidence intervals

Level II
- Lesser-quality randomized controlled trial (e.g., <80% follow-up, no blinding, or improper randomization)
- Prospective comparative study

Level III
- Case–control study
- Retrospective comparative study

Level IV
- Case series

Meta-analysis
"An overview that incorporates a quantitative strategy for combining the results of several studies into a single pooled or summary estimate."[2]

Misplaced modifier
A word or phrase that is not properly located next to the word that it modifies. This error causes confusion for the reader.

Negative trial
A trial "in which the authors have concluded that the experimental treatment is no better than control therapy."[2]

Null hypothesis
"In the hypothesis-testing framework, the starting hypothesis the statistical test is designed to consider and, possibly, reject."[2]

Peer review (refereeing)
Evaluation of submitted manuscripts by selected experts in the field for verification of scientific merit; journals that operate peer review are termed peer-reviewed or refereed journals.

Performance bias
"Unequal provision of care apart from treatment under evaluation."[1]

Plagiarism
"The replication of ideas, data or text without permission or acknowledgement" of the originator.[7]

Plagiarize

"Take and use (the thoughts, writings, inventions, etc. of another person) as one's own." (*The Concise Oxford Dictionary*, 8th edition)

Poster versus podium presentation

Orthopaedic meetings often have poster and podium presentations. In a poster presentation, the investigators prepare a poster summarizing their research methods and outcomes. The poster is displayed during the meeting. Investigators may be asked to give a brief oral summary of their study. They should also be available throughout the meeting to address any questions that the meeting attendees have about their research. In contrast, a podium presentation is a short oral presentation given by the investigator during a scientific session. The presentations are given in front of an audience using PowerPoint. Attendees may ask the investigator questions following their presentation.

Post-hoc hypothesis

A hypotheses developed and stated after data analysis.

Primary outcome

The specific measure that will be used to determine the effect of the intervention(s) receiving the most emphasis in assessment. Include the time frame for taking measurements.[9]

Publication bias

Publication bias occurs when the publication of research results depends on their nature and direction.[2] This typically arises from the tendency for researchers and editors to handle experimental results that are positive (they found something) differently from results that are negative (they found that something did not happen) or inconclusive.

Publication rates

Publication rates represent the percentage of presentations at national meetings that result in a published journal article that can be found in a literature search.

Randomized controlled trial (RCT)

"Experiment in which individuals are randomly allocated to receive or not receive an experimental preventative, therapeutic, or diagnostic procedure and then followed to determine the effect of the intervention.[2]

Redundant publication

A redundant publication is "one which duplicates previous, simultaneous, or future publications by the same author or group or, alternatively, could have been combined with the latter into one paper."[10]

Secondary outcome

"Other key measures that will be used to evaluate the intervention(s) or, for observational studies, that are a focus of the study."[9]

Selection bias

"Biased allocation to comparison groups."[1]

Structured abstract

Text within the abstract is subdivided into predetermined sections.

Systematic review

"A critical assessment and evaluation of research (not simply a summary) that attempts to address a focused clinical question using methods designed to reduce the likelihood of bias."[2]

Time series design

"Typically used in observational studies, time series design monitors the occurrence of outcomes or endpoints over a number of cycles and determines if the pattern changes coincident with an intervention or event."[2]

References

1. Jüni P, Altman DG, Egger M. Systematic reviews in health care: Assessing the quality of controlled clinical trials. BMJ 2001;323(7303):42–46
2. Guyatt GH, Rennie D, eds.ds. User's Guides to the Medical Literature: A Manual for Evidence-based Clinical Practice. Chicago, IL: AMA Press; 2001
3. CONSORT. Available at: http://www.consort-statement.org/. Accessed December 21, 2009
4. Office of Research Integrity. Available at: http://ori.hhs.gov/misconduct/definition_misconduct.shtml. Accessed December 21, 2009
5. Flanagin A, Carey LA, Fontanarosa PB, et al. Prevalence of articles with honorary authors and ghost authors in peer-reviewed medical journals. JAMA 1998;280(3):222–224
6. Wright JG, Swiontkowski MF, Heckman JD. Introducing levels of evidence to the journal. J Bone Joint Surg Am 2003;85-A(1): 1–3
7. Fenton JE, Jones AS. Integrity in medical research and publication. Clin Otolaryngol Allied Sci 2002;27(6):436–439
8. Wittich WA, Schuller CF. Instructional Technology: Its Nature and Use. 4th ed. New York: Harper and Row;1973
9. Clinical Trial Data Element Definitions. Available at: http://prsinfo.clinicaltrials.gov/definitions.html. Accessed December 21, 2009
10. Schein M, Paladugu R. Redundant surgical publications: tip of the iceberg? Surgery 2001;129(6):655–661

Index

Page numbers in *italics* refer to illustrations or tables